teach®
yourself

world cultures:
wales

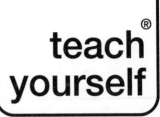

world cultures:
wales
julie brake
and
christine jones

For over 60 years, more than 40 million people have learnt over 750 subjects the **teach yourself** way, with impressive results.

be where you want to be
with **teach yourself**

The publisher has used its best endeavours to ensure that the URLs for external websites referred to in this book are correct and active at the time of going to press. However, the publisher has no responsibility for the websites and can make no guarantee that a site will remain live or that the content is or will remain appropriate.

For UK order enquiries: please contact Bookpoint Ltd, 130 Milton Park, Abingdon, Oxon OX14 4SB. Telephone: +44 (0) 1235 827720. Fax: +44 (0) 1235 400454. Lines are open 09.00–18.00, Monday to Saturday, with a 24-hour message answering service. Details about our titles and how to order are available at www.teachyourself.co.uk

For USA order enquiries: please contact McGraw-Hill Customer Services, PO Box 545, Blacklick, OH 43004-0545, USA. Telephone: 1-800-722-4726. Fax: 1-614-755-5645.

For Canada order enquiries: please contact McGraw-Hill Ryerson Ltd, 300 Water St, Whitby, Ontario L1N 9B6, Canada. Telephone: 905 430 5000. Fax: 905 430 5020.

Long-renowned as the authoritative source for self-guided learning – with more than 30 million copies sold worldwide – the *Teach Yourself* series includes over 300 titles in the fields of languages, crafts, hobbies, business, computing and education.

British Library Cataloguing in Publication Data: a catalogue record for this title is available from The British Library.

Library of Congress Catalog Card Number: on file.

First published in UK 2004 by Hodder Headline, 338 Euston Road, London, NW1 3BH.

First published in US 2004 by Contemporary Books, a Division of The McGraw-Hill Companies, 1 Prudential Plaza, 130 East Randolph Street, Chicago, IL 60601 USA.

This edition published 2004.

The 'Teach Yourself' name is a registered trade mark of Hodder & Stoughton Ltd.

Copyright © 2004 Julie Brake and Christine Jones

Typeset by Transet Limited, Coventry, England.
Printed in Great Britain for Hodder & Stoughton Educational, a division of Hodder Headline, 338 Euston Road, London NW1 3BH by Cox & Wyman Ltd, Reading, Berkshire.

Papers used in this book are natural, renewable and recyclable products. They are made from wood grown in sustainable forests. The logging and manufacturing processes conform to the environmental regulations of the country of origin.

Impression number   10 9 8 7 6 5 4 3 2 1
Year   2010 2009 2008 2007 2006 2005 2004

contents

introduction

This book is designed to give you as full a basic overview as possible of the main aspects of Wales: the country, its language, its people, their way of life and culture and what makes them tick.

You will find it a useful foundation if you are studying for examinations which require a knowledge of the background of Wales and its civilization, or if you are learning the language in, for example, an evening class and want to know more about the country and how it works. If your job involves travel and business relations it will provide valuable and practical information about the ways and customs of the people you are working with. Or if you simply have an interest in Wales for whatever reason, it will broaden your knowledge about the country and its inhabitants.

The book is divided into three sections:

- **The making of Wales**
  Units 1 and 2 deal with the forces – historical, geographical, geological, demographical and linguistic – that have brought about the formation of the country we know as Wales and the language we know as Welsh.

- **Creative Wales**
  Units 3–7 deal with the wealth of creative aspects of Welsh culture from its beginnings to the present day. These units take a look at the main areas or works of literature, art and architecture, music, traditions and festivals, science and technology, fashion and food and drink, together with the people who have created and are still creating them.

- **Living in Wales now**
  Units 8–11 deal with aspects of contemporary Welsh society and the practicalities of living in present-day Wales: the way the political structure of the country is organized, education, the environment, the workplace and how people spend their leisure time. The final unit looks at the country's political, economic and social relations with the wider world, and takes a glance at the future.

Taking it further

Each unit ends with a section entitled 'Taking it further', where you will find useful addresses, websites, suggested places to visit and things to see and do in order to develop your interest further and increase your knowledge.

The language

Within each unit you will encounter a number of terms in Welsh, whose meaning is given in English when they are first introduced. If you wish to put your knowledge into practice, we have provided in each chapter a list of useful words and phrases to enable you to talk or write about the subject in question.

We have been careful in researching and checking facts, but please be aware that sources sometimes offer differing information. Of course a book of this length cannot contain everything you may need to know on every aspect of Wales. That is why we have provided so many pointers to where you can find further information about any aspect that you may wish to pursue in more depth. We trust that you will enjoy this introductory book, and that it will provide leads to further profitable reading, listening and visiting.

Phil Turk
Series Editor

There are 29 letters in the Welsh alphabet including several letter combinations – **ch, dd, ff, ng, ll, ph, rh, th** – which each represent one sound.

a, b, c, ch, d, dd, e, f, ff, g, ng, h, i, j, l, ll, m, n, o, p, ph, r, rh, s, t, th, u, w, y

Pronunciation of consonants

b, d, h, j, l, m, n, p, s, t, th are pronounced as in English. Note the following:

c	ci 'dog':	always a hard 'c' as in English 'cap', *never* as in 'city'
ch	bach 'small':	as in the Scottish 'lo**ch**', rather like the German 'ch', never as in the English word 'mock'
dd	ddoe 'yesterday':	as in the English word '**th**e'
f	haf 'summer':	always a hard 'v' sound as 'f' in English 'of' and 'violin', never as in the English word 'fan'
ff	rhaff 'rope':	as 'ff' in English 'off'
g	gêm 'game':	as in the English word '**g**rand', never as in 'giant'
ng	ngêm 'my game':	as in the English word 'ga**ng**' and 'si**ng**er'
ll	lle 'place':	place tongue to say the 'l' in the English word 'land' and then blow
ph	phen 'her head':	as in the English word '**ph**ysical'
r	ras 'race':	the Welsh 'r' is rolled
rh	rhad 'cheap':	place tongue to say the 'r' in the English word 'red' and blow

Pronunciation of vowels

As in English, vowels – **a, e, i, o, u, w, y** – can be either long or short:

a	(short)	**mam** 'mother':	as in the English word 'cat'
	(long)	**tad** 'father':	as in the English word 'car'
e	(short)	**pen** 'head':	as in the English word 'met'
	(long)	**te** 'tea':	as in the English word 'pear'
i	(short)	**bin**:	as in the English word 'bit'
	(long)	**cinio** 'dinner':	as in the English word 'feel'
o	(short)	**toc** 'presently':	as in the English word 'hot'
	(long)	**llo** 'calf':	as in the English word 'more'
u	(short)	**tun** 'tin':	as in the English word 'pin'
	(long)	**du** 'black':	as in the 'ee' in 'seen', never as in 'cup', or an 'oo' sound
w	(short)	**dwrn** 'fist'	as in the English word 'book'
	(long)	**cwrw** 'beer'	as in the English word 'moon'
y	(short)	**llyn** 'lake'	as in the English word 'pin'
y	(long)	**dyn** 'man'	as in the English word 'peel'

y has two sounds:
'**ee**' or '**i**' in the final syllable or in words of one syllable: **dyn** (man) pronounced 'deen';

and '**uh**' in the preceding one(s): **mynydd** (mountain) pronounced 'muhnithe'.

Long vowels are sometimes marked by the accent ^:

â	**tân** 'fire':	as 'a' in English 'father'
ê	**gêm** 'game':	as in English 'bear'
î	**sgrîn** 'screen':	as in English 'peel'
ô	**môr** 'sea':	as in English 'more'
û	**cytûn** 'agreed':	as in English 'peel'
ŵ	**dŵr** 'water':	as in English 'moon'
ŷ	**ŷd** 'corn':	as in English 'peel'

Diphthongs (vowel combinations)

A diphthong is a combination of two vowels pronounced one after the other in one breath or 'syllable'. As we have seen, some Welsh vowels, like '**i**' and '**u**', sound the same, and so diphthongs like '**ai**' and '**au**' also sound the same.

as in the English 'aisle':

ae	traed	(feet)
ai	gair	(word)
au	dau	(two)

as in 'pay':

ei	cei	(quay)
eu	neu	(or)
ey	teyrnas	(kingdom)

as in 'boy':

oe	ddoe	(yesterday)
oi	rhoi	(to give, put)
ou	cyffrous	(exciting)

aw	**llaw** (hand) pronounced like the 'ou' in the English word 'cloud'
ew	**tew** (fat): a combination of 'e' and 'w' and so sounds like 'eh-oo'
iw, yw, uw	**rhiw** 'hill', **cyw** 'chick', **duw** 'god' as 'ew' in English 'new'
ia	**iâr** (hen)
io	**cofio** (to remember)
ow	**trowch** (turn): as in the English 'oh':
wy	**trwyn** (nose)

Listen to the media or people speaking as much as you can, just to get used to the sounds of the language.

Stress

Emphasis in Welsh words is usually placed on the penultimate syllable: **prifysgol** (university)

The unitary authorities of Wales

1 Ynys Môn (Anglesey)
2 Gwynedd
3 Conwy (Conway)
4 Sir Ddinbych
5 Sir y Ffint (Flintshire)
6 Wrecsam (Wrexham)
7 Ceredigion
8 Powys
9 Sir Benfro (Pembrokeshire)
10 Sir Gaefyrddin (Carmarthenshire)
11 Abertawe (Swansea)

12 Castell Nedd Port Talbot
   (Neath Port Talbot)
13 Rhondda Cynon Taf
14 Merthyr Tudful
15 Caerffili (Caerphilly)
16 Blaenau Gwent
17 Sir Fynwy (Monmouthshire)
18 Torfaen
19 Pen-y-Bont ar Ogwr (Bridgend)
20 Bro Mrgannwg (Vale of Glamorgan)
21 Caerdydd (Cardiff)
22 Casnewydd (Newport)

01

the making of Wales

In this unit you will learn about
- the geography of Wales
- the people of Wales and their history

What made Wales the country it is today? In this unit we will be looking at some of the forces that have contributed to the making of the country. Some events have naturally affected the whole of Britain, but we shall concentrate on those which seem to have been decisive in Welsh history in particular or to have contributed to the richly individual character of the land of Wales and its people.

Geography

Wales is a small country inhabited by some 2.9 million people, who make up approximately 5 per cent of the total population of the United Kingdom. It is only some 64 km wide at its narrowest and 160 km across at its widest. Its maximum length is 225 km. Wales comprises two peninsulas bound in the north by the Irish Sea, in the west by both Cardigan Bay and St George's Channel, in the east by the English counties of Cheshire, Shropshire, Herefordshire, Worcestershire and Gloucestershire and in the south by the Bristol Channel. The Welsh border runs from the mouth of the River Dee in Liverpool Bay in the north, to the mouth of the Wye on the Severn estuary in the south. It roughly follows Offa's Dyke (*Clawdd Offa*), the earthwork frontier fortification built by the powerful ruler Offa of Mercia in the eighth century.

Regions of Wales

Traditionally thought of as being covered in rolling green hills, the geology and geography of Wales are distinctive, offering everything from rugged mountain ranges to rolling upland pastures and sweeping sandy beaches and coves. Moorland dominates Wales, which, together with the mountains, makes up the 'heartland' of the country. Low ground is found mainly along the coast, in the border country, and in the fertile valleys of the south. Wales is often divided into three main geographical regions, each with its own physical character. The mountains of Snowdonia and disused slate quarries dominate north Wales, while the countryside of mid Wales is gentler and the population more sparse. The third region, south Wales, is home to an area of beautiful coastline, as well as numerous mining valleys with their rows of distinctive terraced houses and reclaimed industrial land. This terrain has affected the course of the history of Wales.

Wales

The highlands

Wales is a rugged land. Some four-fifths of the surface of Wales is hard upland with mountainous areas, primarily located in Gwynedd. Of the fifteen peaks in Wales which are over 914 metres, all are located in the county of Gwynedd. Mount Snowdon, at 1,085 metres, is the highest peak in England and Wales. Whilst the mountains of Snowdonia dominate the north of the country, in the south is found the mountain system of the Brecon Beacons and the Black Mountains. The mountains and moorlands offered protection to the Welsh people when invaders attacked. The mountains provided a natural defensive barrier from successive invasions from the east, but they also made communication between different areas difficult, and even today, as noted in Unit 9, there is no satisfactory road link between north and south Wales. The isolated, close-knit communities, which developed as a result of the geography of the country, were an obstacle to unification. The western parts of Wales are generally considered to be the strongholds of the Welsh language and culture today. This is in part due to their isolation, which curbed English influence, thus preserving the Welsh language and culture.

The highest mountain in mid Wales is Cader Idris, which stands at 829 metres. According to Welsh tradition, anyone who stays overnight on the summit will die, become mad, or end up as a poet. In Pembrokeshire, the Preseli Hills are a moorland range from where Stonehenge's Blue Stones originated.

The geographical structure of the country has prevented the growth of a rich agricultural economy. The soil in upland Wales is poor, and the wet and windy climate renders it unsuitable for crop growing. The breeding of animals, particularly hardy mountain sheep, has therefore been the only alternative facing hill-farmers. Poorer soils have been more than adequately compensated for in the past by the rich mineral deposits such as coal, iron and slate.

The lowlands

Lowland Wales is made up of larger river valleys and is far richer agriculturally than other areas. Crop growing predominates in the more fruitful soils of the Vales of Conwy and Clwyd, the Vale of Glamorgan and the border country. Farmers raise beef and dairy cattle in the lowlands, and south-west Wales is the centre of the Welsh dairy industry.

Coastal regions and islands

You are never more than 80 km from the sea in Wales and there is immense variety within the 1,200 km coastline. The coastline consists of many bays, the largest of which is Cardigan Bay. In some places the coastline is rocky with high cliffs and, in others, kilometres of sand dominate. There are many designated Heritage Coast areas, scenic coastline that is managed so that its natural beauty is conserved. The more spectacular of the Heritage Coasts in Wales are St David's Peninsula, St Bride's Bay and the Ceredigion coast. The coastline of Pembrokeshire forms the Pembrokeshire Coast National Park and the Gower Peninsula was the first area of land in Britain to be declared an Area of Outstanding Natural Beauty. The Welsh coast is strewn with islands, many uninhabited. The biggest, Anglesey, the sacred island of the Druids, is some 676 square kilometres and is traditionally known as *Mam Cymru* (the mother of Wales) because of its productivity. Caldey Island (*Ynys Bŷr*) lies some 4.8 km from Tenby harbour and is privately owned by the Reformed Cistercian Order. The monks manufacture perfume, honey, chocolate, yoghurt and dairy products, and boat trips regularly visit the island. One of the islands with the longest history is Bardsey Island (*Ynys Enlli*), which lies beyond the tip of the Llŷn peninsula. A monastery was founded there in 625 by St Cadfan. At one time it was a sanctuary of saints and 20,000 are said to be buried here.

Climate

The weather in Wales is quite similar to that of England, except that because the mountains are so close to the coast, there may be fairly dramatic weather changes over short distances.

Wales is considered to be one of the wettest corners in Europe, having approximately one metre of rainfall per year. Mount Snowdon also boasts the highest annual rainfall in the British Isles with an average of 4,500 mm. The average daily temperature in July is 15.6°C, and in January it is 5.6°C. The south coast is slightly warmer than the north coast. The Dale Peninsula in Pembrokeshire records sunshine levels which equal the highest in Britain, and Pembrokeshire produces the earliest new potatoes in Britain.

Snow has been estimated to cover areas over 900 metres high in Snowdonia for an average of about 100 days a year. There are no peaks in Wales above the permanent snow line, although there are some places where snow does not melt during most summers.

Rivers and lakes

Although not renowned internationally for their size, rivers dominate Wales owing to its regular rainfall and hilly terrain. It has been estimated that there are some 24,000 km of rivers in Wales. The longest that is wholly in Wales is the Usk, which is 137 km in length. The longest river in Britain, the Severn (*Hafren*), starts on the slopes of Pumlumon and travels cross-country to Shrewsbury before following the Welsh border to the Bristol Channel. Two others have their source on Pumlumon, the Wye and the Rheidiol. Three rivers flow to the sea at Cardiff, the capital city of Wales: the Rhymni, Elai and Taff (*Taf*). It is believed that the latter inspired the nickname 'Taffy' for a Welshman (see Unit 12).

There are over 400 natural lakes and over 90 reservoirs in Wales, many supplying the English Midlands, Greater Manchester and Merseyside. The largest natural lake in Wales is Lake Bala (*Llyn Tegid*), 4.38 square kilometres in area. Many fables surround some of the bigger lakes in Wales, Lake Bala is said to be inhabited by a monster not unlike the one dwelling in Loch Ness, and it is said that no bird will ever fly over Llyn Idwal in Gwynedd.

There are also many wetlands or bogs (*corsydd*) in Wales, including seven wetlands of international importance. The biggest of them is *Cors Fochno* on the western coast, but *Cors Caron*, situated near the Ceredigion market town of Tregaron, is also impressive. *Cors Caron* is one of the best examples of a raised mire in Britain and is notable for its rich wetland vegetation and wildlife. The marsh gases produced by these wetlands sometimes lead to spectacular displays. In the seventeenth century, a vapour 'resembling a weak, blue flame' rose from a marsh near Harlech, Gwynedd, setting fire to barns and hayricks in the area. There are also a number of spectacular waterfalls in Wales; Pistyll Rhaeadr near Llanrhaeadr-ym-Mochnant in the Berwyn Mountains is the highest waterfall in England and Wales. Perhaps the most well-visited waterfalls are Swallow Falls between Betws-y-Coed and Capel Curig, the three falls pour down a deep ravine and have been attracting visitors since Victorian times.

The people of Wales and their history

The earliest inhabitants

The first people to inhabit Wales were cave dwellers who trekked across the plains of Europe somewhere between 50,000 and 8,000 BC. The small caves in which these primitive people lived include Goat's Hole cave, at Paviland in Gower where early remains of Cro-Magnon man were found. The skeleton of a young man sported a necklace made of the teeth of mammoth, woolly rhinoceros and a hyena.

Around 6,000 BC, Neolithic farming communities arrived, settling permanently in the western parts of the British Isles, from the Mediterranean area. They constructed huge burial tombs known as *cromlechs*, an example of which is *Pentre Ifan* in Pembrokeshire. The next people to reach Wales were the 'Beaker people', so called because they buried earthenware with their dead. Eventually, stone gave way to metal as the main material used for making tools and weapons with the Bronze age (*c.*2000–500 BC), when the Celts arrived in Wales.

The Celts

The Celts are the people who gave Wales its identity and culture. It is thought that they came to Britain from the Continent in or around 500 BC. The hill forts where they kept herds of animals and grew crops are still evident today. We know surprisingly little about the Celts but we do know that they lived in clans, which formed parts of larger tribes. The great Celtic tribes were the *Silures* and the *Demetae* in the south-east, the *Cornovii* in mid Wales and the *Decaengli* and *Ordovices* in the north. The Celts are generally associated with the Bronze and Iron Ages, and the use of sophisticated iron and bronze implements was widespread during this period. Many implements used by the Celts were discovered in a lake, Llyn Cerrig Bach, on Anglesey. Celtic art and design, consisting of a unique pattern of stylized animals, interwoven with latticework and swirling lines, is found in everything from tools, weapons, jewellery, utensils and clothing dating from this period. There are many examples of Celtic craftsmanship in the National Museum of Wales in Cardiff. Perhaps the most lasting influence of the Celts was their language, which became the basis of the Welsh language. The Celtic tribes, who worshipped nature deities such as *Cernunnos*, the horned god, introduced their own religion to the country and Anglesey became one of the most important places of meeting for the Celtic Druids. Many of the Celtic gods appear as mythological characters in Welsh medieval tales, such as Rhiannon, who features in the *Mabinogi* tales related in Unit 3, who was associated with the horse goddess Epona. Celtic tribes dominated Britain until the Romans invaded the south coast in AD 43.

The Roman era

The Romans conquered Wales with some difficulty, but by AD 80, most of Wales had been conquered. They built great fortresses such as *Isca Silurum* (Caerleon), towns such as Caerwent in eastern Monmouthshire, and roads linking each of their fortresses. One such road was *Sarn Helen*, a road which crossed Wales from Carmarthen (*Moridunum*) to Caernarfon

(*Segontium*) in the north. Caerleon was the headquarters of the Second Legion in Britain and boasts the best-preserved Roman amphitheatre in Britain as well as the only visible legionary baths. The Romans also mined metals on a large scale, especially lead, silver and gold; an example of a Roman gold mine is at Dolau Cothi in Carmarthenshire. After the Emperor Constantine was converted to Christianity in AD 312, Christianity became the official state religion of the Empire, and was introduced to the Celtic tribes in Britain. It took root in Wales, particularly in the south-east, remaining even after the Romans left.

The Dark Ages

The Roman occupation of Britain ended around AD 450. The unity imposed by the Romans disintegrated with the remaining Britons forming a multitude of tiny kingdoms who fought amongst themselves for control of territory. This was an important epoch in Welsh history. Britain was invaded by Germanic invaders, and was eventually divided into the Brythonic west, the area where the Brythonic language, the language of the Celts, was spoken, the Teutonic east where the Germanic invaders had settled and the Gaelic-speaking north-west. These areas later became the nations of Wales, England and Scotland respectively. Wales became more distinct as a geographical area, its identity and language refined and its borders recognisable. The Welsh called themselves *Cymry* meaning comrades or fellow-countrymen. Many legends surround this time in Welsh history including the story of **Merlin** and the two dragons related in Unit 6, which led to the red dragon in the legend being adopted as the symbol of Welsh nationhood.

The Celtic Church was a unifying influence in a Wales made up of warring kingdoms. This period of Welsh history is known as the 'Age of the Saints'. The foremost saint was **St David** (d.589) who became the patron saint of Wales. St David is known as *Dewi Sant* in Welsh and many place names today bear his name, including Llanddewibrefi in Ceredigion.

This was also the age of **King Arthur**, who appears to have led an anti-Saxon rebellion in the sixth century. Little is known about this figure, who was probably Commander-in-Chief of all the combined Celtic forces against the Saxons. The popularity of King Arthur is mostly due to the twelfth-century writer Geoffrey of Monmouth, whose prose work, *Historia Regnum*

Britanniae, became the text on which all later Arthurian traditions were based. Geoffrey is considered to be the creator of the heroic image of Arthur.

It was around AD 770 that **King Offa** of the kingdom of Mercia in England constructed Offa's Dyke, a barrier which separated England from the 'Wealas' (foreigners), from which Wales gets its English name (see Unit 2). The Welsh were to remain on the other side of the dyke, which is one of the oldest national borders in Europe. The Welsh people became a distinct people with their own language, laws and customs. Today, the spectacular 168-mile Offa's Dyke Path attracts walkers from all over Europe.

The ninth-century king of Gwynedd **Rhodri Mawr** became the first Welsh king to unite most of Wales and bring it under his control. Until his death, Rhodri held Wales together and made an alliance with King Alfred of Wessex against the Vikings. Unfortunately, this brief national unity was not to last and his domains were divided after his death. Wales remained a country of individual kingdoms, often at war with each other but also enjoying brief periods of unity. Wales was again united under Rhodri Mawr's grandson **Hywel Dda** (Hywel the Good), who introduced currency and a unifying code of law which you can read more about in Unit 2. This legislation lasted until the Acts of Union with England in 1536. The Welsh laws were based on the rights of the individual member of society and equal protection under the law was accorded to men and women alike. Marriage was an agreement and divorce was permitted if both parties agreed, whereupon the land and possessions were divided equally. A woman could even divorce her husband on the grounds of his *'stinking breath'*. The right of a married woman to own property was not granted in English law until 1883. Illegitimate children had the same rights as legitimate children and there was equal division of land between all children on the death of their parents, a law which had devastating consequences for political unity in Wales. Hywel coexisted peacefully with the English kings despite being advised to ally against them. Close family ties were highly important in this tribal system and on the death of a chieftain his territory was divided, further fragmenting the country. Hywel's death in 950 put Wales into disarray again and the country was harassed by Danish attacks throughout the tenth century. The political fragmentation of Wales had devastating consequences when the Normans arrived.

Norman invaders

Welsh resistance to the Norman invaders was sporadic; the Normans found it easy to play one Welsh prince off against the other and encroached into Wales building castles as they pushed west. Urban settlements grew up around the castles whose ruins are still to be seen in Wales, and powerful Norman lordships or Marches were established on the border with England (see p. 81). Although the Normans held and colonized the lowlands of south and mid Wales, the north and the uplands remained largely Welsh. The Norman marcher lords lived outside the law of the king of England but enforced their own laws over the native Welsh. The death of **Rhys ap Tewdwr**, king of Deheubarth in south-west Wales, in 1093 was seen as an end of independent kingship in Wales, as Welsh rulers thereafter paid homage to the king of England.

The Normans took the most fruitful Welsh farmland and built permanent stone fortresses such as Pembroke Castle keep. By the twelfth century, much of lowland Wales had been conquered and only Gwynedd continued to offer resistance. The period following the death of Henry I of England, however, saw something of a cultural flowering in Wales, poetry and scholarship flourished and folk legends were written down, including the *Mabinogi*. **Llywelyn Fawr**, the Prince of Gwynedd, led a national uprising at the beginning of the thirteenth century and became master of most of Wales. However, he failed to secure a successor, and on his death Wales lapsed into a period of strife and civil war.

The last independent native prince

In the second half of the thirteenth century, the grandson of Llywelyn Fawr, **Llywelyn ap Gruffudd**, went on to gain control of almost the whole of Wales. At the height of his power, in 1267, the Treaty of Montgomery recognized Welsh independence, and England's weak Henry III acknowledged Llywelyn as prince of Wales. However Edward I, who succeeded his father to the throne, was a powerful king who was determined not to let Llywelyn gain more power in Wales. Edward quickly conquered Wales in 1282 and Llywelyn was killed in a skirmish in December of that year. The death of Llywelyn, which possibly came about because of an act of betrayal by one of his own men, is still commemorated today. His infant daughter, Gwenllian, was confined to a nunnery in

Lincolnshire for the remainder of her life. A simple granite plaque at Cilmeri commemorates Llywelyn and the remains of his body (his head was taken to London where it was paraded around the city) lie in the ruins of the Cistercian Abbey of Cwmhir. Edward expanded castle building into the Welsh heartland, building the magnificent castles of Builth Wells, Harlech, Beaumaris, Conwy and Caernarfon. Edward spent half of his crown's annual income in building castles to cut off Gwynedd from the rest of Wales. Welsh independence was at an end. In 1283 Edward confirmed his hold on Wales by the Statute of Rhuddlan, which restructured the administration of the country under a Prince of Wales, whose title from then onwards would lie with the eldest son of the English monarchy. Wales henceforth would be a principality.

After the defeat of Llywelyn ap Gruffudd, Welsh soldiers fought for the English king, even as early as the battle of Falkirk in 1298. The powerful two-metre longbow, which changed the face of European warfare by enabling enemy troops to be killed from a distance, was developed by the Welsh in Gwent and used to great effect, particularly in the wars against the French in the fourteenth century. The crest of the Prince of Wales, the three ostrich feathers and the motto *Ich Dien* date from the Battle of Crécy in 1346 when the fifteen-year-old Prince of Wales took the motto and crest from the fallen King John of Bohemia. In the same battle the Welsh bowmen wore the national colours of green and white and are believed to have taunted the French soldiers by waving the two fingers used to draw the bow in the air, now the infamous V-sign used to show contempt (the two fingers of the draw hand of a captured archer would be cut off to prevent them ever firing an arrow again). In spite of the presence of Welsh soldiers in English armies, rebellion continued sporadically in Wales until 1400, when Wales witnessed an important national uprising.

Owain Glyndŵr (known as Owen Glendower in English)

Social tensions and friction were rife in the period after the Edwardian conquest of Wales. Much of the administration of the country lay in English hands and there was growing discontent amongst the nobility who were subordinate to English administrators. On 16 September 1400, Owain Glyndŵr, who could claim descent from the royal houses of Powys and Deheubarth, was proclaimed Prince of Wales by a small number of his friends and family. They then went on to raid a number of English towns and the raids quickly became a struggle for national independence. Owain's forces gradually took over vast parts of Wales and a peripatetic Welsh parliament, with representatives from all parts of Wales, met at Harlech, Dolgellau, Pennal and Machynlleth. Parliament established a Welsh state, formulating laws, national institutions and foreign policy. Owain also intended to establish two universities, one in the north and one in the south and intended to make St David's an archbishopric, thus making the Welsh church independent of Canterbury. The tide of war eventually turned against Owain and his forces were defeated and scattered. The fate of Owain himself is unknown, there is no elegy to his memory, although he is believed to have died peacefully at his daughter's house. Owain's plans for a modern, independent Welsh state have led to him being regarded as the founder of modern Welsh nationalism. Harsh anti-Welsh legislation was introduced by the English Crown after the uprising making the Welsh second-class citizens in their own country. No Englishman could be convicted on the word of a Welshman, marriage between English and Welsh persons was forbidden, and no Welsh person could serve on juries, bear arms, or be appointed to public office. The Parliamentary Act proclaiming Owain a proscribed traitor was eventually repealed in 1948.

The Tudor era

Henry Tudor's victory over Richard III at Bosworth Field in 1485 led to great expectations from the Welsh. Welsh bards had been claiming for centuries that one day a Welshman would become King of England. When Henry Tudor, a man of Welsh descent, was crowned Henry VII many in Wales felt he was the successor to Owain Glyndŵr. Many Welsh nobles followed Henry to the court in London, others entered local positions of power within Wales. Although Henry allowed more Welsh participation in government and government service, he preferred to concentrate largely on the dynastic, administrative and financial problems which threatened his newly won throne and introduced few reforms in Wales.

The Acts of Union, passed in 1536 and 1543, formally united England and Wales. Wales was practically absorbed by England and denied an independent church, legal and education system, however, Welshmen were given the same rights and liberties as their English counterparts. Land in Wales would henceforth be divided according to the English law of primogeniture, or first-born son inherits all. The English shire system was adopted –

Wales was divided into thirteen counties, administrative boundaries that remained unchanged until 1974. The Acts of Union were seen by many Welsh aristocrats as a means of advancement and many more flocked to London to make their fortune. By the eighteenth century the upper layers of society in Wales had become Anglicized. Although not rich in comparison with England, Wales enjoyed a measure of prosperity during the Tudor era; there was a population increase and a growth in trade as a result of the development of coal and lead mining. In general there was little sympathy for Cromwell and his followers when civil war broke out in England in 1642 and the restoration of the monarchy in 1660 was welcomed.

The Methodist revival

The social life of the people changed profoundly during the eighteenth century. This was the result of a profound religious awakening which swept through Wales and led to Wales becoming a strongly Nonconformist country. The impact of the sixteenth-century Protestant Reformation was not felt in Wales until the Methodist revival in the eighteenth century. Even the increasing number of religious books, including the Welsh translation of the Bible in 1588, had made little impact on religion in Wales. During the Civil Wars (1642–49) and Cromwell's Protectorate, the numbers of Puritans, Quakers, Baptists and Independents had increased in Wales and set up their own churches. Working outside the established Church of England, they became known as 'Dissenters' or Nonconformists. By the early eighteenth century, the number of Dissenters in Wales was growing rapidly and this phenomenon would greatly influence Welsh society for a long time to come.

The first major growth point of the Methodist revival was in west Wales. This was a region where the established Church was poor and where a scattered population had developed informal open-air religion-gatherings. Preaching by charismatic preachers such as **Daniel Rowland** and **Howell Harris**, and the inspirational hymns of **William Williams, Pantycelyn** convinced many Welsh people to become Methodists. In 1811 the Methodist leader **Thomas Charles** of Bala reluctantly led the movement out of the Church of England and Methodism became a separate denomination.

The Methodists were deeply concerned with education. From the 1730s **Griffith Jones** of Llanddowror had set up an innovative system of 'Circulating Schools'. Peripatetic teachers travelled the country teaching children to read during the daytime and adults to read at night. It is estimated that over a period of 25 years around 250,000 Welsh people were educated in these schools. His achievements became the envy of all Europe, and Catherine the Great of Russia sent envoys to Wales to study his methods. Although Jones' main concern was with the spread of religion rather than increasing literacy rates, he played a vital role in making the people of Wales literate in Welsh.

Thomas Charles developed the idea of setting up Sunday schools. By the middle of the nineteenth century, Wales had become a 'Nonconformist country'. The majority of the population were Methodists or belonged to one of the many Dissenting churches. The established Church came to be regarded as the church for the English and the gentry, while the chapels attracted the Welsh people. Nonconformity became a Welsh establishment in its own right, it spread literacy amongst the common people and opened the way for democratic ideas. To some extent, Methodism was seen as a means of protesting against the traditional dominance of squire and parson. Many leading liberals and political orators were Nonconformists and the movement influenced the liberalism which, as seen in Unit 8, would dominate Welsh politics for many years. The extent to which religion influenced politics is illustrated in the 1881 Sunday Closing Act, prohibiting the Sunday opening of pubs. This Act remained in force in parts of Wales until the early 1980s. Methodism in Wales peaked in the period 1904–5 when there was a great spiritual revival.

Industrial Revolution

The coming of industrialization changed the face of Wales for ever. Until the nineteenth century, agriculture formed the basis of the Welsh economy. Most Welshmen relied on agriculture for their livelihood, whether directly as farmers, or indirectly as craftsmen supplying farmers with farm implements and household goods. There was some industry in Wales, but it was on a small scale and contributed little to the wealth of the country. The most important was the woollen manufacturing industry in mid Wales and the lead-mining industry of northern Ceredigion and north-east Wales. Both these industries declined during the Industrial Revolution. In contrast, the iron, copper and coal industries embarked on a period of massive expansion. Society was basically rural in nature and the population was evenly distributed throughout the counties of Wales. There were few towns and these were mainly market centres such as Carmarthen and Tregaron, or ports such as Swansea. Rural society was divided into two unequal sections: a small number of powerful and influential rich landowners and a large number of poor owner-occupiers or tenant farmers. The roads were in poor condition and no new ones had been built in Wales since Roman times. The most important event in rural Wales was the market or fair day, when farmers travelled to town to sell their produce. Cattle and sheep were bought by drovers, who transported hundreds of animals to England to be fattened and then slaughtered. Fairs and markets were also held on festivals such as May Day and All Saints' Day. One of the activities consisted of the holding of mock trials of which the *ceffyl pren* (the wooden horse) was the most famous. In this trial, the unfortunate victim was carried on a wooden pole or ladder to the sound of beating drums.

The rapid industrialization of Wales began with the remarkable growth of the iron industry in south Wales when new techniques increased production. Parts of Wales were rich in both coal and iron. Wales became a vital part of the British economy in the nineteenth century: her coal fuelled commercial steam shipping, her iron was in London Bridge, Swansea produced half of the world's copper by the middle of the century and Llanelli was the tin plate capital of Britain. Wales also produced slate, alcam, silver, and eventually steel in the second half of the century when iron had given way. At the height of industrialization, the whole of Wales seemed to be channelling produce to the south; ponies were sent from Llanybydder in west Wales to work in the coal mines of the south, and the woollen mills of mid and west Wales produced flannel shirts for the miners.

One result of the increasing industrialization was the vast improvement in communication networks in Wales. Roads, canals and railways were built to bring the coal from the south Wales valleys to the ports of Newport and Cardiff. Thomas Telford constructed a road (the A5) which ran through Snowdonia and crossed the Menai Strait by means of a suspension bridge. The opening in 1841 of the Taff Vale railway, a crucial link between Cardiff and Merthyr Tydfil, led to growth for Cardiff as an important dockland town. Improved lines of communication to aid the transportation of produce led to greater social mobility, which gradually eroded the isolation of communities.

The population increased dramatically: in 1801, the four towns of Cardiff, Swansea, Merthyr Tydfil and Newport had only a population of 18,000 between them, by 1921, their combined total was 530,000. The manufacturing industry became more profitable than the traditional agricultural economy and industrial towns grew while the rural scene began to change. Many people left the countryside to work in the industrial areas of the south and most of the country's population was concentrated in the south. At beginning of the nineteenth century, 80 per cent of the Welsh people lived in rural areas but by 1911 only 20 per cent of the population resided there, such was the shift to the industrialized south east.

As the Industrial Revolution gathered momentum, Nonconformity too won greater support in the new communities of south Wales. The first religious census held in England and Wales, in March 1851, showed that nearly 80 per cent of the Welsh people were Nonconformists.

The population explosion resulted in an increase in the poverty of the lower orders of society who often lived in appalling conditions in shanty towns. The old system of parish relief broke down and industrial workers showed their discontent with appalling social conditions in a variety of ways. At the beginning of the century, the most common expression of discontent was a riot or demonstration. Later, workers became organized and formed secret organizations. The most important movement in the south-east was that of the 'Scotch Cattle', who targeted unscrupulous managers and profiteers, and who ensured workers stayed out on strike by intimidation. The 'Scotch Cattle' were gangs of men who would visit the home of strike-breakers disguised by masks or blackened faces and sometimes wearing cattle skins. Furniture would be destroyed and the strike-breaker threatened. They also employed many of their earlier rural traditions such as the *ceffyl pren* in a bid to ensure obedience. Intimidation was seen by many as the only way to ensure solidarity in an age when Trade Unions were forbidden by law. Serious violence broke out in Merthyr Tydfil in 1831, then the biggest town in Wales. Iron and coal workers took over the town for five days and raised the 'red flag' (a sheet soaked in the blood of a calf) of revolution, perhaps for the first time in Britain. In a pitched battle between the protestors and soldiers outside the Castle Inn in August 1831, about two dozen men, women and children were killed when the soldiers opened fire on the crowd. The Merthyr Rising also created the first working class martyr when **Richard Lewis** (Dic Penderyn) was executed for riotous assault and for injuring a soldier. Lewis died protesting his innocence and years later another man confessed to the crime. After a failed Chartist attack on Newport in south Wales in 1839, militancy gave way to Liberalism, the leading force in Welsh politics until the 1930s.

Recent past

The 1880s proved to be something of a turning point in Welsh political life. The Reform Act of 1884 gave the vote to labourers and the number of voters in the Welsh seats increased from 74,936 to 200,373. Wales was dominated by the Liberal party and in 1906 every seat in Wales returned a Liberal with the exception of Merthyr, which elected **Keir Hardie** of the Labour Representative Committee. The predominance of Liberals and Welsh politicians such as **David Lloyd George** (see Unit 8), **Tom Ellis** and **Herbert Lewis** made a new, Welsh presence felt in British politics. These politicians were able to influence Parliament to pass specific bills relating to Wales which reflected their Nonconformity and Liberalism. The Welsh Sunday Closing Act of 1881 mentioned earlier and the Welsh Intermediate Education Act of 1889 are two such examples.

Industrialization continued apace and a distinctive society emerged in the coalfield valleys of the south. Housing was poor, overcrowding common and poverty and ill health rife. Many were attracted to Socialism, particularly during the period between the two wars, and a number of Welshmen went off to fight against Fascism in the Spanish Civil War.

The outbreak of the Second World War helped to raise prosperity in Wales when munitions factories were built near the coalfields. After the war, the workforce found work in the new industries established in Wales attracted by government grants and low-interest loans. Demand for steel expanded and the steel works at Port Talbot became the largest in Europe.

Much of post-war political life was dominated by demands for home rule. Clement Attlee, who during the war had supported 'complete autonomy for Wales' in response to the wishes of his own party in Wales, later opposed home rule in any form. **Aneurin Bevan**, whose career is outlined in Unit 8, became a leading figure in the post-war Labour government. An all-party 'Parliament for Wales' campaign and the forwarding of a home rule bill by Labour MP for Merthyr Tydfil, **S. O. Davies,** helped push the government to set up a Welsh office and a Secretary of State for Wales.

During the 1950s, attentions turned to the issue of flooding Welsh valleys to provide water for England. In 1952, left-wing nationalists blew up a pipeline at the Claerwen dam in mid Wales, which supplied the city of Birmingham. Despite the many protests, the village of Capel Celyn, in the Tryweryn Valley in north Wales was flooded to provide water for Liverpool.

Recession had hit Wales during the 1930s but by the mid 1950s, Wales had almost full employment. However the 1960s also witnessed more and more pit closures followed by a decline in the steel industry and by 1966 most of Wales was classified a 'development area' relying on direct central government.

Cymdeithas yr Iaith Gymraeg, the Welsh Language Society (see Unit 2), was founded in 1962 and demanded official status for the Welsh language. Peaceful demonstrations were held and a campaign of direct action followed. English-only road signs were painted over, selected property damaged, TV transmissions sabotaged and then demonstrations, sit-ins and the occupation of public buildings organized. In 1979, a devolution referendum was held during the administration of Jim Callaghan but Wales voted by a large majority against the proposed devolution. The economic problems intensified during the 1970s and culminated in the bitter miner's strike of 1984. On the 19 November 1998, the UK Parliament passed the Government of Wales Act, making a devolved Welsh Assembly legal and constitutional (see Unit 8). The new Assembly has fired the imagination of many people in Wales who have become inspired with a new confidence. Time alone will tell if their confidence is well placed.

Flora and fauna

Skomer Island, the largest of the islands off the Pembrokeshire coast, is one of the most important seabird breeding sites in southern Britain and is a National Nature Reserve. It also boasts the world's largest population of Manx shearwaters, some 140,000 pairs. Other seabirds nesting on the Welsh coast include the storm petrel, guillemot, puffin, the rare chough, wheateaters, oystercatchers and lesser black-backed gull. Grey seals, porpoises and dolphins are present in the waters around Wales, which include Marine Nature Reserves. It has been calculated that a third of the world's population of grey seals are found around the Pembrokeshire islands and coast.

Wild inland birds and animals native to Wales include the forked-tailed red kite (*Milvus milvus*). This spectacular bird was almost hunted out of extinction; by 1905 only five birds remained, but it is now relatively common, particularly in mid Wales.

Red kite

A type of white trout, *gwyniad*, is found only in the depths of Bala Lake, whilst the British black adder is now only to be seen in Cors Caron. The polecat and pine marten are also on the increase. According to the old Welsh laws, marten fur could only be worn by kings.

Although Wales is home to several acres of ancient woodland, including the Pengelli Forest in Pembrokeshire, many of the ancient woodlands of Wales have long since vanished to provide timber or agricultural land. Vast areas of Wales are now dominated by conifer forests planted for commercial use, which create a dense canopy, smothering the native forest flora,

Snowdon lily

although wild oaks, yew and beech still remain in isolated thickets throughout the country. There are moves afoot to restore the ancient woodlands to their former glory by woodland conservation charities like *Coed Cymru*. There are some species of flower in Wales that are not found anywhere else in Britain. Among the rare alpine plants found in Snowdonia is the Snowdon lily (*Lloydia serontia*), found only in Snowdonia. The bright yellow Welsh poppy can also sometimes be seen in mountainous areas.

Among domesticated species, the most common in Wales is the sheep, which far outnumbers humans; Wales is home to 1 per cent of the human population of the European Union but has 15 per cent of its sheep. There is a multitude of Welsh breeds, one of the more ancient and rare is the *Dafad Rhiw* (Rhiw sheep), which lives only in the Rhiw area of Llŷn and which would probably now be extinct were it not for the efforts of a group of the few remaining breeders who founded a society dedicated to the preservation of the breed in the 1970s. The most numerous and successful is the hardy Welsh Mountain Sheep which can withstand most extremes of the Welsh climate. The most unpopular sheep, at least in the south Wales valleys, is the 'South Walian fighting sheep' which has been interbreeding on roadside verges for generations and descends into the towns and villages at night wreaking havoc, particularly with dustbins. This hardy beast is even rumoured to have mastered the skill of crossing cattle grids by running full pelt at the grid, rolling into a ball at the last minute and then rolling over to enjoy pastures new.

The horse has always been important in Welsh culture and was revered in Celtic literature. There are two important Welsh breeds, the nimble Mountain Pony, which is sold worldwide, and the sturdy Cob. Welsh Black Cattle, descended from the cattle of the pre-Roman era, used to be the prime stock of Welsh farmers. For centuries they were herded along the old drover roads into England for sale, a trade which led to the formation of the first commercial bank in Britain, the Welsh Bank of the Black Ox which later became Lloyd's Bank. Although Welsh Blacks were once a common sight in Wales, they are now outnumbered by species such as the Fresian and Charolais, which were introduced from Europe.

The *corgi* (which translates as 'dwarf dog' in English) was bred short to aid the drovers in herding cattle. It is close to the ground so as to nip the ankles of the cattle whilst avoiding their kicks. The corgi is an extremely old breed and is considered to be one of the more intelligent canine breeds. The English royal family has kept corgis since the days of George VI. One of the best known dogs in Wales is Swansea Jack, a retriever who saved the lives of many in the waters of Swansea Docks in the 1930s. Today Swansea Jack is commemorated by a carved stone on the Swansea waterfront.

GLOSSARY

Geography

mynydd (m.)	*mountain*
mynyddoedd (pl.)	*mountains*
Cymru (f.)	*Wales*
arfordir (m.)	*coast*
rhostir (m.)	*moor*
cwm (m.)	*valley*
bryn (m.)	*hill*
parc cenedlaethol	*national park*
amaethyddiaeth (f.)	*agriculture*
afon (f.)	*river*
llyn (m.)	*lake*
ynys (f.)	*island*

History

rhyfel (f.)	*war*
gwlad (f.)	*country*
trigolion (pl.)	*inhabitants*
Celtiaid (pl.)	*Celts*
goresgynwyr (pl.)	*invaders*
castell (m.)	*castle*
cestyll (pl.)	*castles*
tywysog (m.)	*prince*
diwydiant (m.)	*industry*
Anghydffurfiaeth (f.)	*Nonconformity*
cynulliad (m.)	*assembly*

Flora and fauna

barcut (m.)	*kite*
coedwig (f.)	*wood*
dafad (f.)	*sheep*

Taking it further

Reading

Regions and geography of Wales

Condry, William, *Welsh Country Essays* (Llandysul: 1996)

Howe, G. Melvyn & Thomas, Peter, *Welsh Landforms and Scenery* (London: 1963)

History of Wales

Davies, John, *The History of Wales* (London: 1993)

Gregory, Donald, *Wales Before 1536 – a Guide* (Capel Garman: 1995)

Gregory, Donald, *Wales After 1536 – a Guide* (Capel Garman: 1995)

Hume I, and Pryce, W. (eds.), *The Welsh and Their Country* (Llandysul: 1986)

Jenkins, Philip, *A History of Modern Wales 1536–1990* (London: 1992)

Jones, J. Graham, *The History of Wales* (Cardiff: 1998)

Morris, Jan, *The Matter of Wales* (Harmondsworth: 1984)

Rees, W., *A Historical Atlas of Wales* (Cardiff: 1951)

Williams, Gwyn A., *When Was Wales?* (London: 1985)

Websites

If you have Internet access, you might find these sites useful:

www.britannia.com/celtic/wales/index.html

www.data-wales.co.uk/

www.walesdirectory.co.uk/

02

the Welsh language

In this unit you will learn about
- the history of Welsh
- Welsh in education
- characteristics of the language
- regional variations and dialects
- Welsh in the world
- the Welsh language today

Welsh is the oldest surviving language in Britain, with a history extending over fifteen centuries. It is spoken by over half a million speakers in Wales, around 20 per cent of the population. Welsh is also spoken by unknown numbers in England, the United States of America, Australia and other parts of the world, and by a small bilingual Welsh–Spanish community which was established in Patagonia (in the Chubut province of Argentina) in 1865 (see Unit 12). The Welsh originally called themselves *Brython* or *Brythoniaid* (British), and later, after the invasions of Germanic tribes, *Cymry*, which means 'comrades' or 'fellow-countrymen'. *Cymraeg* is the Welsh language, *Cymru* is Wales, *Cymro* a Welshman and *Cymraes* a Welshwoman. The same '*cym*' element survives in the related form Cumberland, the former name of the county in northern England now called Cumbria. The English words 'Welsh' and 'Wales' derive from a Germanic name for foreigners or for people who have been influenced by the culture of the Roman Empire; there are similar related forms in parts of the old Roman Empire which bordered on the lands of Germanic speakers – the *Walloons* in Belgium, the *Valais* in Switzerland and the *Welsch* of the Italian Tyrol.

The origins of Welsh

Welsh, like most of the languages in modern Western Europe, is an Indo-European language, a language descended from the language now termed 'Indo-European', which was spoken on the steppes of central Asia about 6,000 years ago. As the Indo-European speakers migrated to different parts of Europe and Asia, Indo-European evolved into separate languages. Linguists divide Indo-European into nine different branches e.g. Germanic (to which German, English, Swedish and Norwegian belong) and Italic (to which Italian, French and Spanish belong). The Welsh language belongs to the Celtic branch; the other surviving Celtic languages of Europe are Breton, Irish, Scottish Gaelic, Cornish and Manx, all spoken by communities on the western edge of Europe. The latter two are at present being revived by small but enthusiastic groups of devotees.

The Brythonic language

The Welsh language is derived from the Brythonic form of Celtic (also called British or Brittonic), a language spoken by the Britons who lived in mainland Britain before the coming of the Angles, Saxons and Jutes in the fourth and fifth centuries AD.

Scottish and Irish Gaelic and the Manx language descend from a different form of Celtic, namely Goedelic or Q-Celtic. The closest relatives of Welsh are the other P-Celtic languages, Cornish and Breton, which are also descendants of Brythonic. The distinction between the p- and q- languages is that the Goedelic languages kept the initial Indo-European *kw-* sound (originally written 'q', and now 'c'), while in the Brythonic languages, the *–kw* developed into a *p*. For example, in Irish, the word for 'head' is *ceann*, while in Welsh, 'head' is *pen*. Although there are many words in the Celtic languages today which are very similar, the spoken Celtic languages today are not really mutually intelligible.

Examples of similar words in the modern Celtic languages

Welsh	Breton	Irish	Scots Gaelic
tŷ (house)	*ti*	*teach*	*tigh*
ci (dog)	*ci*	*cu*	*cu*
du (black)	*du*	*dubh*	*dubh*

The history of Welsh

The evolution of Welsh from Brythonic is believed to have occurred by about AD 600. Many of the Latin words, estimated to be around 1,000 in number, which had been absorbed into the Brythonic language during the time of the Roman occupation, are still present in the Welsh of today, including *pysgod* (fish – from the Latin '*piscis*'), *llyfr* (book – from the latin '*liber*'), and *eglwys* (church – from the Latin '*ecclesia*'), cf. French *église*. These borrowed words indicate that Wales during the Roman era was a bilingual country and that Romans and Britons co-existed on relatively peaceful terms thus allowing for a mixture of cultures.

Early and Old Welsh

Conventionally 'Early Welsh' is used to describe the language of Wales, which was in use until around 850, examples of which only survive today in a few inscriptions and notes written on the side of pages in manuscript. One important example of an Early Welsh inscription can be seen in the parish church of Tywyn in Meirionnydd, north Wales. Not many examples of 'Old Welsh', the language of Wales between the ninth and eleventh centuries, survive today. One such example is the twenty-three line *Computus Fragment*, written in about AD 920 and now preserved in the Cambridge University Library. The fragment discusses methods of recording the movements of the moon thus providing evidence that Welsh was being used in the tenth century to discuss 'scientific' topics.

Middle Welsh

Old Welsh evolved into Middle Welsh in the years after 1100 and the term Middle Welsh is used to describe the language spoken from the twelfth to the fourteenth centuries. Welsh had evolved into the language of learning and culture in Wales. Latin religious texts, including biblical passages, were translated into Welsh. The surviving manuscripts of the laws of Hywel Dda date from this period and are proof of a rich legal vocabulary in Welsh during the period. Even after Wales lost its independence in 1282, and Welsh law was supplanted by English, Welsh continued to be used widely in legal texts, and even the Statute of Rhuddlan (see Unit 1) was translated into Welsh. Most of the manuscripts we have of the *Mabinogi* (see Unit 3) date from this period, although the stories themselves are older, having been passed orally down the generations by storytellers. Welsh was also the language of poetry and was used to pen the intricate poems of the *Gogynfeirdd*, or fairly early poets whose work is described in Unit 3. Despite the influx of French and then English speakers from 1066 onwards, Wales remained a predominantly Welsh-speaking country throughout the Middle Ages.

Early Modern Welsh

The poetry of Dafydd ap Gwilym (see Unit 3) is an example of Early Modern Welsh, a term used to describe the language from about the fourteenth to the sixteenth century. This period witnessed a flowering of the arts through the medium of Welsh, including the concise praise poetry of the *Beirdd yr Uchelwyr* (Poets of the Gentry) described in Unit 3, whose work has been judged by some as being the most linguistically intricate in Europe at the time. Although legal documents in Welsh survive from this period, English increasingly became the language of official documents in Wales and the Welsh gentry began to realize that learning English was advantageous. When Henry VII ascended the throne in 1485, therefore, the English language was already playing a dominant role in officialdom in Wales.

The Act of Union 1536

According to the Act of Union:

> ...no personne or personnes that use the Welsshe speche or langage shall have or enjoy any manor, office or fees within the Realme of Englonde, Wales or other of the Kinges dominions upon peyn of forfaitin the same offices or fees unless he or they use and exercise the speech or langage of Englisshe.

This Act, which was the first to refer to the Welsh language, laid down that English should be the only language of the courts in Wales, and that the use of Welsh would debar one from contributing to the administration of the country. Its explicit intention was to get rid of the differences between Wales and England thus creating a uniform administrative system run by a Welsh ruling class fluent in English. Mastery of English was the only way for a Welsh noble to get on in life and they became increasingly assimilated into the English ruling class through education – most went to English public schools and intermarried. One early manifestation of the English influence in Wales was the abandonment of traditional Welsh patronymics ('*ap*' (son of), e.g. Rhisiart ap Hywel) in favour of a fixed surname in the English fashion (see Unit 11). Bishop Rowland Lee, president of the Council of Wales from 1534, tired of the number of 'aps' on juries, ordered the deletion of *ap* and the introduction of English surnames. The surname ap Hywel became Powell, the surname ap Rhys, Price. The Anglicization of the gentry was virtually complete by the eighteenth century and had profound implications for the Welsh language and Welsh literature. Welsh poets were professional, dependent on the patronage of the gentry, the Welsh they used in their poetry was understood by all Welsh speakers throughout Wales. When this system collapsed, it seemed likely that Welsh, having no official status within the country, and not being the medium of official documentation or literature, would deteriorate into a collection of dialects spoken by the peasantry, craftsmen, artisans and other members of the lower orders.

The translation of the Bible

In the event, the danger to the Welsh language was averted by the Protestant Reformation. It was the desire for Welsh speakers to gain access to the new religion that prompted **Sir John Price** of Brecon, in 1547, to publish *Yn y lhyvfyr hwn* (see Unit 3), which included instructions on how to read Welsh as well as religious tracts. Protestantism placed great emphasis on the use of the native languages as the language of worship, which meant, as far as Wales was concerned, that English would be the language heard from the pulpit. However, partly because of governmental fears that Wales would remain Catholic, thus providing a sympathetic back door through which Catholic nations like Spain could invade Britain were religious material not to be provided in a language understood by the majority of the population, an Act was passed in 1563 commanding that Welsh translations of the Bible and the Prayer Book be available by 1567. This task was undertaken by **William Salesbury** (see Unit 3). In 1567 the Prayer Book and New Testament were translated into Welsh with the whole Bible following in 1588.

The translation and publication of the Bible in Welsh in 1588 by **Bishop William Morgan** was something of a turning point for the language. Morgan's adoption of the exalted linguistic standards of the poets and other writers of the Middle Ages meant that his style and vocabulary were highly literary and, even when published, the language of the Welsh Bible was markedly different from spoken Welsh. The Bible in Welsh provided a model of correct and majestic Welsh and introduced the beginnings of a standardized national language based on the speech of the north and north-west of Wales, Morgan's birthplace. The difference between this standardized language and the spoken language was to widen greatly over the following centuries.

Welsh, although excluded from state administration, returned as the language of worship in Welsh churches. This was to play a crucial role in both preserving the language and spreading religious zeal. Welsh was the only one of the non-state languages of Europe to become the medium of a published Bible less than a century after the Protestant Reformation and was alone amongst the Celtic languages in succeeding in bridging the gap between the oral and manuscript traditions of the Middle Ages and the printed word of the modern period.

The sixteenth century was also to witness a 'learning renaissance' in Wales, as in other parts of Europe. A great number of books were published by authors intent on demonstrating the richness of the language and its suitability as a medium of learning and religion. William Salesbury, as well as providing the translation of the New Testament, also published a collection of Welsh proverbs and a Welsh–English dictionary.

Gruffydd Robert, a Welsh Catholic exile in Milan, published the first grammar book written in Welsh.

The eighteenth-century revivals: the spread of literacy

Throughout the seventeenth century, although not the language of high culture, Welsh had been used to advance religious knowledge amongst the Welsh-speaking population of Wales. This continued into the eighteenth century when **Griffith Jones** established his circulating schools, which succeeded in educating 250,000 people, a figure representing over half the population of Wales. Griffith Jones' efforts played a vital role in making many of the people of Wales literate in Welsh.

The Methodist revival

Religion strengthened the position of the Welsh language; during the Methodist revival, the powerful sermons of preachers like **Daniel Rowland**, whose open-air preaching drew thousands from all corners of Wales, created a tradition of religious oratory in Wales. A standard spoken Welsh emerged because of the need of the itinerant Methodist preachers to be understood in all parts of Wales; this standard Welsh later became known as *Cymraeg y pulpud* (pulpit Welsh) and Welsh became the language of all the Methodist administration.

National revival

During the eighteenth century, a national revival was attempted by restoring Wales' ancient history and literature. Druids became fashionable and the Welsh poets were portrayed as being the heirs of the druids. Spurious theories about the origins of Welsh abounded; according to one theory, the Welsh language had been in existence before the Tower of Babel. Another popular theory expounded by the Breton Paul-Yves Pezron was that the Welsh people were descended from Gomer, the grandson of Noah. All the revivals of the eighteenth century gave Welsh an enhanced reputation and stimulated interest in the Welsh language and literature.

Welsh in the industrial age

As well as having an impact on the Welsh economy, the Industrial Revolution also transformed the Welsh language.

Welsh had success in becoming the language of an urban society as Welsh-speaking people moved from rural areas into the towns. By 1851, large numbers of Welsh speakers lived in the towns enjoying activities in Welsh which had not been possible in the sparsely populated rural areas. Many cultural societies were established, as well as choirs and debating societies. Eisteddfodau were held regularly and the publishing of Welsh material multiplied. Welsh started to become the medium of mass communication with the publication of Welsh newpapers and chronicles discussing religion and politics.

New words were coined to meet the needs of the new age, including *cyngerdd* (concert), *pwyllgor* (committee) and *cyfrifoldeb* (responsibility). One of the men chiefly responsible for the new words was **William Owen Pughe** who wrote a grammar book based on his theory that grammar books should not describe a language as it is, but as it ought to be. His grammar book consisted of a new spelling system for Welsh and a new set of verbs and plurals to eliminate irregularity in the language. He also sought to introduce logic into noun gender!

The tide, however, was beginning to turn against Welsh as more and more people migrated to Wales and more and more Welsh speakers began to view Welsh as the language of religion and the hearth and English as the language of every other sphere.

According to the prominent nineteenth-century Welsh industrialist, **David Davies**:

> If you wish to continue to eat barley bread and lie on straw mattresses, then keep on shouting *'bydded i'r Gymraeg fyw am byth'* (May the Welsh language live forever – the chorus of the National Anthem), but if you want to eat white bread and roast beef, you must learn English!

The Treason of the Blue Books

In 1846 an inspection was carried out of Welsh-speaking Nonconformist schools, by three English barristers and Anglican assistants. Their report became know as *Brad y Llyfrau Gleision* (The Treason of the Blue Books) as it labelled standards in the schools as deplorable, and laid the blame for the state of Welsh schools on the Welsh tongue, 'the language of slavery'. According to the report, the language had produced 'no Welsh literature worthy of the name'. As well as criticizing the dirtiness, laziness, ignorance, superstition, and immorality of the Welsh, the report stated, 'The Welsh language is a ...

manifold barrier to the moral progress and commercial prosperity of the people. It is not best to over-estimate its evil effects.'

Attitudes to education

By 1847, only three out of 1,656 day schools in Wales taught any Welsh and in 1852, the Inspector of Schools announced that it was 'socially and politically desirable' that the language be erased. In some schools, a board called the 'Welsh Not' was hung around the necks of children caught speaking Welsh at school. The 1870 Education Act made the English school system compulsory in Wales and, were it not for the Sunday schools, it is possible that many children in Wales would not have been literate in Welsh at all.

Paradoxically, as the use of Welsh declined in elementary schools, the Celtic languages were deemed to be worthy of academic study. The college at Aberystwyth, which opened its doors in 1872, created a chair of Welsh in

'Welsh Not'

1875. Other Welsh colleges also created departments, an important development in the history of the language.

The twentieth century

Wales lost a generation of young Welsh-speaking men through the carnage of the First World War. The post-war depression in agriculture and industry prompted many Welsh people to migrate, mainly to England. This trend continued throughout the century with many young Welsh speakers leaving Wales to enjoy better employment prospects elsewhere. From the end of the twentieth century to the present day, the relatively cheap housing in Wales, particularly in rural Wales, has attracted a wave of incomers, mainly from the south-east of England, leading to the Anglicization of rural life. In the north and west in particular, second homes are seen as a major threat in previously dominant Welsh-speaking villages. Tourism has also been blamed for the decline in the language (see Unit 10). By the 1961 census, only a quarter of the population spoke Welsh.

Education

Slowly, education became available in Welsh, with Welsh-medium schools being established from the 1940s onwards. These schools proved popular with both first language Welsh speakers and non-Welsh speaking children. This was associated with the growth in Welsh-medium nursery education, much of which was provided by *Mudiad Ysgolion Meithrin*, the nursery school movement which is described in Unit 9. Welsh-language schools now exist in most areas and Welsh has also become the medium of instruction in some courses in universities and further education colleges.

Language legislation

Inspired by a speech on the future of the Welsh-language entitled *Tynged yr Iaith* (the fate of the language) given by J. Saunders Lewis and broadcast by the BBC in 1962, *Cymdeithas yr Iaith Gymraeg* (the Welsh Language Society) campaigned using non-violent means of civil disobedience for changes in the status of Welsh. *Tynged yr Iaith* had called for the use of 'revolutionary methods' to preserve the language, and the society forced the English Parliament to pass the Welsh Language Act in 1967. This gave equal status to the Welsh language for the first time since 1536. The Act of 1967 permitted the use of Welsh in courts, giving the right to trial in Welsh or interpretation where appropriate, and made contracts drawn in the Welsh language equally enforceable with those drawn in English. Welsh was also allowed on official documents. A further Act passed in 1993 gave people in Wales the right to deal with public bodies in Welsh. *Bwrdd yr Iaith* (the Welsh Language Board), is charged, amongst other things, with developing and overseeing the implementation of Welsh language schemes by organizations in the public sector. Every official form and document available in English must also be available in Welsh. The obligations of this Act do not extend to the private sector, but some private sector businesses are responding positively to the Act.

Culture

The twentieth century saw an inevitable decline in Welsh publications as the cost of printing rose and readership declined. English daily newspapers became increasingly popular, as did American and English films. The popular monthly Welsh-language community newspapers, *papurau bro* (see Unit 7), are heavily subsidised by the government, as is most Welsh-language activity. In 1922, *Urdd Gobaith Cymru*, the Welsh League of Youth, was founded with the aim of attracting the young to the language (see Unit 10). In 1952, the National Eisteddfod (see Unit 5), which had evolved into one of the pillars of the Welsh language culture, became formally a Welsh-language institution.

Language campaigns

Cymdeithas yr Iaith Gymraeg is also responsible for many of the symbols which have made the Welsh language a natural part of public life in the last half of the twentieth century. Their campaign painting over English words on road signs led to the government introducing bilingual road signs. After considerable public pressure, *Radio Cymru* and the Welsh language television channel *Sianel Pedwar Cymru*, which transmits Welsh during peak hours, were established (see pp. 134–6). New words were coined by television presenters, in particular the sports commentator Eic Davies, who is responsible for many of the sporting terms now used in the media.

What of the Welsh language itself?

The Welsh language is heard as harsh by some ears, mainly because of the 'ch' and 'll' sounds (see Pronunciation guide), while others think it tuneful.

Mutation

A grammatical feature of Welsh (and all other Celtic languages) is the fact that the first consonant of a word may change according to certain grammatical conditions; this change is called 'mutation'. There are three sets of mutation in Welsh: soft, nasal, and aspirate. Visitors to Wales are greeted with a bilingual sign '*Croeso i Gymru*/Welcome to Wales'. The word *Cymru* (Wales) has been mutated softly because it follows 'i' (to), which causes all words following it to mutate softly. Mutations are dealt with in full detail in *Teach Yourself Welsh* and *Teach Yourself Welsh Dictionary*.

Table of mutations

Original Consonant	Soft	Nasal	Aspirate
c	g	ngh	ch
p	b	mh	ph
t	d	nh	th
g	*disappears*	ng	
b	f	m	
d	dd	n	
m	f		
ll	l		
rh	rh		

Mutations in practice

The word *o* (from) causes the soft mutation, so 'from Pontypridd' is '*o Bontypridd*'.

The word *yn* (in) causes the nasal mutation, so 'in Talybont' would be '*yn Nhalybont*'.

The word *a* (and) causes the aspirate mutation, therefore 'and Caernarfon' in Welsh is '*a Chaernarfon*'.

Nouns

Welsh nouns have two genders (masculine and feminine):

Masculine noun: *bachgen* (boy)
Feminine noun: *merch* (girl)

and there are seven different ways of forming the plurals of nouns. Most nouns form their plural by adding an ending:

merched (girls)

but not all nouns form their plurals in this way:

bechgyn (boys)

When learning Welsh, the gender and plural of a word should be learnt at the same time as the word itself. The adjective normally follows the noun:

bachgen da – good boy (*da* = good)

The singular noun is used after the numeral: *tri bachgen* (three boys). The traditional method of counting is based on the number twenty:

un ar ddeg ar hugain = 31 (literally one on ten on twenty) and this is the method of counting used today in time and dates, but there is a growing tendency to adopt the decimal system:

tri deg un = 31 (literally three tens and one)

Word order

The normal word order of a Welsh sentence is verb–subject–object:

Verb	Subject	Object
Tynnodd	*Gethin*	*y llun*

(Gethin drew the picture)

Regional variation

Despite the influence of publication and, in the twentieth century, of broadcasting, there remain substantial differences of dialect between parts of Wales. Regional variation affects the pronunciation, vocabulary and to some extent the grammar of Welsh. Traditionally the principal identifiable dialects are the *Wyndodeg* (Vendotian, of the north-west), *Powyseg* (of the north-east and mid Wales), *Dyfydeg* (Demetian, of the south-west), and *Gwenhwyseg* (of Gwent and Morgannwg in the south-east), however it is common practice to speak of regional variations as being between the Welsh spoken in north Wales and that spoken in south Wales.

Vocabulary

South Wales	North Wales	
tad-cu	*taid*	grandfather
allwedd	*agoriad*	key
llaeth	*llefrith*	milk

See *Teach Yourself Welsh* for further examples.

Wenglish

Wenglish is the name given to the dialect of English spoken in Wales, particularly south Wales. Many of the idiosyncrasies of Wenglish can be traced to the grammar or vocabulary of the

Welsh language. One of the characteristics is bringing verbs to the beginning of a sentence, particularly for emphasis:

Laughed at me he did

Pronunciation

The vowel 'u' is pronounced differently in north and south Wales. In the south, 'u' is pronounced as in the English word 'pin', whereas in the north, the sound is produced by lifting the middle of the tongue towards the roof of the mouth. There is no similar sound to this in English, but it is similar to the French 'u'.

Welsh in the world

Argentina

Welsh has had a modest presence in South America for over a century, ever since a group of Welsh people established a colony in Patagonia on land allotted to them by the government of Argentina. You can read more about the history of the colony on pp. 225–6. Among their reasons for emigrating was the desire to preserve the Welsh language. The language of Parliament, the chapels, the law, and the colony's cultural life was Welsh. Only Welsh school books were used, at a time when the use of Welsh was forbidden in schools in Wales. Bank notes were also printed in Welsh. *Y Dravod*, the newspaper of the Welsh community in Patagonia, was established in 1891 and appeared weekly until 1961 when it became a fortnightly publication, and then a publication that appeared at irregular intervals. The dominance of Welsh was weakened during the early decades of the twentieth century when the Welsh colony's economic success began to attract immigrants from Spain and Italy. Gaiman is considered to be the most Welsh town in Patagonia. There are estimated to be around 5,000 Welsh language speakers living in Patagonia, many of whom are elderly. There is a desire to learn the language amongst the young, and Welsh-language classes are held there, some taught by teachers sponsored by the British Council as part of their initiative to bolster the Welsh language and culture in Chubut Province.

Patagonian Welsh

The Welsh language in Patagonia is a fusion of features from dialects in Wales; it is not uncommon to hear Welsh speakers in

Patagonia using words from both north Wales and south Wales. Spanish influence can be discerned in pronunciation as well as vocabulary; for example, Spanish *sobrino, sobrina* regularly occur for *nai, nith* (nephew, niece).

English influence on the Welsh language

A large number of English words have been absorbed into the Welsh vocabulary, and there is a tendency amongst some Welsh speakers to use English words, particularly nouns and verbs, in Welsh speech. There are growing concerns within some quarters in Wales about the growing use of *bratiaith* or 'debased language' not only amongst the young in Anglicized areas, but also in the media. *Bratiaith* can be defined as a form of Welsh that not only contains extensive English words, but also English idiom and sentence constructions; whole English sentences are often imported into *bratiaith*. An example of *bratiaith* would be the use of the phrase:

dod i fyny gyda syniad

which is a literal translation of the English 'to come up with an idea', instead of the Welsh '*cynnig syniad*'.

Some Welsh words have also been adopted by English: apart from the obvious examples like **coracle** (see p. 200), **corgi,** and **eisteddfod,** we can also add words like **car,** originally a type of chariot which entered English via Latin.

Learning Welsh

It is estimated that there are thousands of people learning Welsh both inside and outside Wales. The University of Wales specializes in Wlpan classes, intensive courses for beginners originally used to teach Hebrew to Jewish immigrants to Israel. The University of Wales providers also specialize in advanced courses for experienced learners. Most Local Authorities in Wales also provide Welsh classes at various levels. Wales has a full-time residential Welsh Language and Heritage Centre at Nant Gwrtheyrn which was opened in 1982. *CYD* (pronounced 'keed'), a national organization with its central office in Aberystwyth, was set up to help people who are learning Welsh by integrating them into the local Welsh-speaking community. Local groups organize various events to help people practise their Welsh in a less formal atmosphere than a class.

The Welsh language today

The Welsh language today would seem, in some respects, to be in a strong position. Visible signs that Wales is a bilingual country are everywhere, from street signs to official forms. The language is used widely on TV and radio: *Pobol y Cwm*, a soap opera, has been running for 30 years and is watched by half of all Welsh speakers. Welsh has a distinct youth culture and Welsh education is on the increase, especially in Anglicized south Wales where a significant number of parents want their children educated entirely through the medium of Welsh. The are also calls for a Welsh-medium college. New vocabulary had been added and is continually being added, e.g. *meicrodon* (microwave) and *sgrîn ben-glin* (laptop). The Welsh language has risen to the challenge of new technologies and has a presence on the internet, the BBC publishes its new broadcasts in Real Audio and has a Welsh language edition of their online news service. There is a digital Welsh language channel. This very visibility of Welsh, particularly on the heavily subsidized Welsh TV channel, has led to a bitterness amongst some non-Welsh speakers and resentment that Welsh speakers are allotted too many of the resources of the country.

Welsh speakers

According to the latest figures, there is a slight increase in the number of those speaking Welsh who are under 14. For the first time since 1891, when a question on language was included on the census form, knowledge of the Welsh language is more widespread amongst children than it is amongst the population as a whole and virtually all children at primary level in Wales have some Welsh lessons. The 2001 census revealed that 16.3 per cent of the population can speak, read or write Welsh, up from 13.6 percent in 1991. Around 28 per cent have some knowledge of Welsh, with the number of speakers estimated to be at least 20.5 per cent – the highest proportion since 1961. Also on the increase is the number of Welsh speakers now living in Wales who were not born there. Many of the 12 per cent of Welsh speakers who were not born in Wales have learned Welsh either through self-study courses such as *Teach Yourself Welsh* or by attending classes.

However, the only areas where substantial proportions of the population speak Welsh are in the west and north-west of Wales, but there is a growing threat to these areas, namely the mobility of people in modern times. In the 2001 census, only 69 per cent of the population of Gwynedd, a traditional stronghold of the Welsh language, were born in Wales. Rural depopulation, emigration, a powerful English language media, increasing facilities for transport and communication, tourism, mixed-language marriages and low social prestige have all contributed and are contributing to the decline in Welsh. A key priority in the revival strategy has been to strengthen Welsh as a community language: raising the profile and facilitating the use of the language locally, causing new activities to be organized, and coordinating existing activities. This has mainly been the responsibility of the *mentrau iaith* or language initiatives.

Welsh, however, remains a language in crisis. The proportion of children being brought up with Welsh as their mother tongue is declining. There are doubts as to the impact that legislation can have. The language is no longer the only clear symbol of Welsh ethnic identity due to the rise of specific Welsh institutions: The University of Wales (established 1872), the National Museum of Wales (established 1907), the National Assembly for Wales (established 1999) etc. so some people fear that the language will be sidelined when, for example, the Welsh Assembly has to decide priorities. In a 2002 Policy Statement, the Assembly declared its commitment to the creation of a bilingual Wales and the revitalization of the Welsh language. A member of the Cabinet, the Minister for Culture, Welsh Language and Sport, has responsiblity for the Welsh language, as well as all the other languages of Wales. The revival of a language, however, is an expensive operation and the long-term prospects look bleak for a language without a large centralized community of speakers, and surrounded by a pervasive Anglo-American culture. Though perhaps, after decades of English influence, the miracle is that it was not swallowed without trace centuries ago.

GLOSSARY	
iaith (f.)	*language*
yr iaith Gymraeg	*the Welsh language*
tafodiaith (f.)	*dialect*
siarad	*to speak*
siaradwr (m.)	*speaker*
dwyieithog	*bilingual*
dylanwad (m.)	*influence*
geirfa (f.)	*vocabulary*
gramadeg (m.)	*grammar*

enw (m.)	noun
ansoddair (m.)	adjective
berf (f.)	verb
treigladau (pl.)	mutations
iaith safonol	standard language
Seisnigeiddio	Anglicization
lluosog	plural
unigol	singular
cyfieithu	to translate
brawddeg (f.)	sentence
cyfathrebu	to communicate
Llydaweg (f.)	Breton
Gwyddeleg (f.)	Irish
Cernyweg (f.)	Cornish
Manaweg (f.)	Manx
Gaeleg (f.)	Gaelic
llythrennedd (m.)	literacy
ymgychu	to campaign
ynganu	to pronounce
Dych chi'n siarad Cymraeg?	Do you speak Welsh?
Dw i'n dysgu Cymraeg	I'm learning Welsh
Sut dych chi'n ynganu...?	How do you pronounce...?

Taking it Further

Reading

Aitchison, J. W. and Carter, H., *The Welsh Language 1961–1981. An Interpretative Atlas* (Cardiff: 1985)

Aitchison, J. W. and Carter, H., *A Geography of the Welsh Language 1961–1991* (Cardiff: 1994)

Andrews, J. A. and Henshaw, L. G., *The Welsh Language and the Courts* (Aberystwyth: 1984)

Davies, Janet, *The Welsh Language* (Cardiff: 1993)

Price, Glanville (ed.) *The Celtic Connection* (Bucks: 1992)

Stephens, Meic (ed.), *The Welsh Language Today,* (Llandysul: 1976)

Saunders, Lewis, 'The Fate of the Language', can be read in translation in *Planet*, 4:13–27.

Learning Welsh

Brake, Julie and Jones, Christine, *Teach Yourself Welsh* (London: 2003)

Lewis, Edwin, *Teach Yourself Welsh Dictionary* (London: 2004)

The **Welsh Books Council** publishes a free catalogue of Welsh language materials for learners every year. Copies are available from: Welsh Books Council, Castell Brychan, Aberystwyth, Ceredigion SY23 2JB; tel: 01970 624151; e-mail: castellbrychan@cllc.org.uk.

The website **www.gwales.com** can be used to check the availability of books and to place orders with Welsh bookshops.

ACEN produce a wide range of learning materials as well as an online beginners' course. For a free catalogue of materials contact: Acen, Tŷ Ifor, 1 Stryd y Bont, Cardiff CF10 2EE; Tel: 02920 300 808; website: **www.acen.co.uk**

The **Welsh Language and Heritage Centre** at Nant Gwrtheyrn in north Wales offers residential courses for all standards all year round. For further details contact: Welsh Language and Heritage Centre, Nant Gwrtheyrn, Llithfaen, Pwllheli, Gwynedd LL53 6PA; tel: 01758 750334; e-mail: nantgwr@aol.com; **www.nantgwr.com**

Cymdeithas Madog, The Welsh Studies Institute in North America, Inc., holds an annual week-long Welsh course. Details can be obtained from Norah Hogoboom, Secretary, Cymdeithas Madog, 27131 NE Miller St, Duvall, WA 98019 USA; e-mail: secretary@madog.org. The Cymdeithas Madog website also offers a number of services for learners including a lending library: **www.madog.org**

Websites

If you have internet access and wish to learn Welsh you will find these sites invaluable:

www.e-addysg.com
contains on-line Welsh courses for beginners and intermediate students and an on-line dictionary

www.bbc.co.uk/wales/learnwelsh
for free online learning materials

www.gwybodiadur.co.uk
a very useful site containing descriptions and reviews of the various dictionaries, grammars etc. available to learners as well as regularly updated information on courses etc.

www.cs.brown.edu/fun/welsh/home.html
a free online Welsh course, spell checker and dictionary.

Further information on the Welsh Language Project in Patagonia is to be found on **www.britishcouncil.org/wales**

Cymru'r Byd – the Welsh language Internet newspaper – can be accessed on **www.bbc.co.uk/cymru**

For information on courses throughout Wales call: Welsh for Adults helpline: 0871 230 0017 **iaith@galw.org**

See also the website: **http:www.elwa.ac.uk**

Watching and listening

Satellite TV has made S4C Digidol available throughout the UK via a dish and the Sky Digital box: channel 104 in Wales, channel 184 in the rest of Britain. The majority of programmes in Welsh carry English subtitles and Welsh subtitles are also available on 889.

BBC Radio Cymru is broadcast world wide on the Internet: **www.bbc.co.uk/radio**

Social events

CYD promotes social activities for Welsh-learners and native speakers in the community and publishes a magazine for its members. For details of local branches contact: CYD Office, 10 Maes Lowri, Aberystwyth, Ceredigion SY23 2AU; tel: 01970 622143.

03

the literature of wales

In this unit you will learn about
- 15 centuries of Welsh literature
- Welsh writing in English

Welsh literature is one of the oldest living literatures in Europe, spanning a period of fifteen centuries. Whilst this long and rich tradition of literature through the medium of Welsh continues to flourish, Wales is of course a country of two languages. As a result of increasing English dominance, the twentieth century saw the emergence and gradual development of a body of writing known as Welsh writing in English. Although many of these early English-language works were not particularly 'Welsh' in outlook, recent writers frequently reflect a sense of nationhood and of Welsh identity, comparable to that of their Welsh-speaking counterparts.

Welsh literature has been called 'the most complete expression of the Welsh mind through the ages'. Many consider it to be the major achievement of the Welsh nation and even nowadays, within Wales, the poet or author appears to be more highly respected than the artist or even the musician.

The sixth to ninth centuries: the origins of Welsh literature

The earliest texts

Much of our early Welsh poetry was actually composed on the borders of England and Scotland! The poet **Taliesin** (late sixth century) was based in the Welsh-speaking kingdom of Rheged (around Carlisle) and his contemporary **Aneirin** (late sixth century), in the Welsh-speaking kingdom of Gododdin (around Edinburgh). They are known as the *Cynfeirdd* (early poets) and their poems can be found in two medieval manuscripts, the *Book of Taliesin* (1350) and the *Book of Aneirin* (1250).

No one knows exactly who Taliesin was, but his earliest poem, dated approximately AD 580, is addressed to Cynan Garwyn, king of Powys in mid Wales. He later moved to the area known as the Old North and became the chief poet of Urien, king of Rheged. In his nine short poems to Urien and his son Owain, he praises Urien for the way he looks after his people both on and off the battlefield. Taliesin's description of the ideal ruler, generous at home and furious in battle, was one which poets made every effort to copy for centuries afterwards. The remainder of the *Book of Taliesin* consists of two other poems attributed to Taliesin and sung to Gwallawg, the leader of the kingdom of Elfed around Leeds, along with a mixture of religious, prophetic and mystical verse by a variety of unknown authors.

Aneirin is the author of a long poem known as *The Gododdin*, which describes how King Mynyddawg Mwynfawr sent 300 of his best soldiers to regain Catterick from the English. There are however no references to this battle in historical sources. The poem tells how they spent a year at Mynyddawg's court, feasting, drinking mead and improving their martial skills before setting off resplendent in all their finery.

The battle was a disaster – one verse states that three plus the poet returned, another says one plus the poet. Nevertheless the poem is not an elegy, instead it celebrates the commitment of these lords to their king. They willingly paid for the hospitality they had received from Mynyddawg with their lives. The mead became their poison, but like true heroes they remained brave and loyal to the end.

Canu Llywarch Hen

The next two centuries were particularly turbulent ones in the history of Wales, as the Welsh were pushed further and further westwards behind Offa's Dyke. Little literature has survived from this period, but the ninth and tenth centuries saw the growth of what is known as saga poetry, based on legends about the past. The three groups of poems known collectively as *Canu Llywarch Hen* (Song of Llywarch the Old) do not tell the story of the events on which they are based, but are dramatic speeches by those involved. Some academics are of the opinion that the prose elements were lost over time. The main figure in the first two group of poems is **Llywarch Hen,** a historical character from the sixth century. Particularly in the second cycle of poems, we see the anonymous poet questioning the nature of war, heroism and cowardice. Maybe the men of the Gododdin were not so wise after all.

The final group of three-lined verses concerns **Heledd.** Once again, although the poems are in the first person, she is not the author. Heledd was the last member of the seventh-century royal family of Powys and here she laments the burning of her home, the destruction of Powys and the death of the King, her brother Cynddylan. Her feelings are clearly conveyed in *Stafell Cynddylan* (The Hall of Cynddylan), where she blames herself not only for the loss of her brother, but for the destruction of Powys. Throughout the cycles runs the belief that fate controls our life and that pride will inevitably lead to a fall.

Medieval Welsh literature

The Mabinogion

This collection of eleven stories preserved in the *White Book of Rhydderch* (c.1350) and the *Red Book of Hergest* (c.1400) is considered by many to be the greatest treasure of Welsh literature and Wales' greatest contribution to European literature. The word *Mabinogion* was adopted by Charlotte Guest as the title of her translation of the tales published in 1846. The first four tales are known as the Four Branches of the *Mabinogi*, a term originally meaning boyhood. These four tales are rather tenuously linked to each other through the character of Pryderi, who is born in the first and dies in the last. Similarity in style suggests that these four tales may have been written by the same author, possibly a cleric from south-west Wales, in the latter half of the eleventh century.

The first branch, which is possibly the most well known, describes three episodes in the life of Pwyll, Lord of Dyfed in south-west Wales. In the first he changes places with Arawn, King of the Underworld, for a year. The second episode is his marriage to Rhiannon and the third is the birth and disappearance of their son Pryderi. Rhiannon is accused of murdering Pryderi and made to sit every day outside the gate to tell her story to passers-by and to offer to carry guests on her back to court. After some years Pryderi is found and Rhiannon reinstated. Pryderi grows up and on Pwyll's death becomes Lord of Dyfed.

The second branch relates the story of the marriage of Branwen, sister of Brân, King of Britain, to Matholwch, King of Ireland. The topic of the third is the marriage between Manawyden, another of Branwen's brothers and Rhiannon, mother of Pryderi, following the death of Pwyll. The last branch is about the family of Dôn in north Wales. King Math will die unless his feet are kept in the lap of a virgin, except for when he is away fighting. In all of the stories, meetings with supernatural characters act as catalysts for much of the action and the central theme in each case is how the mortal characters respond to them.

The other surviving tales are very different in style and pace to the Four Branches. They are:

1 Culhwch and Olwen – the oldest Arthurian legend in any language

2 The Dream of Rhonabwy
3 The Dream of Macsen Wledig
4 Lludd and Llefelys

And the Three Romances

1 Geraint son of Erbin
2 Owain or the Lady of the Fountain
3 Peredur son of Efrawg

which deal with the education of the ideal knight and the tensions and conflict that this can bring.

Lives of the Welsh saints

Another substantial body of literature from this period in Welsh and Latin are the 'Lives of the Saints' written to promote particular churches. For example *Buchedd Dewi* (Life of St David) was written by **Rhygyfarch** (1056?–99) in approximately 1094 to demonstrate David's superiority and to defend and protect the independence of his diocese from encroachment by Canterbury and the Normans.

The poets of the princes

A considerable amount of poetry was produced between the eleventh and thirteenth centuries by poets attached to the courts of independent Welsh princes. They were highly trained professionals whose importance and status were recognized by the laws of Hywel Dda (see Unit 1). The chief bard, who had a special chair in court, was called a *pencerdd* (head-of-song) and was expected to sing two poems – one to God, the other to the King. The poems of these court poets, or *Gogynfeirdd* (not so early poets) as they are also known, are ornate and complicated; a lot of emphasis is put on the use of rhyme, alliteration and archaic words.

The earliest of these poets was **Meilyr Brydydd** (fl.1100–37) who was *pencerdd* to Gruffudd ap Cynan, king of Gwynedd. Other significant poets of the period include **Cynddelw Brydydd Mawr** (fl.1155–95) and **Bleddyn Fardd** (fl.1258–84). **Gruffudd ab yr Ynad Coch's** (fl.1277–82) elegy to Llywelyn ap Gruffudd, the last independent Prince of Wales (see Unit 1), is the most well-known poem of the period. In this powerful poem the poet conveys not only his tremendous sorrow, but also the anguish and sense of despair and loss felt by the whole of Wales at the death of Llywelyn.

The poets of the gentry

With the demise of the independent princes, the native gentry *(uchelwyr)* took over as patrons of the poets. The status of the poets declined considerably as the gentry could not afford to maintain them on a permanent basis and they were forced to travel around from hall to hall.

One particularly significant development during this period was the introduction of the *cywydd* metre, which is based on seven-syllable rhyming couplets. This was much simpler than the *awdl* previously used and gave the poets more flexibility. During the fourteenth century *cynghanedd* became a compulsory element of each line. There are four main types of *cynghanedd*, all of which depend either on internal rhyme, the corresponding of consonants in the beginning and end of a line, or a combination of both. For example, in the case of *cynghanedd groes* each line is split in two, with each half containing the same consonants in the same order prior to the final stress, which is generally on the penultimate syllable.

> *brasgámu* / *brysiog ýmaith* (stride hurriedly away)
> br sg   br s g

One of the first to use the *cywydd* was **Iolo Goch** (c.1325–c.98) who sang to a variety of patrons including Owain Glyndŵr whose career is detailed in Unit 1. *Cynghanedd* is unique to Welsh and still used extensively today.

Dafydd ap Gwilym

Dafydd ap Gwilym (fl.1315/20–1350/70) is generally considered the greatest Welsh medieval poet – if not the greatest Welsh poet of any period. He was born near Aberystwyth to a noble family and is buried in Strata Florida Abbey near Tregaron. Around 150 of his poems have survived, some are religious and others are poems praising his patron Ifor Hael, but the vast majority are love poems in the *cywydd* metre. He did much to develop the use of this new form and to assimilate many European literary influences into the native tradition. His poetry contains elements of courtly love as found in the poetry of the Provençal minstrels or troubadours.

The two women found in the majority of his love poems are Morfudd and Dyddgu, who are known to have been real women. Dark haired Dyddgu is a wise and beautiful unobtainable aristocrat. Fair-haired Morfudd is also a noble woman, whose love affair with Dafydd continues after her marriage to a local merchant nicknamed *Y Bwa Bach* (the Little Hunchback). The poems tell of the various obstacles preventing him from being with her. Nature plays an important role in all these love poems and Dafydd frequently sends wild animals and birds as love messengers.

It is the personal element in Dafydd's poems that make them so effective and different to the more formal, objective poems of the court poets. He tells us of his own feelings and experiences and is willing to poke fun at himself. The *cywydd* entitled *Trafferth mewn Tafarn* (Trouble in a Tavern) shows Dafydd's self-satire at its best. In this poem he seduces a girl at an inn and arranges to visit her room in the night when everyone is asleep. However, he trips up over a stool and bangs his head on a table that has on it a basin and copper pan. The table falls over and the noise wakes up three Englishmen, who think somebody is stealing their things. Dafydd sneaks back to bed and begs God for forgiveness.

Dafydd ap Gwilym has been called many things from innovator, to rebel, to the Charlie Chaplin of his time. The one thing he can not be called is a typical representative of fourteenth- and fifteenth-century verse. Other poets, such as **Tudur Aled** (c.1465–1525), tended to follow the more conservative approach of Iolo Goch.

Gwerful Mechain

Female *cywyddwyr* are few and far between – Gwerful Mechain (fl.1462–1500) is the only one to have left us with a large corpus of verse. Little is known about her except that she came from Powys. She wrote much erotic verse, but her religious poems, particularly her *cywydd* on the sufferings of Christ, are considered her best works, along with a spirited defence of women, in reply to an attack by a fellow poet.

Renaissance literature

The Act of Union of 1536 described in Unit 1 heralded a new era in Welsh literature. Many of the gentry left Wales for pastures new, particularly London, thereby depriving the poets still further of their patronage. At the same time, as the Renaissance swept through Europe, with its emphasis on Greek and Latin and religious literature, many felt that the Welsh language was in danger of being left behind.

Sir John Price

As noted in Unit 2, the first to publish a book in Welsh was Sir John Price. Like most of the Protestants of the time, he was keen to educate everyday folk both spiritually and morally and his collection of basic religious texts such as the Lord's Prayer and the Ten Commandments was published in 1547 under the title *Yn y lhyvyr hwnn* (In this Book).

William Salesbury

The true pioneer of publishing in Welsh however was William Salesbury (c.1520–84). It is thanks to his foresight and vision that the Welsh language survived and developed. He could see that if it were to encompass the ideas of the Renaissance, the Welsh language would need to be enriched and improved. To this effect he produced works such as *A Dictionary in Englyshe and Welshe* (1547) and *Oll Synnwyr Pen kembero Ygyd* (All the wisdom of a Welshman's mind brought together) in the same year, which was a collection of proverbs showing the wealth of wisdom to be found in the Welsh language.

The translation of the Bible

Salesbury was also the first to realize the need to translate the Bible into Welsh if the language was to have any status. In 1551 he published *Kynniver Llith a Bann*, the Epistles and Gospels of the Book of Common Prayer. In 1563 a law was passed ordering that the Bible and Book of Common Prayer be translated into Welsh and in 1567 the *Book of Common Prayer* and the *New Testament* were published. Salesbury was the sole translator of the *Book of Common Prayer*, but **Bishop Richard Davies** (1501?–81) and **Thomas Huet** translated certain books of the *New Testament*.

Unfortunately Salesbury's translations did not live up to expectations, in that he laid great importance on showing the Latin derivation of words and used many archaic forms, so that both the *New Testament* and the *Book of Common Prayer* could only be read by scholars of the language.

The first complete translation of the Bible was made by **William Morgan** (1545-1604) and published in 1588. He adopted the majority of Salesbury's translation of the *New Testament*, but also standardized the spelling, basing his language on the language of the poets. This translation proved a vital link ensuring the continuity of the literary language from the Middle

Ages through to the present day. Some say that the Bible single-handedly saved the Welsh language.

Only minor alterations were made in the revised edition of **Dr John Davies** (c.1567-1644) of Mallwyd in 1620. This was the version generally used in all churches and chapels until 1988, when a new, modern version was launched entitled *Y Beibl Cymraeg Newydd*.

William Morgan, translator of the Welsh Bible

Other humanist writers

Whilst the Bible was the crown of the Renaissance in Wales, there were other important Welsh writers during the period, such as the Catholic exile **Gruffydd Robert** (pre-1532–post-1598). The first part of his Welsh grammar was published in Milan in 1567 and the remainder in 1584. He felt that the language of the poets was too formal and conservative and **Edmund Prys** (1543/44–1623), an amateur poet and relative of Salesbury, was one who took up this cause. The exchange of 54 *cywyddau* between Prys and the professional traditional poet **William Cynwal** (d.1587/8) shows clearly the clash between the old and new ideals.

The seventeenth and eighteenth centuries

Owing to the negative attitudes of many of the traditional poets, the seventeenth century in Wales is a particularly flat period from a literary point of view. The most prolific and talented poet was **Huw Morys** (1622–1709), whose carols and love poems developed the use of *cynghanedd* in free verse.

This century also saw the growth of folk poetry, *hen benillion*, reflecting day-to-day aspects of rural life, frequently sung to the accompaniment of the harp. They are all anonymous, but many are composed from a female viewpoint, suggesting that women preferred the freedom provided by these free metre verses, as opposed to the more constrictive strict metered *cywydd* form.

Morgan Llwyd

The most accomplished seventeenth-century prose writer was Morgan Llwyd (1619–59). He was one of the first to write books in Welsh, rather than translate them from other languages. His most important work, *Llyfr y Tri Aderyn* (The Book of the Three Birds) written in 1653 is considered a classic of Welsh literature. It is a dialogue between an eagle, representing the Government and Oliver Cromwell, a dove, representing the Puritan saints and a raven representing the Church of England.

Ellis Wynne

Another important writer who straddles the seventeenth and eighteenth centuries is **Ellis Wynne** (1671–1734). His best-known work *Gweledigaethau y Bardd Cwsc* (Visions of the Sleeping Bard) was published in 1703. It was based on an English translation of Quevedo's *Visions of Hell*, but became an important work in its own right. In his vivid satire he targets those whom he considers to be sinners, namely doctors, lawyers, vain women, Catholics and Quakers, as they progress through the world to death and finally to hell.

Ballads and almanacs

One of the appealing aspects of Ellis Wynne's work is his use of local dialect, which adds colour to his graphic descriptions. This use of simpler Welsh is also seen in the ballads and almanacs, which became popular during the early eighteenth century as a result of the growth in the number of printing presses. Peddlers in fairs and markets would sell dramatic stories of shipwrecks and murders, religious poems, and crude love songs. The *anterliwt* (interlude) which was a sort of morality play in verse, was also very popular and performed by groups of touring amateurs. There were usually two main characters, a Miser and a Fool. The Fool would carry a large phallic-looking instrument to shock the women in the audience! **Twm o'r Nant** (1730–1810) was one of the foremost Welsh interlude writers, who because of the lack of drama in Wales at the time, gained the somewhat exaggerated title of 'Cambrian Shakespeare'.

Goronwy Owen

One who was particularly scathing of this new interest in folk literature was Goronwy Owen (1723–69). He was one of the main poets of the classical revival of the eighteenth century, which emphasized art and learning above romanticism. His great ambition was to compose an epic and his *cywydd* entitled *Dydd y Farn* (Day of Judgement) was much copied. His finest poems however are those of a more personal nature such as his *cywydd* in praise of his native Anglesey or his elegy on the death of his daughter Elin.

Iolo Morganwg

Iolo Morganwg (1747–1826), a prolific poet and keen promoter of ancient Welsh history, organized a Druidic *Gorsedd* or assembly in London in 1792. In 1819 the *Gorsedd* officially became part of the Eisteddfod (see Unit 5) and has remained so ever since, even though it has now been proved that the bardic degrees suggested by Iolo and the prayers used in the ceremonies were all part of his vivid imagination. Many poems said to be by Dafydd ap Gwilym and 'discovered' by Iolo in local manuscripts have also found to be forgeries. He felt that Glamorganshire, his birthplace, deserved a rich literary history and he was determined to provide it with one!

The Methodist revival

Howell Harris (1714–73) and **Daniel Rowland** (1713–90) began the Methodist movement in Wales in 1735 and in 1737 **William Williams** (1717–91) from Carmarthenshire became converted to their cause. Williams Pantycelyn, as he is best known, is considered amongst the most significant of Welsh writers, in that through his works he helped ordinary people understand Methodism and live by its beliefs. He wrote 1,000 hymns, 71 of them in English. They are simple and straightforward; each one comes across as an expression of his own personal experiences. All emphasize the need to turn away from worldly things towards Christ. Ironically the best known of his English hymns *Guide me o thou Great Jehovah* is now sung regularly at international rugby matches.

The other great eighteenth-century Welsh hymn writer was **Anne Griffiths** (1776–1805) who died shortly after childbirth at the early age of 29. Following her death, her hymns were written down by her maid's husband. They are love songs, full of vivid images and metaphors, reflecting a clear knowledge of the Bible and the beliefs of the Nonconformists. *Rhyfedd, Rhyfedd gan Angylion* (Wonderful, Wonderful in the Sight of Angels) has been described as one of the greatest religious poems in any language.

The nineteenth century

By the nineteenth century, Nonconformity was no longer a radical force, but rather a social institution which dominated all aspects of Welsh culture, including its literature. Preachers and ministers were now the leaders of society and they disapproved of the interludes and the folk verses and these were gradually replaced by hymns and religious biographies.

Some poets such as **Alun** (John Blackwell, 1797–1841) and **Ceiriog** (John Ceiriog Hughes, 1832–87) continued to write on lighter themes and although their works are not rated particularly highly today, they were very popular at the time. Ceiriog worked in England for many years and his poems sentimentally portray Wales as a rural idyll. Unfortunately when he did eventually return, the reality of Welsh rural life was a great disappointment to him and he ended up turning to alcohol for comfort.

Islwyn

In the poetry of Islwyn (William Thomas, 1832–78) romanticism and religion are combined. The death of his fiancée Anne Bowen led him to write the epic *Y Storm* (The Storm) in which he tries to find an answer to the tragedies of life. The shadow of Anne haunted him always and although he later married Martha Davies, he is said to have said on his deathbed: ' thank you, Martha, for all you did for me. You have been very kind. I am going to Anne now'.

The growth of the Welsh novel

Owing to the high status of poetry and the negative attitudes of the Nonconformists towards fiction, the novel was slow to develop in Welsh. **Gwilym Hiraethog** (William Rees, 1802–83) adapted *Uncle Tom's Cabin* into Welsh and several others tried copying English authors such as Dickens with little success. The first to fully realize the potential of the novel was **Daniel Owen** (1836–95). Owing to the popularity of biographies, his first major work *Rhys Lewis* (1885) is the fictitious autobiography of Rhys Lewis, minister of Bethel. *Enoc Huws* (1891), his satirical account of the life of a grocer, is generally considered his finest novel. The story centres on the mystery identity of the grocer's father who turns out to be the roguish Capten Trefor, one of Owen's greatest creations.

Plot construction, however, was not Daniel Owen's strong point! His novels are long-winded and contain many amazing coincidences. Nevertheless this fault was not totally of his making, in that the stories were first printed as serials in magazines, where a somewhat directionless episodic construction was more acceptable. As with Dickens, his strength lay in showing what society was really like and displaying people how they really were. He made great use of irony and satirical comedy and even today he remains unequalled in Welsh literature as an observer of character and society.

The twentieth century

Early twentieth-century poets

The early twentieth century saw a rejection of the moral and cultural standards of the previous century, particularly in the case of poets such as **T. Gwynn Jones** (1871–1949), **R. Williams Parry** (1884–1956) and **T.H. Parry-Williams** (1887–1975). T. Gwynn Jones won the prize for the best poem in a traditional metre at the National Eisteddfod in 1902 for a poem called *Ymadawiad Arthur* (The Passing of Arthur) based on Tennyson's *Morte d'Arthur*. This was the first of many poems based around Celtic myths which he wrote in *cynghanedd* and he is considered the foremost poet of his generation. He hated injustice and oppression and once described himself as 'a pacifist with an emphasis on the fist'.

R. Williams Parry was greatly influenced by T. Gwynn Jones. His poem entitled *Yr Haf* (Summer) which celebrates love and nature and the beauty of the moment was successful in the 1910 National Eisteddfod. As a result he became known as the 'The poet of summer', although he later rejects such romanticism. Many of his later works were inspired by the symbolic burning of the RAF Bombing School on the Llŷn Peninsula in 1936 by members of Plaid Cymru (see Unit 8). His two published collections are aptly entitled *Yr Haf a Cherddi Eraill* (Summer and other Poems, 1924) and *Cerddi'r Gaeaf* (The Poems of Winter, 1952).

T. H. Parry Williams, R. Williams Parry's cousin, introduced a new realism and a more natural style into Welsh poetry. He published collections of essays, sonnets and what he calls *rhigymau* (rhymes) which were deceptively simple rhyming couplets composed in everyday speech. The main themes in his writing are Snowdonia, especially the village of Rhyd-ddu where he was born, and his own family. His poems reflect both a scientific, analytical way of thinking as well as a strong emotional element. Such tensions can be seen clearly in one of his most well known poems entitled *Hon* (This Spot), which has become a classic expression of the ambiguous loyalties facing those born and living in Wales.

He was a conscientious objector during the First World War, and the disillusionment he felt with society at that time is reflected in many of his works, as is the way the natural environment shapes our personalities. Death features strongly in his poems, which frequently suggest a rejection of any meaning and purpose to life. He made a unique contribution to Welsh literature, both as the first 'modern' Welsh poet and as an essayist similar in style and nature to Proust.

The beginnings of Anglo-Welsh literature

Caradoc Evans (1878–1945) has been called the founding father of Anglo-Welsh literature or, as it is known today, Welsh writing in English. He wasn't the first to write in English about Wales, but he was the first to shatter the sentimental view of Wales as a rural paradise. His first collection of stories called *My People* (1915), depicts life in an imaginary village called Manteg and is based on the village in west Wales where he grew up. The volume was well received in England, but many Welsh readers called for it to be banned. It portrays the Welsh as greedy cheats and hypocrites living in squalor and is written in a strange mix of Biblical language and distorted Welsh translations. It attacks many cherished aspects of the 'Welsh way of life' such as the Eisteddfod (see Unit 5) and the chapels and was followed by two similar volumes.

Later in life Caradoc Evans wrote several novels and volumes of short stories, but *My People* remains his best known work. His influence on the next generation of Anglo-Welsh writers was considerable and led to a divide between the two literatures of Wales, with English being associated with hostility towards both the Welsh language and Nonconformity.

Saunders Lewis

One author who laid great emphasis on the Welshness of Welsh literature and who expressed particular concern about the dangers of English-writing in Wales was Saunders Lewis (1893–1985). He was one of the founders of Plaid Cymru in 1925 and joined the Catholic Church in 1932. In all his works he saw Wales as part of Europe and not just as an adjunct to England. Although, as explained in Unit 2, Saunders Lewis' lecture *Tynged yr Iaith* had great importance for the future of the Welsh language, it is as a dramatist that he is best remembered. *Blodeuwedd* (1948) is considered by many to be his greatest play. The theme here is the clash between love and lust as revealed in the character of Blodeuwedd, Lleu's unfaithful wife in the final branch of the Mabinogi. Blodeuwedd is seen as a symbol of present day Wales: rootless, superficial and lacking in any spiritual connections.

In the drama *Siwan* (1955) and his two novels, *Monica* (1931) and *Merch Gwern Hywel* (The Daughter of Gwern Hywel, 1964), he emphasizes that marital harmony is essential for the well-being of society as a whole. In later works, however, his vision of Wales becomes increasingly pessimistic and cynical, as in the play *Cymru Fydd* (Wales To Be, 1967).

Literature and the industrial south

One writer who did not attempt to idealize or sentimentalize Wales in any way was **D. Gwenallt Jones** (1899–1968). He was the first poet to take nationalism and Christianity seriously. His poems contain realistic, vivid images of the poverty of the industrial south Wales valleys and he puts much emphasis on man's sinful state, seeing the Depression as chiefly a spiritual crisis rather than purely an economic one. He published five volumes of poetry, the most important being his first, *Ysgubau'r Awen* (Sheaves of the Muse, 1939), and his third, *Eples* (Leaven, 1951).

Idris Davies (1905–53), who wrote mostly in English, shared Gwenallt's ability to incorporate the whole experience of an industrial community in his poems. *Gwalia Deserta* (1938) which depicts the effect of the Depression and *The Angry Summer* (1943) which discusses the Miners' Strike of 1926, are considered his best works. The pictures he paints are grim and his compassion for his fellow workers is clearly evident.

Many 'Anglo-Welsh' novelists also responded to the struggles and suffering facing these valley communities in the early part of the last century. *Rhondda Roundabout* (1934) written by **Jack Jones** (1884–1970) is considered the first industrial novel of the Depression. **Gwyn Jones** (b.1907) and **Gwyn Thomas** (1913–81) are two other English-language writers to have vividly described the reality of working-class life in south Wales at this time. Writing in Welsh, **J. Kitchener Davies** (1902–52) produced a play entitled *Cwm Glo* (Coal Valley) in 1935, which caused great controversy due to its frank treatment of immoral behaviour in the industrial south.

Possibly the most famous novel published by a Welsh writer in English is *How Green was my Valley*, written by **Richard Llewellyn** (1906–83) in 1939. It depicts an innocent, religious mining community destroyed by an influx of Irish and English settlers. Very much an idealized picture of valley life, it is almost fascist in its stress on racial purity, yet it contains some memorable scenes and characters. It became an instant bestseller and was made into a film in America the following year.

Kate Roberts

The industrial novel begins in Welsh in 1936 with the publication of *Traed mewn Cyffion* (Feet in Chains) by **Kate Roberts** (1891–1985). It tells of the history of four generations of a family based in the slate quarries of north Wales. Kate Roberts is generally regarded as the most distinguished Welsh-language prose writer of the last century. Her short stories and novels concentrate on the struggles of ordinary people, particularly women, and fall into two distinct periods, from 1925 to 1937 and from 1949 to 1981. Those from the second period are more introspective, material hardship is no longer such a problem, but emotional deprivation remains. A particularly good example of this is minister's wife Bet Jones, the main character in her short novel *Tywyll Heno* (Dark Tonight, 1962), who becomes mentally ill having lost her faith.

A lighter side of Kate Roberts' work is shown in her books for and about children, particularly *Te yn y Grug* (Tea in the Heather, 1959). In this collection of short stories, as in her other works, it is her characters that are her strength and whilst they belong to a particular time and place, readers from all generations are able to relate to them.

Dylan Thomas

Although many of the first wave of Anglo-Welsh writers were brought up in the industrial areas of the south, rural west Wales also became an inspiration for many, including the most famous of all Welsh poets writing in English, namely **Dylan Thomas** (1914–53). Dylan Thomas was born to Welsh-speaking parents in Swansea and published his first book, *Eighteen Poems*, at the age of 20. During the 1930s he rejected Wales, which he saw as unsophisticated and narrow-minded and went to live in London.

Towards the end of the Second World War, however, he returned to Wales, where he produced some of his greatest works. These include the poem *Fern Hill* (1945), which describes his childhood visits to his aunt's farm in the rural Carmarthenshire village of Llangain. In 1949 he moved to the Boat House in Laugharne and lived there for the last four years of his life. Whilst there, he wrote the humorous play *Under Milk Wood*. The play tells of life in the imaginary seaside town of Llareggub and is based on Laugharne and New Quay in Cardiganshire, where he lived between 1944 and 1945. (The word 'Llareggub' incidentally, is meant to be read backwards, but it was changed after his death to the less obvious 'Llaregyb'!)

Dylan Thomas' boat house

Dylan Thomas died after a heavy drinking session in New York in November 1953 and his body was brought back to Laugharne for burial. The Boat House later became a Dylan Thomas museum and in 1982 a memorial stone was placed in his honour in Poets' Corner in Westminster Abbey.

Modernism

During the 1950s modernism flourished in Wales and was particularly concerned with both spiritual and national renewal. Three poets who reflected this new modernism were **Euros Bowen** (1904–88), **Bobi Jones** (1926–) and **Waldo Williams** (1904–71). One of the most original poets writing in Welsh in the twentieth century, Waldo did not learn the language until the age of seven. He only published one volume entitled *Dail Pren* (Leaves of a Tree) in 1956. A conscientious objector during the Second World War and later a Quaker, his love of Wales, especially his native Pembrokeshire, features strongly in his works.

The development of the Welsh novel

During the mid-1940s the novels of **T. Rowland Hughes** (1903–49), set primarily in the slate quarries of north Wales, paved the way for **Islwyn Ffowc Elis** (1924–). His novel *Cysgod y Cryman* (The Shadow of the Sickle, 1953), which tells of life on a farm in mid Wales, was a milestone in the history of the Welsh novel due to its fresh and modern approach. A sequel was published in 1956. Islwyn Ffowc Elis was the first novelist to discuss the uncertainty of young people following the Second World War and the loss of traditional values and the desire to forge a new beginning. *Cysgod y Cryman* remains particularly popular – so much so that it was voted Welsh language book of the century in 2000.

The second flowering

Two writers who dominated Welsh writing in English during the second half of the twentieth century were the poet **R. S. Thomas** (1913–2000) and the novelist **Emyr Humphreys**, (1919–), both of whom learnt Welsh as adults. The early works of R. S. Thomas describe the hill farmers of Montgomeryshire, epitomized by the character Iago Prydderch. During the 1960s his poems became more nationalistic in content, with the decline in community spirit and the Welsh language of particular concern to him, along with the survival of Wales as a nation. His collection of religious poems *H'm* (1972) marks a change of direction, with the search for an absent God becoming a major preoccupation, although later volumes such as *No Truce with the Furies* (1995) contain several poignant personal poems. In 1996 he was nominated for the Nobel Prize for Literature.

Emyr Humphreys has produced over 20 novels, a collection of short stories and four volumes of poetry. He has also written many Welsh-language television dramas. His novels are based in the small towns and villages of mid and north Wales and as well as being extremely readable show a clear understanding of contemporary society. *Outside the House of Baal* (1965), which traces the life of a Nonconformist minister, J. T. Miles, is considered by many to be his greatest work. The novel presents a balanced and sympathetic picture of life in Nonconformist Wales, very different to that expressed by Caradoc Evans and earlier Welsh authors writing in English.

This second flowering of Welsh writing in English reached its peak during the 1960s, with the emergence of many new poets. The most nationalistic of these was **Harri Webb**, (1920–94). Other notable names include **John Tripp** (1927–86), **John Ormond** (1923–90) and **Dannie Abse** (1923–).

Welsh-language poetry today

Welsh strict-metre poetry also underwent a revival in the later part of the twentieth century. The revival was begun by rural poets such as **Dic Jones** (1934–) and developed by the likes of **Gerallt Lloyd Owen** (1944–), whose volume *Cerddi'r Cywilydd* (Poems of the Shame, 1972) was a scathing response to the investiture of the Prince of Wales in 1969. **Alan Llwyd** (1948–) is another who has done much to promote traditional metre poetry in recent years. A prolific poet, editor and critic, he also wrote the screenplay for the Oscar-nominated film *Hedd Wyn* in 1994.

The last 15 years have seen a further strict-metre poetry renaissance, with many poets such as **Myrddin ap Dafydd** (1956–) and **Iwan Llwyd** (1957–) regularly performing their poems. Their poems commemorate all aspects of community life as well as national and international events. Humour, often tongue in cheek, is particularly evident in the *cywyddau* of **Emyr Lewis** (1957–) and **Twm Morys** (1961–), son of renowned travel writer and historian, **Jan Morris** (1926–). In August 2000, **Mererid Hopwood** (1964–) became the first woman to win the prize in the National Eisteddfod for a poem in strict metre. She went on to win the Crown at the 2003 National Eisteddfod at Meifod near Welshpool.

In spite of her success however, women still tend to favour prose or free-metre poetry. **Menna Elfyn** (1951–) is Wales' best known feminist poet. Her work is experimental in style and content and is clearly influenced by American writers such as Sylvia Plath. She discusses contemporary issues from both a personal and political viewpoint. She is a firm believer in bringing Welsh poetry to a wider audience and frequently publishes her poems side by side with English translations as in *Cusan Dyn Dall* (A Blindman's Kiss, 2001).

Other well-known free verse poets writing in Welsh include **Gwyn Thomas** (1936–) and **Nesta Wyn Jones** (1946–). **Gwyneth Lewis** (1959–) writes in both Welsh and English, stating that it is the theme that dictates which language the poem should be written in.

English-medium poetry today

Poetry remains a popular form amongst those writing in English also. Nature, landscape, history and the family play an important role in the poetry of **Gillian Clarke** (1937–). For example, her long poem about her memories of her father, *The King of Britain's Daughter* (1993) is based on the legend of Branwen in the *Mabinogi*. She frequently uses characteristics borrowed from Welsh-language writing, such as the rhymes of the strict metre *cynghanedd*. Her *Collected Poems* was published in 1997.

Other significant Welsh poets writing in English today include **Tony Curtis** (1946–), **Peter Finch** (1947–), **Nigel Jenkins** (1949–) and **Sheenagh Pugh** (1950–). Many such as **Mike Jenkins** (1952–) and **Robert Minhinnick** (1952–) focus on the social injustices of life in a post-industrial, capitalist environment.

Novels today

One of the most impressive and unique novels to be published in Welsh since the Second World War is the largely autobiographical *Un Nos Ola Leuad* (One Moonlit Night, 1961*)*. Writing in the first person, the author **Caradog Prichard** (1904–80) tells of life in a deprived slate-quarrying village in north Wales, as seen by a madman reliving his childhood. It was made into a film in 1991.

The novels of Islwyn Ffowc Elis mentioned earlier inspired many new novelists in the sixties, especially women. Two of these were **Jane Edwards** (1938–) and **Eigra Lewis Roberts** (1939–). Jane Edwards tackles the psychological problems of middle-class life in novels such as *Bara Seguryd* (The Bread of Idleness, 1969) and *Cadno Rhos-y-ffin* (The Fox of Rhos-y-ffin, 1984). Eigra Lewis Roberts is more in the Kate Roberts mould, choosing to concentrate on characterization rather than plot. For example, her novel *Mis o Fehefin* (A June Month, 1980) describes the lives of those living in an ordinary street in north Wales during one particular month.

Rhiannon Davies Jones (1921–) and **Marion Eames** (1921–) are two of Wales' most prolific and accomplished Welsh-language authors of historical novels, whilst **Alexander Cordell** (1914–97) wrote many extremely popular, if highly romanticized, English novels about the growth of the industrial communities in south Wales. **William Owen Roberts'** (1960–) unconventional novel *Y Pla* (The Pestilence, 1987) presents a violent and disturbing picture of fourteenth-century Wales and explains how the plague paved the way for capitalism to replace feudalism.

One of the most innovative Welsh prose writers of the present time is **Robin Llywelyn** (1958–) whose novels make particular use of surrealism and fantasy. They are also full of subtle political comment. *O'r Harbwr Gwag i'r Cefnfor Gwyn* (From the Empty Harbour to the White Ocean, 1994) appears to be a tender love story, but can also be seen as a political fable.

Another new prose writer to use elements of fantasy and the unreal in his works is **Mihangel Morgan** (1955–). His characters are often eccentric, living on the edge of society. Irony, satire and humour play an important role in novels such as *Dan Gadarn Goncrit* (Beneath Firm Concrete, 1999) as well as his collections of short stories. To quote another novelist and critic, **John Rowlands** (1938–), 'He is the one who draws a moustache on the face of the Mona Lisa.'

Well known women prose writers writing in Welsh today include **Manon Rhys** (1948–), **Angharad Tomos** (1958–) and **Sonia Edwards** (1961–). Female and feminist issues naturally play an important role in their works, as is true of those women novelists writing in English such as **Siân James** (1932-) and **Catherine Merriman** (1949–). Their subject matter is often particularly hard hitting, as in the case of **Jennifer Rhead's** emotive and disturbing account of three days in the life of an abused young girl, *Y.T. and his holiness* (1998).

Sentimentality is also a thing of the past amongst English language male authors, with traditional themes often looked at in new ways, for example, *Shifts* (1988), **Christopher Meredith's**

(1954–) grim account of the closure of a Gwent steel works; *Glass Shot* (1991), **Duncan Bush's** (1946-) erotic psycho-thriller and *Cardiff Dead* (2000), **John Williams'** description of an ageing rock singer's return to home pastures.

GLOSSARY

awdur (m.)	*author*
awdures (f.)	*authoress*
nofelydd (m.)	*novelist*
llenor (m.)	*writer*
bardd (m.)	*poet*
dramodydd (m.)	*dramatist*
cyhoeddwr (m.)	*publisher*
ysgrifennu	*to write*
astudio	*to study*
darllen	*to read*
cyfansoddi	*to compose*
disgrifio	*to describe*
portreadu	*to portray*
dyfynnu	*to quote*
cyhoeddi	*to publish*
cyfieithu	*to translate*
gwaith (m.)	*work*
llenyddiaeth (f.)	*literature*
barddoniaeth (f.)	*poetry*
rhyddiaith (f.)	*prose*
Eingl-Gymreig	*Anglo-Welsh*
llyfr (m.)	*book*
nofel (f.)	*novel*
stori fer	*short story*
drama (f.)	*play*
cerdd (f.)	*poem*
canu caeth	*strict-metre poetry*
canu rhydd	*free-metre poetry*
chwedl (f.)	*tale*
pennill (m.)	*verse*
llinell (f.)	*line*
cynghanedd (f.)	*metrical consonance*
casgliad (m.)	*collection*
dyfyniad (m.)	*quotation*
crynodeb (m.)	*summary*
cymeriad (m.)	*character*
cyhoeddiad (m.)	*publication*

syniadau (pl.)	*ideas*
cynllun (m.)	*plot*
ystyr (m.)	*meaning*
arddull (m.)	*style*
rwy'n mwynhau	*I enjoy*
mae'n gas gyda fi	*I dislike*
mae'n well gyda fi	*I prefer*

Taking it further

Reading

General books

Brown, Tony (ed.), *The Dragon has Two Tongues* (Cardiff: 2001)

Eames, Marion, *A Private Language* (Llandysul: 1997)

Jarman A. O. H., *et al.* (eds.), *A Guide to Welsh Literature volumes 1–6* (Cardiff: 1976–2000)

Johnston, Dafydd, *The Literature of Wales* (Cardiff: 1994)

Jones, Glyn & Rowlands, John, *Profiles: A Visitors Guide to writing in Twentieth century Wales* (Llandysul: 1980)

Stephens, Meic (ed.), *The New Companion to the Literature of Wales* (Cardiff: 1998)

Texts and translations

Clancy, Joseph, *The World of Kate Roberts* (Philadelphia: 1991)

Conran, Tony, *Welsh Verse* (Bridgend: 1986)

Elfyn, Menna & Rowlands, John (eds.), *The Bloodaxe Book of Modern Welsh Poetry,* twentieth-century Welsh poetry in translation (Tarset: 2003)

Gallie, Menna, *Full Moon* (London: 1993)

Garlick, Raymond, & Mathias, Roland, *Anglo-Welsh Poetry 1480-1980* (Bridgend: 1984)

Jones, Gwyn, *The Oxford Book of Welsh Verse in English* (Oxford: 1977)

Jones, Gwyn, & Jones,Thomas, *The Mabinogion* – Everyman Classics Series (London: 1989)

Jones, Alun R. & Thomas, Gwyn, *Presenting Saunders Lewis* (Cardiff: 1983)

Jones, Gwyn, & Elis, Islwyn Ffowc, *Classic Welsh Short Stories* (Oxford: 1992)

Llywelyn, Robin, *From Empty Harbour to White Ocean* (Cardiff: 1996)

Richards, Alun, *New Penguin Book of Welsh Short Stories* (Harmondsworth: 1993)

Roberts, Elisabeth, *Pestilence* (London: 1991)

Magazines and journals
Golwg – a weekly Welsh-language magazine on the arts and current affairs in Wales.

Planet – a bi-monthly English-language journal covering the arts, culture and politics in Wales.

Poetry Wales – a quarterly English-medium poetry magazine.

New Welsh Review – a quarterly magazine which discusses Welsh writing in English, past and present.

Learners
If you are learning Welsh then you should find that the following two series of novels provide a useful introduction to Welsh literature, as both contain detailed explanatory notes and glossaries:

1 Jones, Christine, & Brake, J. (eds.), *Nofelau Nawr* (Llandysul: 1999–2003)

   This is a series of twelve short novels written especially for those who have only been learning Welsh for a short time. Authors include Mihangel Morgan and Sonia Edwards.

2 Davies, Basil (ed.), *Cam at y Cewri* (Llandysul: 1984–2003)

   This series, for the more advanced learner, contains abridged versions of well-known classics, a volume of short stories and a twentieth-century poetry anthology.

Websites

www.gwales.com provides information on over 15,000 English and Welsh language books which can be ordered from a bookshop of your choice.

www.e-addysg.com the Department of Welsh at the University of Wales, Lampeter, offers a number of accredited literary-based courses online. Subjects available include Early Welsh Literature, Arthur of the Welsh and the Welsh Saints.

04

art and architecture

In this unit you will learn about
- Welsh-subject and Welsh artists
- art organizations
- the story of Wales through architecture

There are now more artists, sculptors and craftsmen working in Wales than ever before and most towns boast at least one gallery. Nevertheless Wales cannot be said to possess a long artistic tradition: little indigenous art of quality can be found dating prior to the eighteenth century and even 30 and 40 years ago, many artists still tended to look towards England and the Continent for inspiration.

It is also true that some native artists described here, such as Augustus and Gwen John, had no great feeling for Wales. Others however, such as David Jones or Ceri Richards, both of whom lived in Wales only briefly, had a strong sentimental attachment to the country as can be seen in their works. This unit therefore looks not only at native Welsh artists, but those 'visitors' and incomers to the Principality, who have made a significant contribution to the visual culture of Wales. One wouldn't, as Dr Gwyn Jones said, 'deny St Patrick to the Irish, merely because he was a Welshman'.

This comment applies equally to the study of Welsh architecture. Whilst the majority of the castles and churches of Wales are Anglo-Norman, they can be said to belong to Wales by domiciliary right. Although much of the architecture we see in Wales derives from styles found in England, English architecture of course is often based on styles from the Continent. Topography, namely the shape of the landscape, climate and social conditions also play their part. For example, generally Welsh buildings are smaller and simpler than their English counterparts, whilst the structure of the rocks affects the type of building stone available.

Welsh art and artists

Topographical artists

A growing interest in topography and nature during the eighteenth century led to the production of many books on these subjects and a need for more illustrators and engravers. Wales suddenly became a popular subject amongst topo-graphical artists. **Samuel Buck** (1696–1779) and his brother **Nathaniel** (1727–53) produced some 500 engravings of Welsh monuments and towns between 1726 and 1753 and published a series of south Wales views in 1740–1 along with a similar series of north Wales views a year later.

Other topographical artists to work in Wales include **Paul Sandby** (1725–1809) and **Samuel Hieronymus Grimm** (1734–94). Paul Sandby toured Wales in the early 1770s and was employed by Sir Watkin Williams Wynn to make drawings of Welsh scenery. Whilst his pictures were very natural in some ways, he also made his landscapes conform to the ideals of the period.

Moses Griffith (1747–1819) was one of the very few Welsh topographical artists. He became manservant to Thomas Pennant and was trained by him to illustrate his account of the people, customs and monuments of Wales entitled *Tours in Wales*. It is believed that Griffith made over 2,000 topographical drawings for Pennant, some of which are now in the National Library of Wales in Aberystwyth.

Thomas Rowlandson (1756–1827) was quite a humourist and an aquatint of his, called *An Artist Travelling in Wales,* shows an artist on a horse, laden with easel, palette, paintbox and kettle, sheltering under an umbrella. The umbrella isn't proving very effective and the rain is dripping off the end of his nose. Obviously the inclement weather proved a barrier then, as is so often the case today! Many of his works, which present a vivid picture of life in rural Wales at the turn of the nineteenth century, can be viewed at the National Library of Wales.

Landscape painters

The best-known native landscape painter of this period is **Richard Wilson** (1713–82), who has been considered by some to be Wales' greatest artist. The son of a clergyman, he was born near Machynlleth and in 1729 was sent to London to study portrait painting. His talents were quickly appreciated and he was commissioned to paint members of the royal family on more than one occasion. In the autumn of 1750 he moved to Italy to continue his studies and remained there for seven years. Whilst there, it is said that he met the popular painter Zuccarelli and that it was he who persuaded him to abandon portrait painting and produce landscapes. On his return to London he painted many pictures of England and Wales in the style of Gellée and Poussin. These Italian-style paintings of familiar places such as Caernarfon Castle and Snowdon proved extremely popular.

However, fashion changes gradually meant that 'the father of British landscape painting' found it increasingly difficult to sell his works or get commissions. In 1776, to supplement his income, he became Librarian of the Royal Academy. He later moved back to Wales when his health failed and is buried in the churchyard in Mold in north-east Wales.

Julius Caesar Ibbetson (1759–1817), a native of Yorkshire, came to Wales in 1789 and again in 1792. Unlike Wilson, he was much more interested in the figures in his paintings than the landscape, which was only put in as a setting for the people. Pictures such as *Aberglaslyn: The Flash of Lightning*, which shows a carriage and its horses terrified by a flash of lightning, clearly reflect this interest. This vivid scene can now be viewed in Temple Newsam House, Leeds.

The greatest of the landscape artists who came to Wales was **J. M. W. Turner** (1775–1851). He made his first visit to Wales in 1792 and visited every year from then on for many years. His sketchbook of his 1795 tour includes drawings of several places including Cardiff, Tenby, Kidwelly, St David's and Llandeilo. However, the only sketch of this tour to become a finished picture was that of Llandaff Cathedral, Cardiff. One of his most elaborate pictures is a large watercolour of Hafod mansion near Aberystwyth, painted a few years later. This is now housed in the Lady Lever Art Gallery, Port Sunlight near Liverpool.

Other renowned watercolour painters drawn to Wales during this period include **Thomas Girtin** (1775–1802), **John Sell Cotman** (1782–1842) and **David Cox** (1783–1859). David Cox first visited Wales in 1814 and was virtually resident in the Royal Oak, Betws-y-Coed during the last 15 years of his life. It has been said that as a painter of Welsh weather he has never been surpassed. He also illustrated Thomas Roscoe's *Wanderings and Excursions in North and South Wales*. His most well-known painting of Betws-y-Coed, *The Welsh Funeral*, is of the burial of a young relative of the innkeeper at the Royal Oak. The old man in the foreground is Cox. This painting is now housed in the Birmingham Museums and Art Gallery.

Pre-Raphaelites

The only Welsh painter close to the Pre-Raphaelites was **Henry Mark Anthony** (1817–86). He had spent some time with the Barbizon School in France in the 1830s and was greatly influenced by Corot. Madox-Brown described him as, 'like Constable only better by far', whilst William Michael Rossetti considered him to be the most 'outstanding landscape artist in England'. The most famous Pre-Raphaelite work in Wales is **Dante Gabriel Rossetti's** (1828–82) triptych *David Rex*, commissioned for Llandaff Cathedral, Cardiff in 1866. It shows a nativity group which includes portraits of the artist's friends as the principal characters.

Six ceramic panels on *The Creation of the World* by **Edward Burne-Jones** (1833–98) can also be seen in Llandaff Cathedral. They were not specifically designed for the Cathedral, but were a later donation. Burne-Jones did however produce some stained glass windows for Llandaff as well as other churches in Wales, such as St Deiniol's Church, Hawarden.

William Goscombe John

One who greatly encouraged the idea of Welsh art in Wales was Goscombe John (1860–1952), the son of wood-carver from Cardiff, who moved to London as a young man to work for the sculptor Thomas Nicholls. He won the Royal Academy Gold Medal in 1889, which enabled him to tour Europe and north Africa. The influence of leading French sculptors, especially Rodin, can be seen clearly in his work. In 1891 he returned to England and his reputation grew steadily. In 1911 he was awarded a knighthood at the Investiture of the Prince of Wales at Caernarfon Castle.

Frank Brangwyn

Another renowned Welsh artist, knighted for his achievements during this period, was Frank Brangwyn (1867–1956). He was actually born in Belgium where his father, a Welshman, was an architect–designer. Frank Brangwyn tended to paint large murals in bright, rich colours – he produced decorative schemes for many buildings all over the world. He was, for example, commissioned by the House of Lords to produce a memorial to those who had died in the First World War. However, the panels that he produced were considered too flamboyant and loud for such a setting and were rejected. He then gave them to the city of Swansea where they still hang in the Guildhall. Although he is primarily remembered for his paintings, his contribution to design in the form of stained glass windows, carpets, jewellery, furniture and metal work is also considerable.

Augustus John

Augustus John (1888–1961) from Tenby in Pembrokeshire brought much that was new to art in Wales through his skilled draughtmanship and use of intense colour. Prior to the First World War he painted a small group of bright landscapes, many of which were of Provence, full of contrast and colour. They made an impression on his contemporaries, particularly **James Dickson Innes** (1887–1914), from Llanelli, who invited him on a painting expedition of north Wales in 1911. Innes loved painting panoramic views of the sea and mountains and on this expedition convinced John of the beauty and potential of his own homeland. The expedition resulted in a brilliant series of landscape studies, one of the most notable of these being John's painting of Llyn Tryweryn. Sadly Innes died of tuberculosis only three years later, whilst John went on, partly for financial reasons, to develop his gift for portraiture.

John's portraits are of particular importance, in that unlike so many of his predecessors, he gave life and character to his sitters. Amongst his best pictures are those of his wife and sons. He also painted several vivid characterizations of many eminent Welshmen. For example, his portrait of David Lloyd George completed when Lloyd George was Chancellor of the Exchequer (see Unit 8), clearly shows a politician greedy for power. It is not suprising therefore to hear that the portrait was not well received by Lloyd George's family.

Gwen John

It is only relatively recently that the talents of Gwen John (1876–1939), the elder sister of Augustus John, have come to be appreciated. Whereas he loved life, people and attention, she was shy, introverted and somewhat of a recluse. Her paintings are always small, often consisting of a single figure set in a simple, grey interior. After she left Wales for the Slade in London in 1896 she rarely returned and never painted there.

In 1903 she went to France and lived there for the rest of her life, becoming mistress to the sculptor Rodin. He encouraged her in her painting and passed on to her the belief that hard work would reap its own rewards. She became a Catholic and after Rodin died in 1917, she became more and more obsessed with her work and religion, withdrawing from her family and friends. She produced numerous delicate, refined paintings and drawings of nuns, women, children and flowers. Her work was held in high esteem by her brother who is reported to have said at an exhibition in London, 'One day someone will say, "Didn't Gwen John have a brother?"'

Art promotion

In the early part of the last century there was a growing interest in the visual arts in Wales. Gwendoline and Margaret Davies, the granddaughters of David Davies of Llandinam, the well-known Welsh industrialist, bought Gregynog Hall, a large mansion near Newtown in Powys, in 1921. They were keen to establish an arts centre there, with regular exhibitions, musical recitals and a printing press. Although their dreams were never fully realized, the Gregynog Press, which is still in operation today, has produced many fine, limited-edition volumes. Through the employment of Welsh artists it has done much to promote art in Wales. The sisters later donated their extensive art collection, which included 14 impressionist paintings and many works by Welsh artists to the National Museum of Wales.

The Davies sisters moved into Gregynog in 1924 and in the same year **Eric Gill** (1882–1940) moved with his family from England to Capel-y-Ffin in the Honddu valley in Breconshire. Gill was keen to set up a Christian self-sufficient community of artists and craftsmen, but within four years the community had collapsed and he returned to England. Whilst in Wales however he did produce a considerable amount of work, including carving, lettering and engraving. Stone carvings he made include *The Deposition, The Sleeping Christ, Mankind* and the lettered font for the church in the monastery on Caldey Island off Pembrokeshire. He designed the *Perpetua* and *Felicity* typefaces and illustrated many books such as G. K. Chesterton's *Gloria in Profundis*.

David Jones

One young artist to be nurtured by Gill at Capel-y-Ffin was David Jones (1885–1974) who, although born in south-east England, was a great admirer of all things Welsh – partly as a result of childhood visits to his grandfather in north Wales. He loved the sea and in his youth he painted many simple landscapes such as *Hill Pastures – Capel-y-Ffin* and *Tenby from Caldey Island*. Later, through the 1930s and 1940s, he began to paint more portraits and flower pictures, using mainly pencil and watercolour, before turning to Welsh literature for inspiration. His love of Welsh mythology, read through translation, contributed considerably to his growth as a painter and calligrapher.

Like William Blake, Jones was also a gifted author as well as a painter; his first book *In Parenthesis* was published in 1937 and was based on his experiences as a soldier in the First World War. Other major works include his long poem *The Anathémata* (1952) and *Epoch and Artist* (1959), a book of essays, which includes discussions on Wales and the role of the artist.

Abstract art

Increasing awareness of abstract art spread in Wales in the early part of the twentieth century through the works of **Ceri Richards** (1903–71), an artist from Swansea, who in an exhibition in London in 1935 was linked with abstract-constructivists such as Henry Moore, Barbara Hepworth and Ben Nicholson. Only a year later, however, he became a member of the British Surrealist Group and the influence of Ernst and Picasso is clear in his later works. Works that have won him an international reputation as one of the most important painters of the twentieth century include a series of paintings based on the poetry of two Swansea poets, Dylan Thomas (see Unit 3) and Vernon Watkins, along with some delicate pen-and-ink drawings of the Gower coast off Swansea. His *La Cathédrale engloutie* series shows not only his fascination with Celtic mythology, especially the story of the disappearance of the township of Cantre'r Gwaelod (see Unit 6), but also his love of music – the title is taken from a prelude of the same name by Debussy.

Another abstract artist who had close connections with Wales was **John Piper** (1903–92). On his marriage in 1937 to Myfanwy Evans from Pembrokeshire, Piper developed an interest in the use of descriptive collage, cutting and pasting fragments of coloured paper to form simple beach scenes such as that of Aberaeron, completed in 1938. His growing interest in Welsh architecture meant that he, like Brangwyn, also moved away from abstract art and chose to study churches, chapels, ruined houses and castles. His later works are characterized by textured walls, dark shadows and dramatic light effects, such as his 1939 oil of Hafod mansion near Aberystwyth.

Graham Sutherland

The Welsh landscape also had a significant effect on the work of Graham Sutherland (1903–80) who first visited Pembrokeshire in 1934. He was particularly struck by the magical quality of the light there and this is clearly reflected in his numerous 'paraphrases' of Welsh landscapes, based on drawings taken on the spot. He found that this was the best way he could capture the feeling for a location, rather than painting *in situ*. In his

Welsh Sketchbook published in 1942, he says of Pembrokeshire, 'It was in this area that I learned that landscape was not necessarily scenic, but that its parts have an individual detachment.' His fascination with the Pembrokeshire landscape continued right through his life and his belief in the ability to detach an image from its source is particularly evident in his later surrealistic still lifes.

In 1976 Graham Sutherland gave 15 paintings, nearly 100 drawings and watercolours and 69 prints to the people of Pembrokeshire and these were housed, under the aegis of the National Museum, in the Graham Sutherland Gallery in Picton Castle near Haverfordwest. In 1995, amidst much local protest, the gallery was closed. Although the aim is to find a permanent home in Pembrokeshire for his works, this has not been achieved as yet.

External influences

In spite of the international success of artists such as Piper and Sutherland, art in Wales during the mid-twentieth century was very provincial in outlook. During the 1950s there was no assemblage art for example and no proto-pop art, as in England. Welsh artists seemed to deliberately detach themselves from international influences. This is particularly true of the writer and painter **Brenda Chamberlain** (1912–71) who chose to live for many years on Bardsey Island off the north Wales coast and later on the Greek island of Ydra. She used the islanders as her subjects and her pictures of children, calm, dignified and remote particularly reflect her attraction to the work of Gauguin and her personal philosophy on life.

Kyffin Williams

Wales' most eminent living artist is **Kyffin Williams** (1918–). During the 1980s it was said that 'you could recognize a Welsh yuppie by the Volvo on the drive and a Kyff on the walls'. He is another artist however who has ignored modern theories of art, choosing to paint primarily not for the public, but for himself. A native of Anglesey, after going to the Slade in 1941, he taught art for a number of years before returning to Anglesey in 1974 and becoming a professional painter. He was elected president of the Royal Cambrian Academy in 1969 and Associate of the Royal Academy in 1970. He was awarded a knighthood for his services to the arts in 1999.

The scenery of his local area has always meant a great deal to Kyffin Williams. He refers to Wales as 'the land that I feel is so very much in my bones'. He is particularly well known for his heavy oil paintings of dramatic, jagged mountain landscapes, bleak snow or rain-filled skies, remote derelict houses and farms and stormy seas. His style is simple, direct and extremely atmospheric. Also a reputed portrait artist, his vibrant, realistic portraits, which, like his landscapes, are always painted in a single day, reflect his love and respect for the people of Wales.

Expressionism

Many painters with an interest in expressionism have contributed to the development of art in Wales, the best-known of these being **Josef Herman** (1911–2000). He left his native Poland in 1938 because of growing anti-Semitism there and fled to Belgium, where he first made contact with the Expressionists, particularly Permeke, whose work strongly influenced his later painting. On a holiday to Wales in 1944 he happened to see a group of miners crossing a bridge in Ystradgynlais near Swansea on their way home from work. This experience was to become the major source of his work for the rest of his life. The political and social philosophies of industrial south Wales were similar to his and he formed a close bond with the people there.

He used a variety of media, including inks, pastels and watercolours, to create representations of a universal mining community. He worked on a dark background, mixing heavy, solid images with isolated slashes of bright colour lavishly applied. He later used similar techniques to these to portray the working people of Spain, France, Israel and Mexico. Towards the end of his life, however, his work became lighter in style, with still lifes and flowers among his motifs.

One of Herman's pupils was **Will Roberts** (1907–2000). Roberts, who was born in north Wales but brought up in the industrial south, also painted in dark, glowing colours, adapting his ideas to Herman's style. The expressive power of his work lay in his ability to isolate and capture everyday experiences, as in his series of large charcoal drawings of men at work in steel and tin-plate mills. Unlike Herman, however, he was not interested in making his paintings vehicles for any form of political message. He was attracted to the industrial remains in the landscape, such as viaducts, chimneys and abandoned railway lines and tried to show how these remains are integrated into the landscape of south Wales.

Although expressionism fell out of favour in London in the early sixties, Roberts never altered or adapted his style, but persevered, exhibiting more and more, primarily in Wales. He never retired as a painter and the large number of paintings he produced give us a clear picture of industrial, pastoral and domestic life in Wales in the second half of the twentieth century.

Art organizations

Royal Cambrian Academy

This was established in 1881, its aim being to set up a permanent institution in Cardiff with galleries, studios and an art school. Lack of funds and a suitable site meant that the dream never became a reality. In 1884 the RCA moved to Plas Mawr in Conwy, a magnificent Elizabethan mansion, leased at a peppercorn rent. It remained there, holding annual exhibitions, until 1993 when a new purpose-built building was created behind Plas Mawr. While the RCA has tried to move with the times, it cannot be said to have had any great influence on the development of art in Wales.

Art awareness

The past 40 years or so have been a particularly fruitful period for the visual arts in Wales, due in part to the establishment of several organizations such as **the 56 Group**. Founded in 1956, this cooperative of leading artists based in Wales has put on exhibitions in Britain, Europe and the USA. There is no '56 style' as such, any similarity between members' works is purely coincidental. Through its enthusiasm and determination not to allow Welsh art to be stereotyped, 56 Group Wales as it is now called has done much to promote a greater understanding and knowledge of the visual arts in Wales.

Another organization which has also increased awareness of Welsh Art is the **Contemporary Art Society for Wales** which was actually founded in 1937. It encourages the purchase of contemporary paintings and presents them to galleries and public institutions for display.

The **Welsh Sculpture Trust,** founded in 1981, has done a great deal to bring three-dimensional works to the attention of all by the founding of an open-air sculpture park at Margam Abbey near Swansea. Wales is not well known for its sculptors, although John Gibson (1790–1866) from north Wales, whose most famous work was *The Tinted Venus*, was one of the most celebrated sculptors of his geneneration. One of the founders of the Welsh Sculpture Trust was the renowned Welsh portrait sculptor Ivor Roberts-Jones (1913–96).

Without doubt, however, the establishment of the **Welsh Arts Council** in 1967 has contributed more than any other organization to the growth of the visual arts in Wales in the period since the Second World War. It has funded artists, exhibitions, schools projects, purchased works of art and so on, thereby encouraging a wider appreciation of the visual arts and nurturing the growth of indigenous art in Wales.

Here and now

As a result of initiatives like those mentioned above, art in Wales is finally getting the recognition it deserves. Unfortunately, there isn't enough space here to describe the paintings of the likes of Arthur Giardelli, Peter Prendergast, David Nash, Shani Rhys James and Aneurin Jones or sculptors such as Robert Harding or David Patterson, but their works can be seen in those galleries listed below and many others.

Whilst Welsh art therefore has never been so varied and vibrant, one cannot afford to be complacent. In November 1999 the beautiful Old Library in the middle of Cardiff was converted into a Centre for Visual Arts. Funded by The Welsh Arts Council, this ranked as Wales' largest gallery space, but within less than a year it had closed because of a lack of visitors. There were frequent complaints about the nature of the exhibitions held there, along with the high entrance fee. Many believed that a gallery of Welsh art would have been more appropriate and the campaign for such a gallery continues.

Architecture

In the words of David Bell, a former curator of the Glynn Vivian Art gallery in Swansea, 'the story of Wales – not only the wars and historical events, but the changing and the unchanging character of people's lives – is written as clearly on the stones and bricks, the stucco and the concrete of its buildings, as in its books'.

Early medieval

Naturally any wooden buildings from this period have virtually disappeared, but there are about 450 memorial stones to princes and nobles, particularly on the west coast on the Llyn, Gower and Pembrokeshire peninsulas. These consist of simple inscribed stones, cross-decorated stones and carved stone crosses with inscriptions in Latin and Ogham, an ancient writing system used by the Celts. Some of the later ones such as those in Nevern and Carew in Pembrokeshire consist of particularly elaborate, intricate patterns.

Romanesque

Castles

Wales is famous for its castles – the remains of almost 600 early castles can be visited today, symbolizing the pressures put upon the Welsh princes by the Norman invaders in the eleventh and twelfth centuries. Most of these early castles, known as motte-and-bailey castles, were constructed from earth and timber. They consisted of a large courtyard (bailey) which was protected by a ditch and an earthen rampart and a flat-topped mound of earth (motte), with a wooden keep on top. Cardiff Castle, built in 1081, is a good example of a motte-and-bailey castle. In the early twelfth century the wooden keep was replaced with one of stone, as was the case in many castles. Chepstow Castle, on the eastern border, was one of the first castles in Wales to be built completely from stone.

There were also simpler ringwork castles, where the motte was sometimes omitted altogether and the keep was on flat ground within a circular bank of earth. Kidwelly Castle was one such castle originally constructed in this way.

Churches

Having established themselves in Wales, the Normans then set about rebuilding many Welsh churches, starting with the cathedral in Llandaff in 1120. Their churches were relatively plain and simple in design with generally only one tower. One of the principal characteristics of Romanesque religious architecture is the use of the semi-circular shape in doorways, windows and chancel arches. Mouldings are richly decorated with bold geometric patterns. St David's Cathedral, the last major Romanesque church to be built in Britain, was completed about 1180.

Gothic

Castles

About two dozen of the stone castles in Wales are of Welsh origin and date from the thirteenth century. Most can be found in north and central Wales, in stony inland areas, particularly in Gwynedd and the Towy Valley. Dolwyddelan Castle has a square keep as has Castell-y-Bere, one of the biggest and most ornate of the Welsh castles situated near Cader Idris. Others such as Dinefwr, near Llandeilo, have round keeps. Carreg Cennen, also near Llandeilo, holds a particularly commanding and dramatic position – 90 metres above a sheer drop into a small rural valley below.

Following the death of Llywelyn ap Gruffudd in 1282, (see Unit 1), Edward I built more English castles along the north Wales coast. These include Harlech, Conwy, Beaumaris and Caernarfon. They were designed by James of St George, an architect from Savoy, and incorporated the latest developments in military technology. The significance of the capture of the Welsh stronghold of Caernarfon is reflected in the lavish design of the castle. The angular towers and banded stonework is reminiscent of the town walls of Constantinople. In 1317 three sculptured Roman eagles were placed on the turrets of the main tower. Ironically the eagle was also the symbol of the great-great-grandfather of Llywelyn ap Gruffudd, the twelfth-century King Owain Gwynedd.

As Wales became more settled and prosperous, the need for large military fortifications such as Caernarfon gradually declined and fortified manor houses replaced castles. In north Wales the best known example of a fortified house is the four storey Gwydir castle built by John ap Maredudd in the sixteenth century.

Religious architecture

One of the principal characteristics of religious Gothic architecture is the use of pointed arches for windows, doorways and vaulting. Pointed-arch windows were initially individual tall, narrow lancets, whilst later windows were placed in pairs or groups to provide more light. Fourteenth and fifteenth-century windows were particularly elaborate and highly decorated, as is the case in Tintern Abbey.

Many of the more important churches were enlarged during this period by the addition of aisles and towers to serve as look-out posts. Very rarely were spires added. With the introduction of the Perpendicular style in the late fifteenth/early sixteenth centuries, windows became wider and arches flatter and vertical and horizontal lines predominated. St Giles' Church, Wrexham, is one of the best examples of a perpendicular church in Wales.

A feature of many of the later churches were the elaborate timber ceilings. At Tenby the 169 bosses are all carved with humorous designs whilst in St David's Cathedral, the bosses of the panelled ceiling were developed into huge decorative pendants. Intricately carved rood screens have also survived in some late medieval churches, particularly in Powys and Gwent.

Tudor

After the dissolution of the monasteries (1536–40) very few churches were built and domestic building dominated the next three centuries. There was great emphasis on comfort and warmth with fireplaces everywhere and flat ceilings replaced open roofs. Decorated plaster and wooden panelling were used extensively.

Sir Richard Clough (1530–70), who built two houses near Denbigh, introduced new architectural ideas into north Wales, based on Dutch Renaissance designs. His style of gables became a popular feature of other large houses in the area such as Plas Mawr in Conwy, one of the best-preserved examples in Britain of a Tudor town house which was until 1993, as noted earlier, home to the Royal Cambrian Academy.

Renaissance

Renaissance ideas were slow to spread in Wales and there are very few good examples of seventeenth-century classical architecture remaining. The biggest Renaissance house in Wales is Tredegar House near Newport, built in red brick around 1670 and surrounded by formal gardens, which complement the house's symmetrical design. The Gilt Room on the first floor contains carvings, paintings and sculptures copied from European examples, along with an elaborately painted gold stucco ceiling.

The eighteenth century

The eighteenth century was a period of increased prosperity which resulted in the building of many more mansions and the growth and development of many market towns. Elegant and well-proportioned Georgian and Regency houses with tall sash windows were built in towns such as Abergavenny, Welshpool and Montgomery.

One of the most interesting buildings of the period is the elegant Orangery at Margam Park, which was designed by Anthony Keck in 1787 to protect the orange trees during the winter. Considered both one of the finest buildings of its type in Britain and one of the largest in the world, it has a floral centre parapet and ornate windows.

The eighteenth century also saw a rejection of the formal, classical-style gardens of the Renaissance. Landscape gardeners such as 'Capability' Brown showed a great interest in 'natural' landscapes, creating artificial lakes, grottoes and follies. One of the best known romantic follies in Wales is the neo-Gothic sham castle Clytha Castle, built near Abergavenny in 1790.

In 1784 the eminent architect **John Nash** (1752–1835), who is thought to have been born in west Wales, set up an office in Carmarthen. Whilst there he developed his romantic Classical style and designed a number of small country houses, as well as the gaols at Carmarthen and Cardigan. It is also said that he planned the layout of the new town at the port of Aberaeron in 1808. Although there is no written evidence to support this fact, he certainly designed several houses in this area of west Wales, such as Llanerchaeron in 1794.

Vernacular architecture

Vernacular architecture is the term given to those buildings built without the guidance of an architect. Up to the middle of the sixteenth century, one of the most common forms of house in Wales was the **cruck-truss hall-house**. Construction of these single-storey houses was based on rows of trusses, each formed out of a pair of boomerang-shaped crucks. Hall-houses contained a large room in the centre – the hall or living area – which was heated by an open fire. The kitchen would be at one end of the hall and the sleeping area or parlour at the other.

In upland areas the *tŷ hir* (long house) was also common. This was a long rectangular single storey building, with the family living in one half and the animals the other. A passage through the centre would serve both parts of the house. The end where the animals lived would be at a slightly lower level and would have an earthen floor, whereas the end where the family lived often had a floor of stone slabs.

Another form of simple dwelling was the *bwthyn croglofft* (rood-loft cottage). In one or two-roomed cottages, extra accommodation was provided over the sleeping area by a loft in the roof space, reached by a ladder. Frequently these smaller thatched Welsh cottages in moorland areas and in the west were made of earth or clay *(clom)*, reinforced with stones or rushes and colour-washed or whitewashed.

Ruins of *tai-un-nos* (one-night houses) can be seen in upland areas. According to an ancient custom, you could erect a dwelling on common land and keep the surrounding land, provided that the house, usually of prepared turf, was built during one night and had smoke coming out of the chimney the following morning.

Another popular custom was to move, along with the animals, from the main farmhouse, the lowland *hendre*, to a less substantial upland house known as the *hafod* during the summer. Many of these were probably built in the same way as the *tai-un-nos*. Whilst few *hafodydd*

Thatched one-bedroomed cottage

remain today, you will find both *hafod* and *hendre* common in farm names all over Wales.

By the late sixteenth century, storeyed houses became more common and the internal layout varied from area to area. For example, in mid Wales and on the English–Welsh border, the fireplaces were generally back to back in the centre of the house. On the other hand, in the north-west, fireplaces were placed on the end walls, resulting in gable chimneys.

The growth of heavy industry

As explained in Unit 1, the Industrial Revolution transformed the Welsh landscape and although most buildings were basically functional structures, some were particularly distinctive, such as the stone colliery winding houses which frequently resembled Nonconformist chapels, with their regularly positioned windows picked out in red or yellow brickwork. Weaver's Flour Mill in Swansea was built in 1897 to a French design and was the first multi-storey reinforced concrete building to be erected in Britain.

Long lines of two-storey terraced houses followed the contours of these industrial valleys, the classic example being the Rhondda Fawr with a built-up area 16 kilometres long and a kilometre wide. In the south most terraces are built in red-brown sandstone with entrances at the back and front.

Nonconformity

The earliest chapel to have survived intact is Maes-yr-Onnen near Hay-on-Wye which was built in 1696. During the eighteenth century over a hundred chapels were built, mostly on a similar design to Maes-yr-Onnen, with a pulpit in the middle of one of the long walls, either between or facing the two entrances. Women and children used one of these entrances, men the other.

As the Nonconformist movement grew, the number of chapels increased. Lack of space in the new industrial towns meant that most nineteenth-century chapels were built at right angles to the road, with a single entrance at the pine-end. Windows were tall and rounded and a plaque giving the date when the chapel was built usually placed above the door. Sometimes a first-floor gallery provided additional seating. Later chapels are characterized by the frequent use of neo-classical features such as pediments, columns, cornices and balustraded parapets. Many of these were designed by professional architects such as John Humphreys, who was responsible for Tabernacle chapel in Morriston, Swansea. This vast chapel built in 1873 is aptly known as 'the great Cathedral of Welsh Nonconformity'.

By 1905 there were 1,600 chapels in industrial south Wales alone. Although many of these have been forced to close due to dwindling congregations, there are still more chapels in south Wales than in any other part of the British Isles.

Anglican churches

Anglican churches built in Wales during this period were generally either neo-Romanesque or neo-Gothic. The iron masters when building churches for their workers naturally tended to choose the cheaper Romanesque style as in Tredegar in 1836. Llandaff Cathedral was rebuilt between 1843 and 1867 in

'Early Gothic' by the Welsh architect **John Pritchard** (1817–86). Decorated Gothic later became fashionable and a fine example is St Margaret's Church, Bodelwyddan near Abergele, known as the Marble Church due to it being built in white limestone.

Public and educational buildings

Many of the most interesting examples of nineteenth-century architecture in Wales are public and educational buildings such as the neo-classical old Shirehall in Brecon or the University of Wales, Lampeter designed by C. R. Cockerell in 1827 in the form of a stuccoed quadrangle with small cupola towers on the corners. In 1864 a large extravagant-looking neo-Gothic hotel was begun on the seafront at Aberystwyth. The money ran out before the hotel was completed and in 1872 it became the first college of the University of Wales. Although much of the building was destroyed by fire in 1885, the triangular southern wing, the northern wing and the round staircase tower at the rear remain. The 'Old College' as it is known today, is now the home of the university's Welsh Department.

Castellated mansions

The rich industrialists demonstrated their new found wealth and power in the design of their homes. Cyfarthfa Castle near Merthyr, which is an overpowering mixture of Late Norman and Gothic styles built in 1825 for the 'Iron King' William Crawshay, is an excellent example of this. However, the most ostentatious of the nineteenth-century 'castles' is without doubt Castell Coch. This was a ruin, extravagantly reconstructed by William Bruges for the Marquis of Bute in French Gothic style, complete with working portcullis and drawbridge. It is a true fairy-tale style fantasy castle – not really the sort of building you'd expect to see on a wooded hill just outside Cardiff.

The twentieth century

The Arts and Crafts movement of the late nineteenth and early twentieth century, pioneered in England by William Morris, emphasized craftsmanship and the use of traditional building methods. Mounton House near Chepstow and Harlech College in north Wales are two of the larger Welsh buildings that reflect the beliefs of this movement through their simple, natural designs and restrained use of detail.

Both Arts and Crafts and Art Nouveau influences are apparent in the work of the architect John Coates Carter who had a practice in Cardiff between 1885 and 1914. Art Nouveau was concerned primarily with decoration and was typified by curving asymmetrical lines and stylized flowers and leaves. Carter was also influenced by the German Romanesque style, as can be seen in his design for the Monastery at Caldey which was built between 1910 and 1912.

Public buildings prior to the First World War continued to be built in some form of classical style. The most notable example is the Civic Centre in Cardiff, where every building is influenced by a different source. For example the City Hall was greatly influenced by Austrian Baroque, whilst the National Museum reflects North American versions of classical Greece. Those public buildings built during the inter-war years, however, lack the colour and variety of their predecessors. Many such as the Guildhall in Swansea (1934) and the Temple of Peace in Cardiff (1938) have been called stark and emotionless, although they are now seen as fine examples of their time. Both of these buildings designed by **Sir Percy Thomas** (1883–1969) show a watering-down of classical motifs under the influence of the modern movement.

Modernism

The modern movement believed that the functional aspects of a building were of particular importance and that this should be reflected in its appearance. The 1951 Brynmawr Rubber Factory in the eastern valleys, which was recently demolished, clearly demonstrated this principle. Every part of the factory was covered with a different form of roof, in line with the belief that 'form follows function'. To create a feeling of space, nine shallow shell concrete domes covered the main production area.

Urban architecture

One of the most significant post-war developments in Wales has been the birth of many new well-designed, carefully landscaped towns, such as Cwmbran in the south during the 1950s and Newtown in mid Wales in the 1960s. They represent successful architectural, economic and social experiments.

As well as the development of new towns, many others have been given a new lease of life following the decline of heavy industry, through schemes such as the Valleys' Initiative. The transformation of the old dock at Swansea into a bustling marina with restaurants, a maritime museum, arts centre and flats is an excellent example of urban renewal.

Another major example of such regeneration is the transformation of Cardiff docks by the now defunct Cardiff Bay Development Corporation (see Unit 10). The kilometre-long Cardiff Bay Barrage, central to this scheme, was completed in 2001. The 12 kilometre long freshwater lake is surrounded by shops, restaurants, a hotel and Crickhowell House, the temporary home of the National Assembly for Wales. The main showpiece of the development was originally meant to be a national Opera House and a competition was held in the late 1980s to find a suitable design. This was won by the Iraqi architect Zaha Hadid with a radical design known as the 'crystal necklace', a square of angular glass with a central courtyard. In the early 1990s, however, opposition to her design and to the idea of a so-called elitist opera house grew, fuelled by the Welsh Press. Although Hadid modified her design in 1995, rugby ruled the day, with the Millennium Commission deciding not to fund the project, but choosing instead to support the building of a 70,000 capacity Millennium Stadium in the centre of Cardiff.

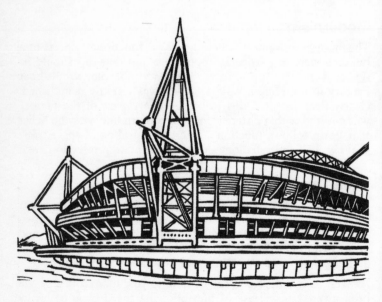

Millennium Stadium

Recently another architect involved with the Cardiff Bay Development has caused further controversy. The eminent British architect **Lord Richard Rogers** (1933–) had accepted a commission to design a permanent home for the National Assembly in the Bay and work had begun on his slate, steel and primarily glass structure. However, escalating costs led to the abandonment of the project and the sacking of Lord Rogers in the summer of 2001. In the autumn of 2002 the Auditor General of Wales stated that Lord Rogers was entitled to £448,000 from the Assembly as payment for disputed invoices. In July 2003, however, Assembly members approved a fixed price contract of £40.997 million with Richard Rogers Partnerships as lead designers. Behind the proposed National Assembly site, the Wales Millennium Centre, a multi-purpose arts complex, is due to be completed at the end of 2004. Whilst its remit is much wider than just opera, it is somewhat more conventional in design than the doomed opera house.

GLOSSARY

celfyddyd (f.)	art
y celfyddydau cainn (pl.)	the fine arts
arlunydd (m.)	artist
paentio	to paint
peintiwr portreadau	portrait painter
llun (m.)	picture
tirlun (m.)	landscape
tirluniwr (m.)	landscape painter
bywyd llonydd	still life
lliw (m.)	colour
paent olew	oils
dyfrliiwiau (pl.)	watercolours
dull (m.)	style
surrealaeth (f.)	surrealism
moderniaeth (f.)	modernism
celfyddyd haniaethol (f.)	abstract art
arddangosfa (f.)	exhibition
oriel (f.)	gallery
pensaerniaeth (f.)	architecture
pensaer (m.)	architect
patrwm (m.)	design
clasurol	classical
cerflunydd (m.)	sculptor

adeiladu / codi	to construct
adeilad (m.)	building
cerfio	to carve

Taking it further

Reading

Bell, David, *The Artist in Wales* (London: 1957)

Halsam, Richard, *Powys* in the *Buildings of Wales Series* (Cardiff: 1979)

Hilling, John, *The Historic Architecture of Wales: An Introduction* (Cardiff: 1976)

Hilling, John, *What Style is it? A Pocket Guide to Architecture in Wales* (Cardiff: 1995)

Lord, Peter, *Gwenllian: Essays on Visual Culture* (Llandysul: 1994)

Lord, Peter, *The Visual Culture of Wales* (Cardiff: 2000)

Newman, John, *Gwent / Monmouthshire*, in the *Buildings of Wales Series* (Cardiff: 2000)

Rowan, Eric, *Art in Wales 2000BC–AD1850* (Cardiff: 1978)

Rowan, Eric, *Art in Wales: An Illustrated History 1850–1980* (Cardiff: 1985)

Williams, Kyffin, *Across the Straits* (Llandysul: 1974)

Williams, Kyffin, *A Wider Sky* (Llandysul: 1991)

Williams, Kyffin, *The Land and the Sea* (Llandysul: 1998)

CD-ROM
Lord, Peter, *Visual Culture of Wales – Industrial Society*, (Cardiff: 2000)

Places to visit

Museums and art collections
The National Museums and Gallery, Cathays Park, Cardiff, CF10 3NP; Tel: 02920 397951 contains extensive examples of the work of virtually all the artists detailed here. Curators will arrange to show you any work that is in store but not on

display. For further details telephone 02920 573104 or send an e-mail to art@nmgw.ac.uk. Online images of most of the paintings in the Museum can be found on the website: www.nmgw.ac.uk

National Library of Wales, Penglais, Aberystwyth, Ceredigion, SY23 3BU; Tel: 01970 632800. Over 4,000 digitized examples of framed works of art can be viewed on: **www.llgc.org.uk**

Cyfarthfa Castle Museum & Art Gallery, Brecon Road, Merthyr Tydfil CF47 8RE; Tel: 01685 723112

The Ffotogallery, 31 Charles Street, Cardiff CF1 4EA; Tel: 02920 341667

Glynn Vivian Art Gallery, Alexandra Rd, Swansea, SA1 5DZ; Tel: 01792 655006

Oriel Mostyn, 12 Vaughan Street, Llandudno, LL30 1AB; Tel: 01492 879201

Oriel Plas Glyn-y-Weddw, Llanbedrog, Pwllheli, LL53 7TT; Tel: 01758 740763

Oriel Ynys Môn, Rhosmeirch, Llangefni, Anglesey LL77 7TQ, Tel: 01248 724444

Royal Cambrian Academy, Crown Lane, Conwy, LL32 8BH; Tel: 01492 593413

The Museum of Modern Art, Wales, Y Tabernacl, Heol Penrallt, Machynlleth, Powys, SY20 8AJ; Tel: 01654 703355

Museum of Welsh Life, St Fagans, Cardiff, CF5 6XB; Tel: 02920 573500

Information

The National Trust, Trinity Square, Llandudno, Conwy, LL30 2DE; Tel: 01492 860123

CADW: Welsh Historic Monuments, Crown Building, Cathays Park, Cardiff CF10 3NQ; Tel: 02920 500200

Websites

www.gallery4wales.com twentieth-century and contemporary Welsh art can be viewed and bought on-line.

05

Welsh music

In this unit you will learn about
- the Welsh musical tradition
- famous Welsh composers, musicians and singers

Many writers have remarked on the musical talents of the Welsh. Dylan Thomas for example, famously declared, 'Praise the Lord! We are a musical nation.' Wales is frequently known as *Gwlad y Gân* (the Land of Song) and those from outside of Wales often appear to think that if you are Welsh, then you must be able to sing. Sadly this is not always the case.

Equally ironic is the fact that whilst many Welsh people throughout the centuries may have reflected their love of music vocally, either through folk songs, choral music or pop songs, Wales was until comparatively recently very much a 'musical nation' without music. Only recently has Wales produced classical composers of world renown and as far as popular music is concerned, until the early 1990s, Tom Jones and Shirley Bassey were the main representatives of Wales abroad.

During the last ten years, however, pop groups such as The Manic Street Preachers, Catatonia and Stereophonics have given a new vitality and youth to Welsh music and culture, resulting in what became known in the mid–late 1990s as the 'Cool Cymru' phenomenon. Whilst this 'trend' has now peaked, the injection of energy and enthusiasm it brought with it has spread through all aspects of the musical life of Wales.

Early instruments

We don't know a great deal about early Celtic music. In the case of Wales, there are no manuscripts of music dating earlier than the reign of Charles II. The Celtic bardic tradition was essentially an oral one, although **Gerald of Wales** (1146–1233), (see Unit 11) does tell us that three instruments were popular in Wales during the twelfth century, namely the **harp,** the *crwth* and the *pipau* or pipes.

The harp

The harp has always been considered the principal instrument of the Welsh, although its origin is uncertain. A primitive sort of harp was used in Egypt centuries before the birth of Christ. The laws of the tenth-century king Hywel Dda (see Unit 1), note that both a king's harp and that of the *pencerdd* or chief court poet, were worth 120 pence each. He also notes that a sheep was worth four pence.

Whilst schools of Welsh harpists were in abundance in medieval Wales, the only major source of their music to survive is the famous *Musica* or *Beroriaeth* which Robert ap Huw copied in 1613. Five scales were used, but no one is really sure how they should sound. Recent composers have suggested that it was also virtually incomprehensible to harpists of the day. With the ascendancy of the Tudors to the English throne, harpists tended to look eastward for patronage and their music tended to imitate English and continental models.

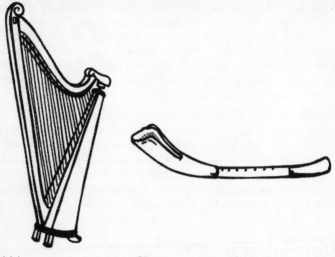

Welsh harp   Pibgorn

The simple early harps were ousted in the seventeenth century by the introduction of the *telyn deires* or triple harp, which produced a rich and unique sound. It was considerably more complicated, with two parallel rows of strings sounding the same note and a row of accidentals between them. It was extremely popular, but in the second half of the nineteenth century, it too was replaced in the popularity stakes by large chromatic pedal harps designed by Hockbrucker and Sebastian Erard.

Although originally from Italy, the *telyn deires* has always been regarded as the traditional Welsh harp, because it was in Wales that it developed. Whilst most loved for its lyrical, haunting qualities, it has not been without its critics. After a visit to Llangollen in north Wales, Mendelssohn commented:

> Now I am in Wales, and dear me, a harper sits in the hall of every reputed inn playing incessantly so-called national melodies; that is to say, most infamous, vulgar, out of tune

trash ... It is distracting and has given me the toothache already!

Amongst those renowned for playing the *telyn deires* today are Robin Bowen, Osian Ellis and Elinor Bennett, who have played to audiences all over the world – thankfully to better effect than the poor Llangollen harpist!

Crwth

The *crwth* was a rectangular six-stringed instrument with holes each side of the keyboard. It was played with a bow, but could also be plucked. It was generally more popular in north Wales than south and it gradually died out in the eighteenth century.

Pipes

Two popular forms of pipe were the *pibgorn* and the *picawd*. The *pibgorn* was a cow's horn played by blowing through a reed, whilst the *picawd* was a primitive Welsh bagpipe. Both of these also declined in popularity in the eighteenth century, although certain modern folk bands, such as *Ar Log* (For Hire), have both pipers and *crwth* players.

The choral tradition

As mentioned in previous units, extensive chapel building occurred during the period of the Industrial Revolution and these new chapels nurtured Welsh cultural identity. Hymn singing played an important part in the chapel service and singing schools were established. Chapels would come together to arrange *cymanfaoedd* (singing festivals), which remain popular today.

Ordinary people were keen to embrace tonic solf-a, pioneered in Wales by Eleazar Roberts, and most towns and villages had active choirs. Many of those still flourishing today, such as Côr y Penrhyn, were established in the later part of the nineteenth century. Others such as the Ystalyfera Choir were established in the early part of the twentieth century. In 1926 a choir known as the Welsh Imperial Singers was established in north-east Wales and toured Britain and North America extensively between 1926 and 1939. The success of many of these choirs was often due to the training they had received in their local chapels. Crowds of 20,000 or more regularly attended competitions between them. Their status can be compared to that enjoyed by top-class British football teams today.

Many of these choirs had well over 100 members and the oratorio became particularly popular. The first half of the twentieth century saw countless performances of the *Messiah* and *Elijah* in workingmen's clubs and village halls throughout Wales. It has been said that Handel contributed more than any other composer to the development of music in Wales, as Welsh composers began to compose anthems and choruses in a similar style.

The gradual decline in chapel attendance has meant that the days of the very large mixed choirs have come to an end, although male voice choirs, women's choirs and youth choirs of all sizes continue to prosper. Many of these, such as Morriston Orpheus, Treorchy, Pontarddulais and Rhosllannerchrugog, have made several recordings and tour extensively abroad.

Cerdd dant

The ever-increasing interest in choral works meant that the piano became more popular than the harp in the nineteenth century. *Cerdd dant* was now only heard in rural, isolated areas. This form of performance, whereby the harpist leads with one tune while the voice or voices sing a counter one, is unique to Wales. Making sure everyone ends together on the final note is no mean feat! Without the efforts of the blind harpist **David Roberts** (1875–1956), this tradition might well have died. He collected 49 musical arrangements and published them under the title *Y Tant Aur* (The Golden String) in 1911.

Revived interest in *cerdd dant* amongst harp teachers following the publication of these tunes led to the founding of the Welsh Cerdd Dant Society in 1934. Members were keen to sustain and develop this enthusiasm for singing traditional Welsh poetry to the accompaniment of the harp, and the society has grown from strength to strength. *The Gŵyl Cerdd Dant* (Cerdd Dant Festival) is held annually, alternating between north and south Wales. Whilst *cerdd dant* is possibly more limited in its appeal than other forms of music, new arrangements are continually being devised, ensuring both the preservation and continuation of this ancient Welsh art.

Opera

The traditional Welsh love of singing and of the oratorio in particular led to the founding of many amateur operatic companies at the turn of the last century. One of the most popular operas of the time was *Blodwen* by **Joseph Parry**

(1841–1903). Parry, from Merthyr, was the most talented composer of his age, who composed nine operas in all. One of his most well-known choral pieces, the tender love song '*Myfanwy*', is still regularly sung by male-voice choirs, although few of his other works are now performed. He was extremely highly thought of in his day – the National Eisteddfod gave him £600 in 1896 in recognition of his contribution to music in Wales.

The growth in amateur operatic companies provided a natural source for a national opera company. In 1946 the **Welsh National Opera** (WNO) was set up by Idloes Owen from Glamorgan, who left the mines to become a professional musician. His aim was to set up four amateur choruses in Cardiff, Swansea, Aberystwyth and Bangor. A group of professional soloists was established to take the principal roles and to sing with these choruses in turn.

Being familiar with ambitious choral works, the Welsh audiences strongly supported the WNO and its popularity grew and grew both at home and abroad. By the mid-1970s it had its own fully professional chorus and orchestra as well as an opera school. Whilst the WNO is highly respected internationally, the lack of a purpose-built opera house (see pp.88–9), has meant that many Welsh people have been deprived of hearing many of their great native opera singers such as Dame Gwyneth Jones, Margaret Price, Sir Geraint Evans, Dennis O'Neil and Stuart Burrows.

Wales' best known opera singer at present is **Bryn Terfel** (1965–) who has been called international opera's hottest property. He made his professional debut in 1990 at the WNO as Guglielmo in Mozart's *Così Fan Tutte*. Since then his popularity has soared and he has sung all over the world, achieving particular acclaim for his portrayal of Falstaff in Verdi's opera of the same name. Terfel's roots in north Wales are very important to him. As he himself once said, 'I have half a mountain in Wales – what more do I need?' He organizes and takes part in the three-day open-air Faenol Music Festival there every August.

Silver and brass bands

Singing was not the only form of music to increase in popularity as a result of the Industrial Revolution. Silver and brass bands became increasingly popular. Every procession would be led by a band, especially on special occasions such as May Day. Most of these bands were linked with the heavy industries of the times, as their names often suggest, e.g. the Cory Workmen's Band or the Melingriffith Works Band. Inevitably, cultural and social changes following the Second World War led to the demise of a great many of these bands, although in certain former industrial areas both adult and children's bands continue to flourish. In 2001 Ammanford Town Silver Band were crowned British Champions at the National Championships – the first time in ten years for a Welsh band to win the coveted title.

Composers

As noted at the start of this unit, Wales until relatively recently has lacked classical composers of world renown, primarily because of the lack of financial support and facilities available to them. It has been suggested that, if Joseph Parry had been born in Milan or Munich, then he could possibly have gone straight to work in an opera house and developed as a Verdi or a Wagner.

One who would have made a significant contribution to the growth and development of music in Wales, had she not died of appendicitis at the young age of 25, is **Morfydd Llwyn Owen** (1893–1918). As stated in German on her gravestone, 'the indescribable happened here'. The few compositions of hers which were published before her death show her ability to compose vocal works of lasting quality and beauty such as 'Slumbersong of the Madonna' and 'To Our Lady of the Sorrows'. As well as composing, she was a popular and successful singer.

Welsh women composers were, and still are to a certain extent, less well known than their male counterparts. **Grace Williams** (1906–77), however, was the first composer of either sex to have any lasting impact outside of Wales. She used and adapted her knowledge of traditional Welsh folk material in compositions such as *Fantasia on Welsh Nursery Tunes* and *Penillion for Orchestra*. She composed a variety of works, choral pieces, two symphonies, a violin concerto and a one-act opera, *The Parlour*.

Another early ambassador for Welsh music was **Daniel Jones** (1912–93) who composed ten piano sonatas before he was nine years old! He was a close friend of Dylan Thomas and composed one of his many symphonies in memory of him, as well as writing a book entitled *My Friend Dylan Thomas* in

1977. Essentially an instrumental composer, he also composed several operas and and cantatas such as *The Country Beyond the Stars*.

Other less well-known early composers include **Mansel Thomas** (1909–86) and **Arwel Hughes** (1909–88), whose son **Owain Arwel Hughes** has followed in his father's footsteps to become one of Wales' most eminent conductor–composers. **Meirion Williams** (1901–76) was a particularly gifted and prolific composer of vocal music and his compositions such as 'Aros mae'r Mynyddau Mawr' and 'Y Blodau ger y Drws' remain extremely popular.

The two most celebrated Welsh composers of the last 50 years, however, are **Alun Hoddinott** (1929–) and **William Mathias** (1934–92), who have succeeded largely because of their individual and independent styles. Both have done a great deal to raise the profile of Welsh music on an international level.

Hoddinott's work is the more powerful and dramatic of the two, whilst Mathias is frequently labelled the composer of the dance, due to infectious compositions such as *Dance Overture* and *Celtic Dances*. Hoddinott's first opera, *The Beach of Falesa* was performed by the WNO in 1974 and he followed this with television operas, a chamber-opera and a children's opera, *What the Old Man Does is Always Write*. His catalogue of orchestral and instrumental music is equally extensive and includes the highly acclaimed *Star Children*, a symphony for organ and orchestra.

Mathias' instrumental output is considerably less prolific, but he is held in particular high regard as a writer of choral music. Major works of his include *St Teilo, This Worldes Joie* and *World's Fire*. In 1981 he was commissioned to write an anthem for the wedding of Prince Charles and Lady Diana Spencer. Mathias is particularly popular in America as a composer of church music and festivals of his music are held there regularly.

Many classical composers have followed in their wake. Some such as Jeffrey Lewis reflect the influences of the likes of Stockhausen and Ligeti, but in contrast to Hoddinott and Mathias, lack a particular Welsh identity. Others to have made a significant contribution to Welsh music in recent years include Ian Parrott, John Metcalf, Gareth Glyn and Pwyll ap Siôn. Despite an increased interest in classical music and improved facilities, however, no single Welsh composer can as yet be said to be as well known either in Wales or beyond as Hoddinott or Mathias.

Professional orchestras

In 1928 the **National Orchestra of Wales** played its first concert in Cardiff City Hall under the baton of Sir Henry Wood. However, despite much initial enthusiasm, the orchestra sadly was soon disbanded, owing to a lack of financial support.

A few years later a small studio orchestra was formed by the BBC. This time with Welsh Arts Council funding, the orchestra went from strength to strength. By the mid 1970s it had developed into a full-sized symphony orchestra. It has since been renamed the **National Orchestra of Wales** and tours and broadcasts extensively abroad. Its success also led to the founding of the **Welsh Philharmonic Orchestra** in 1985, which concentrates on pieces especially composed for small orchestras, as well as promoting new Welsh composers.

Following the Second World War the **National Youth Orchestra of Wales** was established. This has provided a valuable training ground for young Welsh musicians. Along with this there is also a thriving **National Youth Brass Band** and a **National Youth Choir of Wales**.

Competitions and festivals

Festivals play an important role in the musical life of Wales. *Eisteddfodau,* a term that originally meant a meeting of the bards, are held in villages and towns all over the country, offering a wide variety of literary and musical competitions. The **Royal National Eisteddfod** is Wales' largest annual event, whilst the **Urdd National Eisteddfod** is the biggest youth festival in Europe. Although the National Eisteddfod of Wales can be traced back to 1176, it was during the nineteenth century that it became a large-scale folk festival. In 1880, the National Eisteddfod association was formed and given the responsibility of staging the annual festival to be held in north and south Wales alternately. Since this date, a national eisteddfod has taken place every year with the exception of 1914 and 1940. The Royal National Eisteddfod is held during the first week in August.

The **Llangollen International Music Eisteddfod**, which is held every year in July, has extended the concept of the Eisteddfod to a wider audience. It is a particularly colourful event with choirs, folk singers and instrumentalists from all over the world frequently competing in national costume.

Feelings have been known to run high in Eisteddfod competitions. There are many newspaper accounts of furious choristers getting on stage and refusing to allow adjudicators to leave. It comes as little surprise therefore to read that when the famous nineteenth-century conductor, Sir Frederick Cowen, was asked what was the most dangerous moment of his career, he cited the time he adjudicated a choral competition in an Eisteddfod. His choice of winner so annoyed the supporters of rival choirs that they attacked the hotel where he was staying. Luckily he escaped their wrath by swapping clothes with a local policeman!

Thankfully such behaviour is a thing of the past and is certainly not a feature of the **Cardiff Singer of the World** competition. This competition was set up in 1983 and it has become increasingly important. In 2002 there were 500 hopeful singers from all over the world at the auditions. The winner receives £10,000 and an additional concert with a BBC Orchestra. There is also the Song Prize of £2,000 and an additional concert with a BBC orchestra, which is awarded to the singer with the best performance of *Lieder*, art song or folk song during the competition. The winners of the Song Prize have gone on to careers as successful as the overall winner – Bryn Terfel, the 1989 winner, being the perfect example.

There are many professional musical festivals held annually throughout Wales such as the **North Wales International Musical Festival**, the **Vale of Glamorgan Festival**, and the **Fishguard Festival**. They do much to encourage new composers, as does the **Guild for the Promotion of Welsh Music** founded in 1950. Other annual festivals include the **Pontardawe Folk Festival** and the **Brecon Jazz Festival**. This jazz festival, started in 1984, is now reputed to be the biggest of its kind in Europe. It is estimated that 50,000 people visit Brecon throughout the three days of concerts every August. You will find on p. 201 a fuller list of festivals held in Wales.

Stars of the stage

Ivor Novello (1893–1951), one of Wales' most well-known and most loved silent movie actors, was first and foremost a composer, who composed and produced numerous romantic musicals such as *Glamorous Night* and *King's Rhapsody*. Novello, from Cardiff, was born David Ivor Davies and took his stage name from his mother, Madame Clara Novello Davies. In 1914 he composed the popular First World War song, 'Keep the Home Fires Burning', which made him famous overnight.

Another particularly charismatic personality of stage, TV, and film was **Sir Harry Secombe** (1921–2001), who as well as being one of the founders of the comedy show *The Goons,* was a singer with a fine classical tenor voice.

His chart hits included 'This is My Song' and 'If I Ruled the World'. A native of Swansea, between 1963 and 1965 he took the part of Mr Pickwick in *Pickwick Papers* in the West End and later went with the production to Broadway. He hosted the popular religious Sunday night TV show *Highway* for ten years between 1983 and 1993.

Many Welsh singers have followed Harry Secombe to the West End. Two of the best known are **Jonathan Pryce** (1947–), and **Peter Karrie** (1946–). Pryce has won particular acclaim for his role as Juan in *Miss Saigon* whilst Peter Karrie has made the role of Phantom in the *Phantom of the Opera* very much his own.

Early success

One who lists performing in a West End musical as one of her greatest ambitions is the young soprano from Cardiff, **Charlotte Church** (1986–) She has already put Wales on the map in a number of ways. Her first album *Voice of an Angel* released in 1998 made her the youngest artist ever to have a number 1 in the UK classical album charts. She is also the youngest ever British artist to have a Top 10 album in the United States. In January 2003 she achieved a top 5 hit with *Jurgen Vries*. She has sung for the Pope at the Vatican, the Clintons in Washington, the presidential inauguration of George W. Bush and the 50th birthday party of the Prince of Wales – no mean achievement for one so young! Another to gain success at an early age was boy soprano **Aled Jones** (1971–), with his popular recording of 'Walking in the Air'. Now a well-known broadcaster and presenter, he returned to singing as a baritone with two highly successful albums, *Aled* and *Higher*.

Folk music in Wales

Many English-medium folk singers and groups have earned greater recognition outside Wales than in Wales itself. **Huw** and **Tony Williams** from Gwent, who are extremely popular on the British folk-club circuit, are a good example of this. Likewise the folk band **Calennig Dŵr**, who mix lively Welsh dance sets with Anglo-Welsh folk songs. They tour regularly in Europe and America, but at home remain relatively unknown.

Within Wales, the Irish-influenced trio known as the **Henesseys** are particularly popular in the Cardiff area and have been playing together for over 20 years. **Max Boyce** (1943–) is another folk singer and entertainer whose career goes back a long way. His valleys background and his ten years as a miner influenced many of his early songs such as 'Rhondda Grey', whilst later songs are lighter in tone, many celebrating the successes of the 1970s Welsh rugby team. His 1975 album *We all had Doctor's Papers*, is the only comedy album to have reached number 1 in the album charts. After a successful career in TV in the 1980s, many new younger fans have recently 'discovered' the singing talents of Max Boyce. His legendary 1973 album, *Live at Treorchy Rugby Club* was re-released in 1998 and his 1999 TV show, *An Evening with Max Boyce* broke BBC records. It even achieved higher viewing figures than the 1999 Wales *v* England rugby international – usually one of the most avidly watched programmes in Wales.

Dafydd Iwan (1947–) is without doubt the father of Welsh language folk music. He first came to prominence during the 1960s as a protest singer and active member of the newly formed *Cymdeithas yr Iaith Gymraeg* (Welsh Language Society). In 1969 he founded the *Sain* record company along with Huw Jones and is now its managing director. He has released 17 albums and has been described as a country/folk/rock singer with attitude. He finally retired as a regular performer in 2000, but continues to record new compositions. One of his most popular songs, 'Yma o Hyd' (Still Here), celebrates the recovery in the use of the Welsh language as revealed in the 1981 census returns. Past heroes such as Macsen Wledig, Arthur and Llywelyn Fawr are summoned to join in the celebrations and pledge themselves to the struggle. The chorus, '*er gwaethaf pawb a phopeth, dyn ni yma o hyd*' (in spite of everyone and everything, we are still here), is frequently cited.

Another singer who began his career in the early 1960s and was heavily influenced by the likes of Bob Dylan is **Meic Stevens** (1941–) from Solva in Pembrokeshire. Singing a mixture of folk and acoustic rock, he still performs regularly both in Wales and beyond and songs like 'Môr o Gariad' (A Sea of Love) and 'Cân i Walter' (Song for Walter) are as popular now as when they were first released.

One of the most active folk bands of the moment are the **Moniars** who have frequently stated that their aim is to show what fun there is to be had with traditional instruments. Their popularity is testimony to their success. The same could also be said of **Bob Delyn a'r Ebillion**, whose blend of contemporary Welsh and Breton influences have won them considerable admiration. Their frequently surreal lyrics are sung to a combination of blues, jazz and classical elements. Along with the likes of the harpist and singer **Siân James** (1962–) and the bands Mabsant and Ar Log, they have taken Welsh folk to an international audience.

Nearer home, the guitar-playing duo **John ac Alun**, who sing original compositions in a gentle country genre, are the best-selling Welsh medium recording artists in Welsh today.

At the same time, the revival of many traditional folk songs through the successes of many of those mentioned above, has also led to a revival in traditional dance. **Dawnswyr Nantgarw** and **Dawnswyr Talog** are just two of several dance troupes that have turned Welsh dance into a flamboyant and theatrical art form.

Pop music in Wales

Until relatively recently the only two Welsh pop artists who could claim to be household names worldwide were **Tom Jones** (1940–) and **Shirley Bassey** (1937–). Tom Jones, the slick 1960s sex symbol from Pontypridd, remains a crowd puller today. So much so that he was chosen to headline the 1999 Voice of a Nation concert in Cardiff Bay, to celebrate the opening of the National Assembly. Jones first landed a record contract with Decca back in 1964, after being discovered a year earlier whilst playing the workingmen's clubs of south Wales with his band Tommy Scott and the Senators. His second single 'It's Not Unusual' was an international hit and was followed in the 1960s and 1970s by hits such as 'What's New Pussy Cat', 'Delilah' and 'Green, Green Grass of Home'.

In 1987 a cover version of 'Prince's Kiss', recorded with the British techno-pop group, The Art of Noise, sparked off a new interest in his music. In 1992 he participated in a stage performance of Dylan Thomas' *Under Milk Wood* directed by Sir Anthony Hopkins – as well as appearing as himself in the animated cartoon show *The Simpsons*. He later went on to record the Randy Newman hit song, 'You can leave your hat on' for the British Oscar winning film *The Full Monty*.

One reason for Tom Jones' continued success is his ability to redefine himself for each new generation of music fans, often through collaboration with the in-groups of the day. His 1999 duet album, *Reload*, included contributions from Stereophonics and Cerys Matthews, the former lead singer of Catatonia. He enjoyed further success with the 2002 album *Mr Jones*, a collaboration with Wyclef Jean.

Shirley Bassey

Shirley Bassey's career has also spanned many decades. The daughter of a Nigerian seaman brought up in Tiger Bay, the docklands of Cardiff, she first reached the UK charts in 1957 with 'Banana Boat Song'. Her recording of the James Bond theme song, 'Goldfinger', in 1965 was her big breakthrough overseas and countless hits followed, such as 'Big Spender' and 'Diamonds are Forever'. Recent chart successes have included 'Disco La Passione' in 1996 and 'History Repeating' in 1997. *Diamonds are Forever – the Remix Album* saw some of her biggest hits reworked by new artists in 2000. In the same year she was made a dame for her contribution to the music industry. Two of her most recent performances in Wales were at the Voice of the Nation concert and the opening ceremony of the World Cup in 1999 – where her dramatic dress made of a giant Welsh flag caused quite a stir.

It is important to stress however that Tom Jones and Shirley Bassey were not the only Welsh contributors to the international music scene in the 1960s and 1970s. **John Cale** (1942–), a classically trained pianist from south-west Wales, was a founder member of **Velvet Underground**, one of the most influential and avant-garde rock groups of the 1960s. After they disbanded he produced many solo albums, both rock and folk, as well as classical collaborations with symphony orchestras. More recently he has worked with the reformed Velvet Underground.

Another Welsh singer to gain fame during this period was **Mary Hopkin** (1950–) from Pontardawe near Swansea. After appearing on the talent show *Opportunity Knocks*, the model Twiggy recommended her to Paul McCartney, the former Beatle, who produced her first single 'Those were the Days', which reached number 1, both at home and in America in 1968. She also sang 'Knock Knock Who's There?' Britain's 1970 Eurovision Song Contest entry which got to number 2 in the charts. After a couple of relatively successful albums, she retired to bring up her family, but recently sang with the young Welsh band **The Crocketts**, on their single 'Chicken Vs Macho'.

Amen Corner, a seven-piece band from Cardiff and Newport were another sixties success story. Their first record 'Gin House Blues' was released in 1967 and six more hits followed, including 'Bend Me, Shape Me' a year later, which reached number 30 in the British charts. They were the first Welsh band to top the charts in the UK with 'If Paradise is Half as Nice' in 1969. They split up later the same year, but their lead singer **Andy Fairweather Low** (1948–), went on to solo success in 1975 with the song 'Wide Eyed and Legless'.

The Welsh rock band **Man** was also formed during the late 1960s and still performs occasionally today. They were produced by Cardiff-born singer and guitarist **Dave Edmunds** (1943–) whose band **Love Sculpture** had a chart hit in 1968. His chart-topping hit 'I hear you knocking' sold over 3 million copies in 1970 and was followed by another top 30 hit 'Baby I love you'. A few years later in 1977 the rock band **Racing Cars**, achieved fame with their single 'They Shoot Horses Don't They'. Although they had two hit albums, a change in musical tastes and possibly a lack of exposure meant that their success was relatively short lived.

One who hasn't suffered that fate is **Bonnie Tyler** (1953–), the rock ballad singer from Swansea, who has been described as a female Rod Stewart owing to her husky, deep voice. Her first UK hit 'Lost in France' was released in 1976 and 'It's a Heartache' became her first American success two years later. In the mid 1980s she successfully teamed up with Jim Steinman who wrote many songs for Meatloaf and she continues to tour extensively and release successful albums today such as *Heart Strings* (2003).

Whilst the name **Shakin' Stevens** (1948–) is known by many, worldwide, not so many realize that Shakey, alias Michael Barrett, is one of a family of 12 children who was brought up in Cardiff. When he left school he was told by one of his teachers, 'I hate your voice, but keep singing – someone else might be fool enough to like it.'

After years in a band called Shakin' Stevens and the Sunsets, he joined the West End musical *Elvis* in 1977 and, on leaving 19 months later, he cashed in on 1950s musical nostalgia with cover versions of hits of the period and similar sounding original songs. His first hit was 'Hot Dog' and this was followed by many others such as 'Green Door' and 'You Drive me Crazy' which sold in their millions. In 1984 he joined up with Bonnie Tyler on the hit single 'A Rockin' Good Way'.

One of the premier Welsh groups to gain both British and American success in the 1980s was the **Alarm,** a folk–punk band from Rhyl. They were formed in 1981 and produced seven albums between 1984 and 1991, many of which achieved gold status. They were frequently supported by Welsh language bands, proving that Welsh could be more than just a medium for religious choral works. Their lead singer **Mike Peters** (1958–) learnt Welsh and successfully relaunched his solo career in 1994.

Cool Cymru

During the 1990s a variety of pop bands took Welsh music one vital step further; as a result it is now internationally recognized as making a significant contribution to the contemporary music scene, independently of the rest of Britain. **The Manic Street Preachers**, from Blackwood in Gwent, are without doubt Wales' most successful rock group. Formed in 1989, just 300 copies of their debut, punk rock style, single 'Suicide Alley' were produced. However, in 1991 they struck lucky with a 10 album deal with Columbia and a string of hits followed such as the militant 'Motor cycle emptiness'. In February 1995 the guitarist and lyricist Rickey Edwards disappeared on the eve of a promotional visit to America. A fortnight later his car was found, but his whereabouts remain a mystery to this day. In December the band made their live comeback without him and their anthemic album, *Everything Must Go* reached number 2 in the charts the following summer. *This is my truth, tell me yours* (1998) proved even more successful and included their first UK number 1 single, 'If you tolerate this then your children will be next'.

On Millennium Eve they played to an audience of 52,000 in Cardiff's Millennium Stadium and in February 2001 played a 'come-back' gig in Cuba with President Fidel Castro in the audience. They won a variety of awards in the 1990s and have been labelled by many as Wales' answer to U2. Their greatest hits album, *Forever Delayed* was released in October 2002.

Cerys Matthews' (1969–) gift for writing memorable lyrics played an important part in the success of Cardiff based **Catatonia,** whose first chart success, 'You've got a lot to answer for' reached number 35 in the British charts in 1996. Their first album was released the same year. However, it was their second album, *International Velvet* (1998), which made them a household name. The chorus of the title track, 'Every day when I wake up, I thank the Lord I'm Welsh,' has become an unofficial national anthem. However, in September 2001, after two quiet years with cancelled tours and disappointing sales of a fourth album, Catatonia announced that they were calling it a day. Despite a loud, wild party image, emphasized by slogan T-shirts such as 'fastrising, beersoaked, riproaring poptart', the fame that goes with success appeared to be too much for Cerys and the band to take. However, in May 2003, Cerys returned with a solo album of folk music entitled *Cock-a-hoop* which included a version of a Welsh hymn.

The indie band **Super Furry Animals** were formed in 1993 and were signed to Creation after their first London show. All band members had been in Welsh-language bands before coming together as the SFA and the importance of Wales and the Welsh language to them was apparent in their contract with Creation. This allowed them to record in Welsh and never to work on St David's Day. Their debut album *Fuzzy Logic* received much acclaim in 1996, but the harder, rockier follow-up *Radiator* in

1997 was not so popular. *Guerilla* (1999) was a lighter and much more accessible album, but was followed by the collapse of Creation in March 2000. The SFA responded to this by producing an all-Welsh album *Mwng* (Mane) in May of the same year, on their own label Placid Casual Records. Their fifth album *Rings Around the World* in 2002 included cameo appearances by Paul McCartney and John Cale and was the first ever album to be released simultaneously on DVD and CD. Through their emphasis on a bilingual identity, the SFA have, in the words of one critic, 'enlarged the sense of what is possible, of what one world finds of interest in another'.

The rise of the three-piece rock band **Stereophonics** has been meteoric. Their songs are very much based on their experiences growing up in Cwmaman, a small village in the Cynon Valley (the rugby related anthem 'As long as we beat the English' being an obvious example). Their first limited edition single 'Looks like Chaplin/More Life in a Tramp's Vest' was released in 1996 and their debut album a year later. Each successive release has done better than the last and they have toured with the likes of the Manics and the Who. Tom Jones made a special guest appearance with the band in August 2000. Their album, *Just Enough Education to Perform* released in Easter 2001, reflected a move away from the no-nonsense rock feel of other works and displayed a wider range of styles and images, whilst *You Gotta Go There to Come Back* released in 2003 takes a more electronic direction. Drummer **Stuart Cable** left the band in September 2003.

Perhaps one of the most experimental and adventurous of the contemporary Welsh bands is **Gorkey's Zygotic Mynci**. Formed back in 1991, this bilingual psychedelic pop band from west Wales has been tipped for imminent stardom for years. However inspite of some excellent, well-received albums such as *Gorkey 5* (1998) and *Spanish Dance Troupe* (1999), they are still waiting for their big break.

Gorkey's, like the SFA, have been heavily criticized by some fans for singing in English. Some feel that such groups turn to English only to gain greater commercial success. **Beganiffs,** a successful Welsh-language pop band from Caernarfon, renamed themselves **Big Leaves** and had considerable success with their single 'Fine' which became record of the week on Radio One. An EP *Animal Instinct* was released in June 2001 and was followed by a Welsh language EP *Siglo* (Swaying). Big Leaves demonstrated what popular music in Wales could and should be like, but unfortunately they split up following the release of their second album *Alien and Familiar* in March 2003.

Two other groups to have gained success recently are **Melys** (Sweet) and **Feeder** – named after the leader singer's goldfish. Feeder achieved their first big hit in January 2001 with 'Buck Rogers', which got to number 5 in the UK charts and is a backing track in the Hollywood blockbuster *Behind Enemy Lines*. Tragically their heavy touring schedule put great pressures on the band, resulting in the suicide of drummer John Lee in January 2002. The two remaining members of the band joined with Mark Richardson to release a new album *Comfort in Sound* in October 2002.

Welsh-language rock music

It was in the 1980s that the Welsh-language rock scene really began to take shape. Prior to that there had been some rock groups such as the **Trwynau Coch** (Red Noses) and **Edward H. Dafis**, but most Welsh-medium pop music had been very middle-of-the-road. **Anrhefn** (Disorder) was one of the first Welsh punk bands. In 1983 the group set up Recordiau Anrhefn, producing what they called, 'dodgy compilations of up-and-coming left-field weirdo bands'. This new wave of Welsh underground bands included **Y Cyrff** (The Bodies), and **Datblygu** (Develop), possibly the most diverse and varied of all these new Welsh-language bands. The Radio One DJ John Peel invited Datblygu and other Welsh bands to do sessions on his show, thereby introducing Welsh music to a Europe-wide audience. Datblygu responded to the increased interest in their music by including sleeve notes in English on their albums released between 1985 and 1995. Super Furry Animals recently covered a Datblygu song 'Y Teimlad' (The Feeling) on their album *Mwng*, which has generated new interest in the band.

By the late 1980s Welsh-language pop music had established a firm infrastructure of bands, many of whom frequently toured with English bands. In 1983 the glam rock group **Ceffyl Pren** (Wooden Horse) became the first Welsh band to tour North America and the first to tour the Far East in 1987. More and more young bands have naturally led to the development of many new labels. One of the most innovative and prolific of these is *Ankst*, whilst another, *Fflach*, has a subsidiary, *Semtexx* for heavy-rock bands. *Sain* also has a subsidiary label entitled *Crai* Records, set up in 1989 to concentrate on Welsh-language pop.

One of the first bands to sign up with *Ankst* in 1988 was the indie band **Ffa Coffi Pawb**. The name translates as Everyone's Coffee Beans, although many mistakenly thought it really meant something else! HTV Wales refused to caption Ffa Coffi Pawb when they appeared on stage and made them change the billing to FCP. Undeterred, they went on to bigger and better things – their lead singer, Gruff Rhys, is now lead singer of the Super Furry Animals.

One of the first Welsh groups to attempt to make a living solely by singing in Welsh were **Jess**. Jess frequently toured with The Alarm in the early 1990s and members of the band later played in Mike Peters' new band **Poets of Justice**. Most of those singing solely in Welsh cannot however survive just on their music. For example, Bryn Fôn, the lead singer of the extremely popular 1990s folk-rock band **Sobin a'r Smaeliaid**, is a well-known Welsh actor.

Many Welsh bands go back a long way. **Anweledig** (Unseen) is a band who have been together for around 20 years and are still extremely popular. Another 1980s band that is still releasing records is the punk twosome **Llwybr Llaethog** (Milky Way); they are also producers for Anweledig and **Tystion** (Witnesses), one of the first Welsh rap bands formed in 1997. The Welsh-language music scene has also had its share of boy bands, **Mega** being one of the most well-known recent examples. The young indie pop/rock band **Gwacamoli** released their first album *Clockwork* to much acclaim in 2001 whilst other names to look out for in the future include **Maharishi**, **Epitaff** and **Vanta**.

In a recent interview, Gruff Rhys aptly summed up the significance and importance of the thriving pop culture in Wales today:

> There's always been good music in Wales. But before, the ones who made it did it by having no relevance to anything… I suppose the one thing we're all fighting against is this romanticized comedy view of Wales. We're introducing people to different kinds of heroes… who maybe don't live in that clichéd leeks and rugby view of Wales.

GLOSSARY

canwr (m.)	*singer*
cantores (f.)	*female singer*
côr (m.)	*choir*
côr ieuenctid	*youth choir*
cân (f.)	*song*
canu	*to sing*
llais (m.)	*voice*
unawd (m/f.)	*solo*
deuawd (m/f.)	*duet*
cerddoriaeth (f.)	*music*
cerddoriaeth glasurol	*classical music*
canu offeryn	*to play an instrument*
canu gwerin	*folk music*
canu roc	*rock music*
canu gwlad	*country music*
dw i'n hoffi	*I like*
dw i ddim yn hoffi	*I don't like*
gwrando ar	*to listen to*
twmpath (m.)	*ceilidh, barn dance*
opera (f.)	*opera*
cymanfa ganu	*singing festival*
dawns (f.)	*dance*
dawnswyr (pl.)	*dancers*
cerddorfa (f.)	*orchestra*
telyn (f.)	*harp*
cryno disg (m.)	*compact disc*
record (f.)	*record*
cyfansoddwr (m.)	*composer*
cyfansoddi	*to compose*
cyngerdd (m/f.)	*concert*
tôn (f.)	*tune*
emyn (f.)	*hymn*
symffoni (f.)	*symphony*
pibau (pl.)	*pipes*
bandiau pres	*brass bands*
offerynol	*instrumental*
pianydd (m.)	*pianist*
cystadleuaeth (f.)	*competition*
gwyl (f.)	*festival*
beirniad (m.)	*judge, adjudicator*

Taking it further

Reading

Cale, John, *What's Welsh for Zen?* (London: 2001)

Crockett, Kate, *Y Sîn Roc* (Talybont: 1995)

Herbert, Trevor & Stead Peter (eds.), *Hymns and Arias* (Cardiff: 2001)

Wright, Brian, *To Hell and Back with Catatonia* (London: 2001)

Websites

www.landofsong.net contains general information regarding the current music scene as well as biographies, concert listings and links to various other music-related sites in Wales.

www.welshbands.com

www.pluckandsqueeze.com lists English-language folk evenings in south and west Wales and has links to several other Welsh folk-music sites.

www.choir.demon.co.uk lists male voice choirs in Wales with links to the home pages of some of them.

www.eisteddfod.org.uk is the website for the National Eisteddfod.

Information on events

The Friday edition of the national newspaper *The Western Mail* contains details and contact numbers for all major musical events in Wales during the coming week.

Golwg, the Welsh-language arts and current affairs magazine, frequently contains features on Welsh bands and gives weekly listings of Welsh-language pop concerts and folk nights.

Taplas, the English-language bi-monthly magazine of the folk scene in Wales can be obtained from 182 Broadway, Roath, Cardiff CF2 1QJ; Tel: 02920 499759

Record companies

All of the following have extensive mail order catalogues. It is also possible to buy online from Sain on **www.sainwales.com**

Sain, Canolfan Sain, Llandwrog, Caernarfon, Gwynedd LL54 5TG; Tel: 01286 831111

Fflach Records, Llys y Coed, Tenby Road, Cardigan, Ceredigion SA43 3AH; Tel: 01239 614691

Ankst Records, 106 Cowbridge Road East, Cardiff CF1 9DX; Tel: 02920 235453

Festivals

For further details of those festivals already mentioned and others such as the Gŵyl Ifan Dance festival, Sesiwn Fawr Dolgellau or the St David's Cathedral festival contact the **Welsh Tourist Board,** Brunel House, 2 Fitzalan Road, Cardiff, CF24 0UY; Tel: 02920 499909. Their website **www.visitwales.com** also contains an extensive events list.

06

Welsh traditions, festivals and customs

In this unit you will learn about

- seasonal festivals and customs
- customs associated with courtship and marriage
- emblems, flags and crests
- Welsh folklore, national costume and folk stories

Like all countries, Wales has a rich tradition of celebrations and festivals but like many other modern societies, a number of the old cultural traditions are being forgotten as people turn to the ready-made entertainment of the mass-media and urbanization transforms community life. In addition to preserving the Eisteddfod, the *Noson Lawen* (community-based evenings of entertainment provided by local people), the *twmpath dawns* (barn dances) and the *Cymanfa Ganu* (Singing Festival), Wales has also managed to keep alive other old traditions, though some of these are now confined to particular areas. Many folk customs relate to the calendar or are seasonal.

Seasonal customs

Dydd Calan: New Year's Day 1 January

The church celebrated New Year's Day (*Dydd Calan*) on 12 January until 1752 when the Gregorian calendar was introduced in Britain. Since then this day has been celebrated on 1 January. In Wales, as in many other parts of the world, Christmas and the New Year are a time of celebration and rejoicing. New Year is a time to express good wishes for the coming year. One of the customs still practised in Wales at New Year is that of *calennig* (a small New Year gift). Very early on New Year's Day, groups of children visit all the houses in their village and sing or chant a short verse that celebrates the letting in of the New Year and wish health and prosperity to all in the household. In return, they are given money or sweets. The practice of giving *calennig* is an ancient custom and originally the children would carry an apple or orange into which sprigs of holly, oats or corn had been inserted. The apple/orange was fixed on three short wooden skewers. The custom is practised from the early hours until noon after which it is considered very unlucky indeed.

There used to be many superstitions associated with the New Year, it was thought that if you had not paid all your debts by this date, you would remain in debt throughout the whole year. It was also considered very unlucky to lend anything on New Year's Day, even a candle. How one behaved at New Year was an indication of how one would behave throughout the coming year: if for some reason you rose early on 1 January, you would be an early riser for the rest of the year. It was also thought that good or bad luck would be brought to the household by the first visitor of the New Year. In some areas, it was considered unlucky for a man to see a woman first; in others, it was thought unlucky for a woman to see a man first. Some people believed that you would suffer misfortune if the first person you saw at New Year was a red-haired man. In general, a dark-haired person was preferred as the first visitor to a house on 1 January. *Nos Galan* (New Year's Eve) is generally more widely celebrated in Wales than New Year's Day.

Living in the past

Even to this day, numerous areas continue to celebrate *Dydd Calan* on either 12 or 13 January, adhering to the old pre-Gregorian New Year. Before the arrival of the Romans, this night was one of Wales' fire festivals and was celebrated across the Celtic world. Celtic people believed that life was a continuous circle and that rebirth followed death. The celebration of the old new year, or *Hen Galan* as it is called in Welsh, is particularly prevalent in the Gwaun valley in Pembrokeshire. *Hen Galan* was originally celebrated as a matter of 'principle'. There was general mistrust of the new Gregorian calendar when it was introduced in 1752, and riots were widespread throughout Wales when the calendar was first adopted. To accommodate the new calendar, 12 days had to be 'dropped' from the year and people were worried that almost two weeks of their life had been stolen from them.

Mari Lwyd (grey mare)

One custom associated with the end of the Christmas season, which was formerly carried out in all parts of Wales, is that of the *Mari Lwyd*. The custom is ancient and has its roots in other pre-Christian customs. This tradition now only survives in a few areas, although the practice is now being revived in many places where it had formerly died out. The *Mari Lwyd* is a horse's skull, decorated with reins and bells, and covered with a white sheet bedecked with colourful ribbons. The skull is carried around on a tall pole by someone concealed under the sheet. The horse's jaw is fitted with springs which enable it to open and close and make a snapping sound. The *Mari Lwyd* is carried from door to door accompanied by people dressed as Sergeant, Merryman, Punch and Judy. At the house doors, the team

engages in a battle of wits with the people inside in order to gain entry. Verses are recited by the team as they beg for admittance. Those inside the house reply, also in verse, refusing entry. One such opening verse is:

Mari Lwyd

Wel, dyma ni'n dwad,
Gyfeillion diniwad
I 'mofyn am gennad i ganu

Well here we come
Simple friends
To ask for permission to sing

The *Mari* and her companions sing until they inevitably win the contest and are permitted to enter. Once inside the house, the *Mari* chases the young ladies, snapping its jaws. Judy pretends to sweep the hearth and Punch engages in all kinds of mischief until food and drink are offered.

Twelfth Night (the evening of 5 January)

Twelfth Night was celebrated as the end of Christmastide. This is the date when the decorations, including holly and mistletoe, were taken down. The ashes of the Christmas log were removed from the fireplace and stored until spring when they were buried along with the seeds planted to ensure a good harvest. Nowadays, it is still considered bad luck to leave Christmas decorations up after Twelfth Night.

Dydd Santes Dwynwen (St Dwynwen's Day) 25 January

St Dwynwen's Day is 25 January, when Welsh lovers send cards to each other. Dwynwen, the patron saint of Welsh lovers, was the daughter of Brychan, King of Wales, during the fifth century. She was known to be beautiful, religious and pure and a man called Maelon fell in love with her and wanted to marry her. Even though Dwynwen loved him, she rejected him because she wanted to become a nun. In a dream, she took a potion that saved her from his attentions, but this resulted in him turning to ice. She knew Maelon loved her so she prayed that he be restored to life. Dwynwen then became a nun and went to live on Llanddwyn Island. Nowadays, on the Isle of Anglesey, lovers walk along a route which goes along the beach to Llanddwyn Island to the ruins of a church dedicated to St Dwynwen.

Dydd Gŵyl Dewi (St David's Day) 1 March

1 March, AD 589 is the traditional date of the death of St David, the patron saint of Wales. He was a Celtic monk, who became the Archbishop of Wales and was one of many early saints who helped to spread Christianity among the pagan Celtic tribes of western Britain by establishing churches. Dewi was born near Capel Non (Non's chapel) on the south-west Wales coast near the city of St David's. Little is known about his early life. He was educated in a monastery called *Hen Fynyw*, by a blind monk named Paulinus. There are many stories about Dewi. According to one of them, at a synod of the church in Llanddewibrefi, he stood up to address a congregation. The crowd shouted that they were unable to see or hear him, so Dewi produced a handkerchief and placed it on the ground. He then stood on it and the ground rose underneath him so he could be seen by everyone. It is said that Dewi lived for over 100 years and was buried in the grounds of his own monastery, where the Cathedral of St David now stands. Eisteddfodau are held in schools throughout Wales on this date and children wear national costume. There is a movement within Wales campaigning to make 1 March a national holiday.

Sul y Blodau (Sunday of the Flowers)

Palm Sunday is known in Welsh as *Sul y Blodau* (Sunday of the Flowers) and on this day it is the custom to decorate the graves in the churchyards with flowers as a preparation for Easter.

Graves are often cleaned, weeded and whitewashed before being decked with garlands of spring flowers.

Calan Haf 1 May

In Celtic times, the year was divided into two dominant seasons, summer and winter. In Wales, the first day of May is known as *Calan Mai* or *Calan Haf*, which means the first day of summer. *Calan Haf* marked the beginning of summer and was a time for celebration and courtship. The celebrations would start on May Eve, the evening before *Calan Mai*. The tradition of lighting midsummer bonfires happened annually in south Wales until the middle of the nineteenth century. Maypole dancing was also a feature of *Calan Haf* and this is still practised today.

Calan Gaeaf 31 October

Calan Gaeaf was the traditional beginning of winter in the old Celtic year. *Nos Galan Gaeaf* (All Hallow's Eve) is thought of as being the time of the year when spirits come to life and supernatural beings are visible to mankind. On stiles or entrances to footpaths, ghosts of the dead were said to appear at midnight. One such supernatural being which is said to manifest itself on this day is the *Hwch Ddu Gwta* or short black pig. This terrifying tailless pig is said to chase people. The *Hwch Ddu Gwta* used to be associated with bonfires which were lit at dawn on hillsides. Apples and potatoes were thrown into the fires for roasting and men would dance or leap through the flames for good luck. Stones were thrown into the fire, then, when the flames died down, everyone would run for home to escape the *Hwch Ddu Gwta*. The next morning, at daybreak, searchers would try to find their stones. For those who found their stone, the coming year would bring good fortune. If you could not find your stone, then bad luck or even death would follow. Many of the rituals on *Nos Galan Gaeaf* consisted of ways to foretell the future. In some areas, a mash was made of nine ingredients: potatoes, carrots, turnips, peas, parsnips, leeks, pepper, salt and new milk. In the mash was hidden a wedding ring. The young woman who found the ring would be first married. Apples have always played a large part in Halloween festivities. Apple bobbing is still a very popular Halloween game. Six or eight perfectly round fruit are placed in a large bowl of water set on the floor. Then, with both hands tied behind one's back, one tries to pick up an apple with only one's teeth. Apples play a large part in many other customs, too. It is thought that if you peel an apple in one single piece and then throw the peel over your shoulder, the letter of the alphabet it most closely resembled when it hits the ground will be the initial letter of your future partner in marriage.

December

As in many other European countries, there are many traditions connected with Christmas in Wales, some religious and some entirely secular. Generally Christmas was of lesser importance than New Year. In many parts of Wales up until quite recently, it was the custom to get up very early on Christmas morning to attend the Church service known as *Plygain* held between three and six a.m. *Plygain* means Cockcrow and the *Plygain* service is unique to Wales. To pass the time during the long overnight wait on Christmas Eve, young people would make treacle toffee and decorate their houses with freshly gathered mistletoe and holly and play divining games. Green plants, especially evergreens, were seen as symbols of the return of spring. The mistletoe was considered both a magical plant and a powerful protector of the home from evil. The holly, a symbol of eternal life, was also prominently displayed, along with ivy, rosemary and bay leaves. These plants also had the added advantage of having pleasant scents to disguise household smells that had built up during the winter months when doors and windows were not opened. The method of cooking the toffee caused it to twist into curly, letter-like shapes. These toffee shapes were then used for the divination of future loves. Others would spend the time dancing and singing until it was time to go to the *Plygain* service. The churches would be lit with beautifully decorated candles. The *Plygain* itself was often a short form of morning service in which carols were sung by visiting soloists and groups of singers. Many of the carols and songs are very old indeed, and are traditionally sung by men without accompaniment. *Plygain* music is still very popular and recorded material is still available, and several places around Wales still hold the service.

O little town of Bethlehem

One relatively recent Christmas tradition is the sending of Christmas cards to the post office in the small village of Bethlehem near Llandeilo to be franked with the name 'Bethlehem'. People from all over the world send their Christmas mail to the post office.

Nos Galan (New Year's Eve)

The night before *Dydd Calan* (see the beginning of this unit), the activities of the Christmas season came to a climax at the New Year when there was, and still is, much merry-making.

Courtship and marriage

The Welsh love spoon

One courting tradition in Wales that has been in practice since the sixteenth century is the carving of a wooden love spoon. The spoons, which are carved from a single piece of wood, were originally made by young men as a love token for their sweethearts (or to present to girls with whom they hoped to start a relationship). To accept the spoon meant that the girl welcomed the giver's advances, returning the spoon indicated that she was not interested in him at all. The carving of love spoons was a particular pastime enjoyed by farm labourers during the winter. Some of the spoons had intricate designs and

various symbols, such as hearts, keys, chains, bells or small, loose balls were carved into the spoon. Some of the designs can be interpreted as follows: two bowls sprouting from one handle signifies the unity of two lovers, keys or keyholes signifies sharing a home. Many spoons are carved with a swivel or chain attachment with the number of links showing the number of children desired. Naturally, many have the heart or entwined hearts motif, some bear the initials of the lovers. The spoons were given long handles and could be hung on the wall as reminders or as decorations. The finest display of love spoons is now on permanent exhibition at the Museum of Welsh Life, St. Ffagans. Love spoons are still being given by lovers today, and are now made by craftsmen for sale and are a favourite tourist souvenir.

Love spoon

Wells

There are holy wells and wishing wells all over Wales into which people still throw money. Some wishing wells are said to help your love life, others, according to tradition, can heal the sick. The most visited holy well in Wales is Saint Winifrid's Well in Holywell, north Wales where many of the local residents keep a bottle of water from the well in their homes in case they become ill. Winifrid was the niece of the seventh-century Saint Beuno. Winifrid was a beautiful and godly woman who had dedicated her life to God. She was beheaded by a local chieftain named Caradog at a place called Sychnant after she refused his advances. The head rolled down a hill towards Beuno's chapel and the well is said to have sprung from the exact spot where Winifrid's head landed. St Non's Well in Pembrokeshire, named after the mother of St David, is another well-known holy well in Wales which is also said to possess remarkable curative powers. Another Pembrokeshire well is St Govan's Well which has been regarded as a place where wishes come true as long as the wisher does not change his mind before turning round to go.

Marriage customs

One traditional marriage custom is the prevention of the bride from reaching the church by means of a rope placed over the road. A variation on this is the prevention of the newly married couple from leaving the church grounds until the groom has paid a fine.

Emblems, flags and crests

Flying the flag

Wales is part of the United Kingdom, yet it is not represented on its flag, the Union Jack. The standard of Wales consists of a red dragon on a background of green and white horizontal stripes. Green and white are the traditional colours of Wales and were worn by Welsh bowmen at the battle of Crécy (1346). The national symbol for Wales, *y ddraig goch* (the red dragon) goes back to a time long before the Union Jack was ever put together. The Welsh red dragon is thought to be of Chinese origin and to have been introduced to Britain by the Romans some 1,800 years ago, and was perhaps initially a military standard. By the early fifth century, the red dragon had been adopted by the early Britons to symbolize their authority after the Roman occupation. By the seventh century, it was known as the Red Dragon of Cadwaladr, and was to be forever after associated with the people of Wales.

Historia Brittonum, the manuscript attributed to the ninth-century historian **Nennius**, mentions the red dragon and it was also referred to by **Geoffrey of Monmouth** in his *Historia Regum Britanniae* (1135). Geoffrey names **Uther Pendragon** as the father of **King Arthur**. Uther dreamed of a dragon appearing in a comet and had two dragon standards made when he became king. The English word 'dragon' and the Welsh word *draig* both come from the same Latin root 'draco' and *draig* was used in Welsh poetry to symbolize a leader.

The red dragon is also associated with **Merlin**. According to the legend, sometime during the post-Roman period, Britain was ruled by **Vortigern** (or *Gwrtheyrn* in Welsh). Vortigern was under attack from the Saxons, and decided to build a fortress at Dinas Emrys in Snowdonia, the ancient seat of Welsh power. Every time the fort walls were built they fell down. He consulted wise men who advised him that it was the work of a bad spirit, and that a fatherless child should be sacrificed and its blood poured on the foundations to placate the spirit. The castle could then be built in peace. Men were sent in all directions to seek such a child. A boy, **Myrddin Emrys**, the Merlin of the Arthurian legend, was found and brought to Dinas Emrys. Merlin disclosed the reason why the walls kept falling. He said that two dragons (one white and one red) lived in a lake under the hill, and it was their fighting that was causing the walls to fall down. The white dragon represented the Saxons and the red one the Welsh, and if they were released they could fight elsewhere so that the castle could be built. Merlin was proved right and the dragons were found. He also said that although the white dragon was winning, the red dragon would be triumphant in the end. The king found another site for his stronghold which is still named after him – Nant Gwrtheyrn (Vortigern's Valley) on the Llŷn Peninsula, which is now home to the Welsh Language and Heritage Centre.

Although Owain Glyndŵr (see Unit 1) adopted the red dragon as his standard in 1400 as a symbol of revolt against the English Crown, the dragon continued to be used by the Tudor monarchs. It signified their direct descent from one of the noble families of Wales. Henry VII decreed that the red dragon flag on its white and green background was to be the official flag of Wales. During Henry VIII's reign the red dragon on a green and white background became a favourite emblem on many of the Royal Navy ships. The red dragon lost its popularity under the Stuarts who favoured the unicorn. The red dragon reappeared as the royal badge for Wales in 1807, but wasn't officially recognized as the national flag until 1959 when the Queen was successfully petitioned for its national use by the Gorsedd Beirdd Ynys Prydain (see Unit 10). The red dragon did make an appearance, however, at the 1911 Caernarfon Investiture of Edward, the Prince of Wales. The red dragon flag now flies over public and private buildings all over Wales. The Welsh flag, therefore, has remained unchanged for 1,000 years and was accepted as the oldest flag in the world at the international conference of flag makers in South Africa in 1987. Also gaining popularity in Wales is the flag of St David, a gold cross on a white background.

Crest

The Welsh crest of three white feathers and the motto *Ich Dien* was adopted by the Black Prince at the battle of Crécy. The crest has been adopted by the Princes of Wales since this date and used to be on the international rugby shirt.

The leek

The leek and the daffodil are both emblems of Wales. The leek has been recognized as the emblem of Wales since the mid-sixteenth century but its association with Wales can be traced back to the seventh-century battle of Heathfield. The leek was reputedly adopted after the battle in which Welsh forces wore leeks in their hats to distinguish themselves from their Saxon enemy. According to one legend, it was St David who persuaded the Welsh to wear leeks to distinguish friend from foe although this connection could have been made purely because St David was vegetarian. The leek was also once regarded as an essential ingredient in the diet of Welsh saints, particularly during Lent. It was also a symbol of purity and immortality and was widely used in divination and in folk medicine. Shakespeare notes in Henry V that the Welsh archers wore leeks at the battle of Agincourt in 1415. Since 1984, British pound coins have featured different reverse designs for each of the four parts of the United Kingdom. The leek appears on the reverse of £1 coins to represent Wales.

Leek v daffodil

The daffodil is another national emblem of Wales, which, like the leek, is worn on St David's Day and at international rugby matches. Some people believe that the daffodil became confused with the leek because the Welsh word for leek, *cenhinen* is so similar to the Welsh word for daffodil, *cenhinen Bedr*. The daffodil is said to have gained popularity during the nineteenth century, partly because it was considered to be a more fragrant option to be worn at St David's Day dinners amongst London-based Welsh people.

Folklore and folk stories

Folklore abounds in Wales. We have already mentioned the famous wizard **Merlin**, **Myrddin Emrys**, who was famous as a poet and prophet in Welsh folk tales long before he became Arthur's counsellor. An ancient tree, known as 'Merlin's Oak' used to stand in Priory Street in Carmarthen, surrounded by iron railings. According to folklore, Merlin had uttered a dire prophecy regarding the oak:

When Merlin's Oak shall tumble down,
Then shall fall Carmarthen town

In spite of this, in 1978, the council removed the tree, by then merely a leafless stump, in order to make room for road improvements. Carmarthen remains intact and pieces of the tree are on display in Carmarthen Museum.

In common with other Celtic countries, there has always been a close relationship between folk customs and folk tales and a strong tradition of storytelling around the *aelwyd*, or hearth. One classic folk story from Wales is that of Melangell and the hares. Brochwel Ysgythrog, a sixth-century prince of Powys, was hunting when a hare ran in front of him and hid between the feet of a beautiful young woman. Both the hare and the young woman begged Brochwel not to kill the hare. One of Brochwel's hunting companions tried to blow the horn to summon the dogs to the scene, but no sound came out of the horn which became stuck to his lips. The woman said her name was Melangell and that she had fled from Ireland to avoid marriage to a certain Irish chieftain. She had come to Wales to find peace to worship God. Brochwel realized Melangell was a holy and virtuous woman and gave her some land on which to build a church, where she stayed until she died. Melangell became the patron saint of hares and in Powys, where this incident is said to have taken place, hares are sometimes called *ŵyn bach Melangell,* or Melangell's little lambs. It was also considered unlucky to kill a hare there.

Another tale featuring an animal is the story of Gelert, the faithful dog of **Llywelyn the Great** (1173–1203).

Hunting was one of the favourite pastimes of princes and the gentry. One morning, Llywelyn the Great was setting out with his huntsmen and hounds to chase deer, leaving behind his infant son and heir at the castle. Amongst the Prince's pack of hounds was his favourite, a strong, loyal dog named Gelert. Gelert was a present to Llywelyn from his wife's father, King John. Llywelyn called for Gelert, but Gelert did not appear and no one could find him. Llywelyn went to hunt without his faithful hound. After the hunt, the hunters returned to the castle. Llywelyn immediately went to visit his young son. In the boy's room the prince was horror stricken to see Gelert lying exhausted on the floor with bloodstained mouth and paws. The baby's cradle lay upturned and there was no sign of the infant. Llywelyn was sure Gelert had killed his son and in his anger, he drew his sword and plunged it into the hound. He then heard a faint cry from behind the upturned cradle. There he saw his son lying unharmed and safe. He also found the bloodstained body of a huge wolf which had been torn to pieces. Llywelyn was grief-stricken when he realized that, had it not been for his faithful hound Gelert, his baby would surely have been slain. In order to honour his hound's memory, Llywelyn had Gelert buried in a beautiful meadow just below the precipitous side of Cerrig Llan. The grave consists of a slab lying on its side and two upright stones and to this day the place is called Beddgelert (Gelert's grave). It is still possible to go and see Gelert's grave at Beddgelert. However, it is now known that Gelert's grave did not exist 200 years ago; it was erected by a South Walian hotelier, **David Pritchard** who became the landlord of the Royal Goat Hotel in 1800 and who wished to attract tourists to the area.

There are many Welsh folk tales about lakes and drowned cities. Cantre'r Gwaelod (literally the lowland hundred) is the name of land once, according to legend, in Cardigan Bay that was submerged by a sudden flood. Cantre'r Gwaelod was ruled by King Gwyddno Garanhir. The land was protected from the sea by an embankment with sluices, which were the responsibility of a man called Seithennin. One night, after a great feast, Seithennin forgot to close the sluices and the town and its inhabitants were drowned. According to the legend, the sound of the church bells of Cantre'r Gwaelod can still be heard ringing under the sea.

National costume

The popular image of Welsh 'national' dress, a woman in a *betgwn* (gown), *ffedog* (apron), *pais* (petticoat), *siôl* (shawl), and tall black hat with lace cap underneath is an extension of clothing which was worn by Welsh countrywomen during the late eighteenth and nineteenth centuries. The tall hats were the same as those worn by men of the period. The Welsh national costume, then, is in fact the common dress of farm servants and cottagers. The style of *betgwn* varied, some were coat-like loose gowns, others had a fitted bodice and long skirts and others were short and of a similar style to a riding habit. At first plain shawls with a woven patterned border attached were the most common. Later the paisley pattern became very popular in Wales along with home-produced woollen shawls with checked patterns. Original costumes can be seen in the Museum of Welsh Life at St Ffagans. The adoption of this dress as the national costume of Wales was mainly due to the activities of **Lady Llanover** (1802–96), the wife of an iron master in Gwent. Lady Llanover was passionately interested in everything to do with Welsh culture – music, folk dancing, costume, cookery and poetry and was a fervent believer in keeping what she considered to be Welsh traditional culture alive. To her, the wearing of an identifiable Welsh costume was important in order to present a national identity, so she designed a new costume based on the clothes worn in the eighteenth and nineteenth centuries. Servants at her estate in south Wales were issued with her new Welsh costume and she published a series of pictures of costumes which were supposed to be typical of the various Welsh counties.

GLOSSARY

dathlu	to celebrate
gŵyl (f.)	festival
traddodiad (m.)	tradition
draig (f.)	dragon
chwedl (f.)	legend
cymdeithas (f.)	society
Blwyddyn Newydd Dda	Happy New Year
Nadolig (m.)	Christmas
Nadolig Llawen	Happy Christmas
diwylliant (m.)	culture
ofergoel (f.)	superstition
arfer (m./f.)	custom

cenhinen (f.)	*leek*
cennin Pedr	*daffodils*
baner (f.)	*flag*
noson lawen	*'merry evening'*
straeon gwerin	*folk tales*
gwerin (f.)	*folk*
het (f.)	*hat*
Pasg (m.)	*Easter*
gwisg (f.)	*costume*
blodau (pl.)	*flowers*
ffynnon (f.)	*well*
coelcerth (f.)	*bonfire*

Taking it further

Reading

Barber, Chris, *More Mysterious Wales* (London: 1987)

Gwyndaf, Robin, *Welsh Folk Tales* (Cardiff: 1999)

Humphreys, Emyr, *The Taliesin Tradition: A Quest for the Welsh Identity* (London: 1983)

Jones, T. Gwynn, *Welsh Folklore and Folk-Custom* (Cambridge: 1979)

Jones, Francis, *The Holy Wells of Wales* (Cardiff: 1992)

Owen, Trefor M., *A Pocket Guide – The Customs and Traditions of Wales* (Cardiff: 1991)

Ross, Anne, *Folktales of Wales* (Stroud: 2001)

Websites

If you have access to the internet, you will find the following sites useful:

www.data-wales.co.uk

www.bbc.co.uk/wales/about/events-customs.shtml

www.informationwales.co.uk

www.worldwidewales.tv/html/movie-150.php: a film of the *Mari Lwyd*

07

creativity in other spheres

In this unit you will learn about
- famous Welsh scientists and inventors
- the media, cinema
- famous Welsh actors
- Welsh fashion and food and drink

Scientists and inventors

Wales is often thought of as a land of musicians and writers and the contribution of the Welsh to science and technology is less well known. One person who has successfully embraced both disciplines is forensic pathologist and barrister **Bernard Knight** (1931–) from Cardiff. In 1994 he was the pathologist involved in the identification of all 12 women, many of whom had been missing for many years, in the Fred West murder inquiry in Gloucester. As well as being involved in cases all over the world, he has written many medical textbooks and popular, non-fiction medical books. He also enjoys an international reputation as a detective writer and historical novelist and has written numerous TV storylines and radio plays.

Another example is award-winning TV scriptwriter **Elaine Morgan** (1920–), who first received international recognition with her book, *The Descent of Woman* (1972). This heralded the start of her research into the Aquatic Ape Theory, as discussed in later volumes such as *The Aquatic Ape* (1982), *The Scars of The Descent of the Child* (1994) and *Aquatic Ape Theory* (1999). She is now recognized as the principal figure associated with this theory which suggests that man's ancestors passed through a semi-aquatic existence before returning to a predominantly terrestrial lifestyle.

Other scientists with Welsh connections who have contributed to the discussion on evolution include **Alfred Russel Wallace** (1823–1913) and **Steve Jones** (1944–). Alfred Russel Wallace from Monmouthshire was acknowledged by Darwin as theory co-founder in his *On the Origin of Species* (1859), whilst Steve Jones, renowned geneticist, prolific broadcaster and best-selling author of popular science books such as *The Language of Genes* (1993), was born in Aberystwyth.

Many people are also unaware of the fact that three important mathematical symbols were invented by Welshmen. **Robert Recorde** (1510–58) from Tenby in Pembrokeshire was the founder of modern algebra and the first to use the symbols + and =. He was also one of the first in Britain to believe Copernicus' theory that the planets moved around the sun. He wrote several books and was physician to King Edward VI and Queen Mary.

The other mathematical genius was **William Jones** (1675–1749) from Anglesey, who in his book *Synopsis Palmariorum Mathesios* (1706) was the first to use the sixteenth letter of the

Greek alphabet, namely pi (π), to represent the ratio of the circumference to the diameter of a circle. He was also interested in navigation and used mathematics to calculate positions at sea as described in his book *A New Compendium of the Whole Art of Navigation.*

If asked to name a Welsh scientist, **Edward Lhuyd** (1660–1709) would be the obvious choice of many Welsh speakers. The society that bears his name, *Cymdeithas Edward Llwyd*, organizes weekly Welsh-language nature walks throughout Wales as well as regular study sessions and workshops. Lhuyd, who became curator of the Ashmolean museum in Oxford, specialized originally in botany and geology but later concentrated on studying antiquities and philology in a scientific way. He compiled a catalogue of British fossils *Lithophylacii Britannici Ichnographia* (1699), but his greatest work was his *Archaelogica Britannica* (1707), which inaugurated the study of comparative Celtic philology.

Wales has also made an important contribution to the field of wireless communication. **David Edward Hughes** (1831–90), who emigrated with his family to Virginia as a young boy, was the first to transmit and receive radio waves, although due to a lack of support he was never able to develop his discovery, which was later explored further by German scientist Heinrich Hertz. Hughes also invented the carbon microphone and the printing telegraph adopted by the American Telegraph Company, which was later used all over Europe and was introduced into Britain in 1863.

William Henry Preece (1834–1913) from Caernarfon was sceptical of Hughes' discoveries, but he too showed that it was possible to transmit signals over or through land and water by using the earth's magnetic field. He did many experiments near Porthcawl in south Wales, where Marconi in 1897 transmitted messages without the use of wires to the island of Flat Holm off the Somerset coast. A short time later Preece created the world's first practical wireless system for commercial use. As well as introducing to Britain the monograph, or early gramophone, he was also a pioneer in the use of electricity on the railways.

Evan James Williams (1903–45) from Llanybydder in west Wales is considered one of the greatest physicists of the twentieth century and his death at the age of 42 was a great loss to scientific development. In 1939 he discovered a new particle, meson, only to find that scientists in California had made a similar discovery a month earlier. It was Williams however who showed through experimentation how meson turned into an electron. Although a Japanese scientist had already published this theory, it was not proved until Williams made his discovery.

The media

The press

Wales has a wide range of local and regional newspapers such as the *South Wales Evening Post*, the *Wrexham Evening Leader*, and the *South Wales Argus*. *The Western Mail*, founded in 1869, claims to be the 'national newspaper of Wales'. It contains a mix of local, Welsh and British news and is very pro-Conservative in outlook. Many derogatorily call it *Llais y Sais* (The Voice of the English), whilst another popular name for it is 'The Western Wail'.

The London-based papers are still the most popular in Wales, particularly the tabloids such as the *Sun*. The *Welsh Mirror,* a Welsh edition of the *Daily Mirror,* was launched in 1999 but ceased production in 2003. The Liverpool based *Daily Post* has a strong following in north Wales.

The only national Sunday paper in Wales is *Wales on Sunday,* which was launched in 1989. A populist tabloid, it did not live up to the expectations of many hoping for a more serious broadsheet. Nevertheless its detailed coverage of Welsh sporting events has been its salvation and sales have been consistently good.

There are many English-language magazines on the arts in Wales and some of these are described in Unit 3. Others include *Cambria* and *One Wales. Cambria,* a glossy bi-monthly containing a wide variety of articles on Welsh culture past and present, subtitles itself the 'national magazine of Wales'. *One Wales*, a quarterly publication, concentrates on contemporary Wales with short features on anything from the arts, to sport, to travel or business.

There is no daily newspaper in Welsh, neither is there a Sunday paper. A weekly general interest newspaper called *Y Cymro* (The Welshman), which first appeared in 1932, has a readership of around 5,000. In 1988 the arts and current affairs weekly *Golwg* (View) was founded. *Lingo* is a bi-monthly magazine for Welsh learners and *WCW a'i ffrindiau* (WCW and friends), is a comic for the under sevens. *V* is a magazine for the 16–25 market, produced by *Golwg*.

There are also approximately 50 Welsh-language monthly local magazines or *Papurau Bro*. These first appeared during the 1970s to help halt the decline in the reading of Welsh. It is estimated that between them these magazines sell approximately 70,000 copies each month. They are produced by volunteers with the help of grants from the Welsh Language Board.

The radio

The first radio station in Wales was opened in Cardiff in 1923 and another was opened in Swansea in 1924. Virtually all the programmes were in English, although there were a few items in Welsh, such as a series of Welsh lessons. In 1935 a studio was opened in Bangor which broadcast more Welsh-language programmes. Two years later Wales received its own wavelength, known as 'the Welsh region'.

With the introduction of VHF, the BBC decided to have an English-language service for Wales on medium wave and a Welsh-language service on VHF. By the late 1970s Radio Cymru and Radio Wales were born, leading to a comprehensive service in the two languages.

Radio Cymru now broadcasts 20 hours a day and offers a variety of easy-listening music shows along with an extensive news and sport service. Many listeners have criticized the decision to include English pop music in many of the music shows, especially those late at night geared for younger audiences. It is available on satellite on channel 904.

Radio Wales is similar to Radio Cymru in content. Amongst its most popular programmes is the daily current affairs programme, *Good Morning Wales* and the music and chat show presented by Roy Noble, one of Wales' most well-known media hosts. There is also a daily programme for Welsh learners called *Catchphrase*.

As well as all the usual UK radio stations, there are a number of commercial stations specific to Wales. For example, Red Dragon FM serves the Cardiff area, whilst Swansea Sound extends as far west as Pembrokeshire. Commercial stations in north Wales include Champion FM around Caernarfon and Bangor and Radio Maldwyn in north Powys.

Growth of Welsh-language television

The BBC first began transmitting programmes in Welsh in 1952. The first programme entirely in Welsh was a religious service from Cardiff, broadcast on St David's Day 1953. As there was no word for television in Welsh, a competition was held to devise one. Over 1,000 suggestions were generated and the word *teledu* eventually selected. One of its merits was that it could be used as a noun and a verb. It is derived from tel as in television and *darlledu*, the Welsh verb for to broadcast. (It was noted however that it was also the name of the stinking badger of Sumatra.)

By the early 1960s the BBC and commercial TV were producing about 12 hours of programmes in Welsh every week. These tended to be shown late at night or in the afternoon. By the late 1960s, however, many people began to call for a substantial increase in Welsh broadcasts, particularly during peak viewing times. Nevertheless, at the same time, many non-Welsh speakers were deliberately choosing aerials which didn't receive programmes produced in Wales, so as to avoid Welsh-language programmes. It became clear that the only way to keep everyone content was to set up a separate Welsh-language channel. In 1974 the Crawford Committee recommended this to the Labour government, who accepted its decision.

Five years later however, a new Conservative government reversed this decision, choosing instead to improve the existing provision, in spite of having supported the idea in their manifesto. Thousands of viewers in Wales angrily responded by refusing to renew their licences, with a small minority raiding transmitters. The most effective protest however was that of Gwynfor Evans, the President of *Plaid Cymru*, who threatened to go on hunger strike if a Welsh channel wasn't created.

The protests had their desired effect and on 17 September 1980 the Government agreed that all Welsh language broadcasts should be concentrated on one channel called *Sianel Pedwar Cymru* (Channel 4 Wales). S4C, as it is known, began broadcasting on 1 November 1982, the first channel within the European Community to concentrate on broadcasting in a 'lesser-used' language. Initially it was on the air for 70 hours a week, 22 of which were in Welsh. The remainder of the hours consisted of some of Channel Four UK's more interesting programmes.

S4C today

S4C now broadcasts around 150 hours a week of which around 40 are in Welsh. The majority of these are scheduled in prime viewing time. By far the most popular Welsh programme is the soap opera *Pobol y Cwm* (People of the Valley). Based around the fictional village of Cwmderi in south-west Wales, it is broadcast five times a week. Most of the Welsh-language programmes are subtitled in English on Sbectel 888 and simplified Welsh subtitles are available on 889. In November 1998 a new Welsh-language digital channel was set up and S4C programmes are now available throughout Europe by satellite on channel 104.

Other TV stations

The majority of programmes shown on BBC One Wales and BBC Two Wales are the same as those shown throughout the UK. There are however news and sports programmes particular to Wales such as *Wales Today*, and *Scrum Five,* along with certain education and political programmes. Harlech Television (HTV) is the present holder of the licence to broadcast on the commercial ITV network. Channel 5 UK is available in some, but not all, parts of Wales.

Cinema

Silent film days

Two significant figures who played an important role in the development of the screen industry in Wales were **Arthur Cheetham** (1864–1936) and **William Haggar** (1851–1925). Arthur Cheetham made around 30 simple documentaries and opened the first permanent cinema in Rhyl, north Wales, in 1906. William Haggar made approximately 60 high-quality films which embraced most genres and his bioscope or travelling cinema introduced the world of the cinema to many rural communities in mid and west Wales.

Mining films

The Proud Valley (1940) is seen by many as the archetypal mining film. It is also virtually the only British film of the period to feature a black actor, Paul Robeson, as the lead character. Robeson plays the part of an unemployed seaman who arrives in a Welsh village looking for work. His excellent singing voice wins him a place in the local choir and a job in the mines. A fire leads to the closure of the mine, but the miners, aided by Robeson, persuade the owners to reopen it. The film ends on a celebratory note with a rendering of the Welsh national anthem in English by the local choir and brass band.

A year later saw the release of *How Green was my Valley* which won five Oscars. The story is told through the voice of Huw, who is 50 years old and about to leave the area. The film tells of life in the valley prior to the coal mines and slagheaps, which have destroyed the beauty of the place. In spite of the fact that the valley doesn't look a bit like a Welsh valley, the rooms in the houses are much too big and the Irish and English cast have strange Welsh accents, it is a powerful and moving film.

Other significant mining films include *Fame is the Spur* (1947) and *Blue Scar* (1949), which was directed by Jill Cragie, the only woman director of the time.

Contemporary images

In 1997 *Twin Town* became the most commercially successful 'Welsh' film since *How Green was my Valley*. The picture it presents of Wales however is very different to that of its romantic predecessor. *Twin Town* is a black comedy based in Swansea and tells the tale of Julian and Jeremy, unemployed, drug-taking twins who steal cars and generally cause mayhem in their 'pretty shitty city'. The terraced house is replaced by a caravan, the male voice choir by karaoke in the local pub and insensitive mine owners by corrupt businessmen.

It is a brave and confident film that shows it is possible to ignore the obvious ways to be Welsh or to laugh at them from within. Similar in approach to the British *Carry On* films and labelled by some as a Welsh version of the Scottish film *Trainspotting*, it was criticized by many, including the clergy, the Welsh Tourist Board and Swansea City Council. Sadly its satirical message was missed by many of its critics.

House of America (1997) also questions the idea of a Welsh identity. The story is based around a family living in the upper Swansea Valley. The children believe that their father is in America and all that he has left behind is a Harley Davidson bike, Jack Kerouac's 'On the Road' and some albums by the 1960s Welsh band *Velvet Underground*. The brother and sister have no money, so they can't go to America, but they pretend that they are Jack Kerouac and his girlfriend. Their American dream gives them hope for the future.

The desire to escape is once again apparent in the highly successful *Human Traffic* (1999). The film is set in Cardiff and documents a weekend in the lives of five friends who, through partying, clubbing and drug-taking, escape the humdrum of their everyday existence. This is not a second *Twin Town* however, the film is at pains to show that these are ordinary young members of society. Whilst knowing the risks, even 'nice kids' do drugs in Wales today and enjoy themselves too. Although the film takes no moral stance, conventionality wins the day – ultimately, falling in love makes life's stresses and anxieties easier to bear.

Welsh-language films

The first Welsh-language talkie *Y Chwarelwr* (The Quarryman, 1935) was made by Sir Ifan ab Owen Edwards, founder of the *Urdd*, the Welsh League of Youth (see Unit 10). The film tells of a young man who, following his father's death, sacrifices the chance of a university education to earn enough money in the quarries so that his younger sister can go to college.

Apart from *Y Chwarelwr*, *Yr Etifeddiaeth* (The Inheritance, 1949) and *Noson Lawen* (Merry Evening, 1949), there were very few Welsh-language films until the founding of the Welsh Film Board in the 1970s. Since the founding of S4C the Welsh-language film industry has flourished, producing many high-quality films such as *Hedd Wyn* (1992) and *Gadael Lenin* (1993). *Hedd Wyn* tells the tragic life story of the poet Elis Evans, killed in action in 1917, days before being awarded the main prize at the National Eisteddfod. It became the first Welsh-language film to be nominated for Hollywood's Foreign Language Film Oscar. The year 2000 saw another Welsh film receive an Oscar nomination: *Solomon and Gaenor* is a tale of forbidden love between Gaenor, the daughter of a poor, highly religious Welsh family and Solomon, a young Jewish cotton seller. It was made in Welsh, English and Yiddish.

Oed yr Addewid (Do not go Gentle) won the best fiction category at the Festival International de Programmes Audiovisuels in Biarritz in 2001. A tragicomedy set during the weeks leading up to the 1997 British general election, it charts an old man's descent into senility.

Some stars of the screen

Ivor Novello (1893–1951), in the 1920s (see Unit 5), was the first in a long tradition of Welsh actors to make his mark on the international stage. The 1950s were a particularly fruitful period and saw the likes of Stanley Baker, Glyn Houston, Meredith Edwards and Rachel Roberts becoming household names. But by far the most famous of this prolific group was **Richard Burton** (1925–84) from Pontrhydyfen, whose film debut *The Last Days of Dolwyn* (1947) was made by Welsh director Emlyn Williams.

Following an Oscar nomination for his role in *The Robe* (1953), Burton had starring roles in films such as *Prince of Players* (1955) and *Alexander the Great* (1956). However, it was his performance in *Cleopatra* (1963) and his much-sensationalized affair with co-star Elizabeth Taylor that truly launched him as an international superstar. One of his greatest performances was playing George opposite Elizabeth Taylor in *Who's Afraid of Virginia Woolf* (1966). His strong theatrical voice also led to several notable stage performances such as that of Hamlet on Broadway in 1964.

Many criticized him in the 1970s for wasting his talent by taking part in films simply for money, which he spent on alcohol or on the many women in his life. One of his greatest later performances was in the title role in *Wagner* (1983) completed a year before his death from a brain haemorrhage. At his request a copy of the complete works of Dylan Thomas was placed in his grave.

Although principally a stage actress, **Siân Phillips** (1934–), is another Welsh name to come into prominence during the 1950s. She married Peter O'Toole in 1959 and acted alongside him in several films such as *Becket* (1964), *Goodbye Mr Chips* (1971) and *Under Milk Wood* (1971). More recently she appeared in *The Age of Innocence* (1993) and *House of America* (1997). She has played the lead in countless TV dramas, but is probably best remembered as Livia in *I Claudius*.

Like Siân Phillips, **Anthony Hopkins** (1934–), was a successful stage actor before achieving big screen success with *The Lion in Winter* (1968). Born only ten miles from the home of Richard Burton, he is frequently labelled as his successor. He won an Oscar for his portrayal of serial killer Hannibal Lecter in *The Silence of the Lambs* (1991) and since then hasn't looked back. He went on to star in films such as *Nixon* (1995), *Meet Joe Black* (1998) and *Instinct* (1999), gaining another three Oscar nominations during the 1990s. He moved into directing with *August* (1996), an adaptation of Checkhov's *Uncle Vanya*, filmed in Wales. He also acted in the film and composed the musical score.

In 2001, he returned to his alter ego, psychopath Hannibal Lecter in *Hannibal*, which made 100 million dollars in just nine days. *Red Dragon*, the first volume in the Lecter trilogy by Thomas Harris, was released in 2002. The year 2003 saw the release of *The Human Stain* in which Hopkins played the part of Coleman Silk, a professor whose career and reputation was in ruins.

After appearing in the popular British TV series, *The Darling Buds of May*, in the early 1990s, Swansea-born **Catherine Zeta Jones** (1969–), moved to the USA to forward her career. Her role in a docudrama *Titanic* led Steven Spielberg to choose her for the lead in *The Mask of Zorro* (1998). Other highly acclaimed performances followed including *Entrapment* (1999) with Sean Connery. Her fairy-tale rise to Hollywood celebrity status continued with her marriage to Michael Douglas in November 2000 and the birth of their son Dylan. She co-starred with Douglas in the Oscar-winning movie *Traffic* (2000) and Julia Roberts in *America's Sweethearts* (2001). In March 2003, a month before the birth of her second child, Cerys, she won the best supporting actress Oscar for her portrayal of ruthless murderess Velma Kelly in the film musical *Chicago*.

Titanic – the Kate Winslett version this time – also launched the film career of Cardiff-born **Ioan Gruffudd** (1973–). Following his portrayal of Harold Lowe in the film, he then went on to star in *Solomon and Gaenor* (1999) and as the innocent shop owner in Disney's *102 Dalmatians* (2000). Frequently playing the romantic, heroic lead, he has done a great deal of TV work including *Hornblower* and *The Forsyte Saga* – roles far removed from his first small screen part as shy schoolboy Gareth Wyn in the Welsh soap *Pobol y Cwm*. His latest part is Lancelot in Disney's *King Arthur* to be released in December 2004.

Other leading young Welsh actors include **Mathew Rhys** (1974–) and **Rhys Ifans** (1968–). Matthew Rhys starred as Demetrius in the film *Titus Andronicus* (2000) and played opposite Kathleen Turner in *The Graduate* (2000) in the West End. Other recent films include *The Lost World* (2001) and *Death Watch* (2002). Rhys Ifans, of *Twin Town* fame, starred as Hugh Grant's flatmate Spike in the highly successful *Notting Hill* (1999) and as Puff in the romantic comedy *Human Nature* (2002).

Animation

Over the last 20 years, S4C and the European Commission have done a great deal to promote the animation industry in Wales. As a result the Welsh animation scene has grown steadily and received much international recognition. The first major success was *Super Ted*, the adventures of a magical bear and his alien friend Spotty, which was commissioned by S4C in the early 1980s. *Super Ted* was sold to 45 countries and dubbed into 17 languages. It was quickly followed by many other highly popular children's series such as *Sam Tân* (Fireman Sam) and *Wil Cwac Cwac*.

Recently, in order to avoid direct competition with the likes of Disney, S4C in its commissioning strategy has tried to identify gaps in the animation market. *Animation Classics*, an ambitious series including adaptations of Shakespearean plays, famous operas, biblical stories and Welsh folk stories, has proved extremely successful and has been sold worldwide. Symbolic of Wales' position in this field is the fact that the International Animation Festival is held annually in Cardiff.

Fashion

The name **Laura Ashley** (1925–1986) is known throughout the world. A native of Merthyr Tydfil, she created country-style clothes and wallpapers based on nineteenth-century designs. These became particularly popular in the 1970s and by 1981 there were 5,000 Ashley outlets worldwide. Following her premature death in 1986, the company's fortunes took a turn for the worse, which resulted in the closure of its five Welsh factories. Recently, however, sales on the home furnishing front in particular have gradually improved.

Two other Welsh designers to make their mark in the 1970s and 1980s were **Jeff Banks** (1943–) and **David Emanuel** (1952–). Jeff Banks launched the *Warehouse* chain and later set up the mail-order firm *Warehouse Utility Clothing Company*. He was the instigator and presenter of the first mainstream fashion programme on British TV, *The Clothes Show*. David Emanuel, along with his wife Elizabeth, specialized in vibrant, luxurious evening wear and in 1981 they achieved worldwide fame as the designers of Lady Diana Spencer's wedding dress – an extravagant silk gown with an eight-metre train.

The big Welsh name in the fashion industry today is **Julien MacDonald** (1972–) also from Merthyr Tydfil. He has worked for several leading designers such as Alexander McQueen and Karl Lagerfeld and was appointed Chanel's knitwear designer as well as being responsible for revamping the Spice Girls. After being voted Glamour Designer of the Year at the 2001 British

Fashion Awards, he was appointed artistic designer at the House
of Givenchy.

Food and drink

When it comes to food, until recently Welsh cuisine cannot be
said to have been particularly well known internationally.
However, **Taste of Wales**, set up by the Welsh Development
Agency and the Welsh Tourist Board, has done a great deal to
remedy this. It actively promotes Welsh food at home and
abroad and encourages standards of excellence in the
preparation, presentation and sale of Welsh produce. Look out
for the 'Taste of Wales' logo on guesthouses, tea rooms, pubs
etc. Leeks, lamb and laver bread are making a comeback and the
Welsh food scene has never looked so healthy!

For starters

The traditional Welsh first course is *cawl*, which is considered by
many to be the national dish of Wales. Although there is no exact
translation for the word *cawl*, it is best described as broth in
which the meat for a main course is cooked, together with a
variety of vegetables such as leeks, cabbage and herbs. Recipes for
cawl vary from area to area and from season to season depending
on what vegetables are available. While *cawl* now tends to be
eaten as an all-in-one stew, in the past the broth was usually
served first, followed by the meat and vegetables.

Oysters (*wystrys*) used to be caught in great quantities along the
Gower peninsula near Swansea, but are now extremely rare.
Cockles *(cocos)* however remain prolific and in Gower villages,
such as Penclawdd, these are still gathered daily. Swansea
market is one of the best fish markets in Wales and fresh
Penclawdd cockles sprinkled with pepper and vinegar are a
popular lunch-time snack.

Laver bread *(bara lawr)*, described by Richard Burton as 'the
Welshman's caviar', is also found primarily on the Gower
peninsula. This dark green edible seaweed was traditionally
mixed with oatmeal and fried with bacon and served for
breakfast or supper. Nowadays many restaurants also serve it as
a first course or as a main meal with meat or fish. Extremely
high in protein, it should ideally of course be eaten fresh, but it
is also available in tins, so there is no excuse not to give it a try.

Main course

Herring *(pennog)* and mackerel *(macrell)* have always been an important part of the Welsh diet, especially in the west, and the most common method of preparing them – soused in herbs and spices – is still popular. Another favourite is sewin or Welsh sea trout *(brithyll-y-môr)* which is similar in appearance to salmon but has less of an oily texture and a paler, pink flesh.

Although lamb *(cig oen)* is of course considered the meat of Wales, in the past it would have been reserved for holidays and special occasions. Pig *(cig moch)* used to form the mainstay of the diet and at one time every house in the country had a pig or two. A *twlc* or pigsty at the bottom of the garden was also a common sight in the terraced mining valleys of the south. One of the native breeds of beef cattle in Wales is the Welsh Black whose meat is extremely tender and flavoursome.

A traditional vegetarian option often available in cafés and restaurants today are Glamorgan sausages *(selsig Morgannwg)*. They contain cheese, breadcrumbs, leeks and herbs. Although the cheese from which they got their name is no longer made, the crumbly white cheese, Caerphilly, is an adequate substitute.

Puddings

There are not many puddings that are particular to Wales. Flummery, a sort of modern-day muesli, consisting of oatcakes crumbled into a bowl of buttermilk, used to be very popular. The word 'flummery' derives from the Welsh word *llymru*. Rice pudding *(pwdin reis)* too has been a consistent favourite and would often be served after a roast dinner.

Cheese

Cheese making has a long tradition in Wales. So much so that cheese *(caws)* is specifically mentioned in the tenth-century laws of Hywel Dda (see Unit 1). Following a divorce, any cheese in brine went to the wife and any cheese that was hung up to the husband. During the last 30 years, cheese production has increased dramatically and wherever you go you are sure to find a wealth of hard and soft cheeses, some of which are made using ewe's and goat's milk. Names to look out for include Llanboidy, Llangloffan, Teifi, Caws Cenarth, Pencarreg and Pant Ysgawn.

Baking

No visit to Wales would be complete without some *bara brith* (speckled bread) which is a rich tea bread. *Teisen lap* (moist cake) is a simple, shallow fruitcake, which is another traditional popular favourite. One extremely important cooking device is the griddle, a cast-iron bake stone used to make pancakes *(crempog)* and Welsh cakes *(pice ar y maen)*, moist scones containing currants readily available today in cafés and bakeries throughout Wales.

Drink

Wrexham used to be the brewing capital of Wales with a multitude of breweries, including the first lager brewery in the British Isles. Sadly these have now all closed. The Cardiff brewery Brains dominates the beer market in the south-east, whilst beers *(cwrw)* such as Double Dragon from the Felinfoel brewery near Llanelli can be found all over south Wales. Felinfoel was the first brewery in Britain to produce canned beer for public sale in March 1936.

First cone-shaped can of Felinfoel beer

There is a growing range of Welsh spirits, although some of these are not as Welsh as they seem. It was recently discovered that one popular so-called Welsh whisky was actually imported from Scotland and only blended and bottled in Wales. The Welsh Whisky Company was set up recently and the first Welsh whisky to actually be made in Wales went on sale in 2003.

The weather in Wales does not lend itself to wine *(gwin)* production although there are a few vineyards such as the Cwm Deri Vineyard in Pembrokeshire. A variety of Welsh spring waters *(dŵr)* such as *Tŷ Nant* and *Brecon Carreg* are also available everywhere. The attractive recyclable blue and red glass *Tŷ Nant* bottles are particularly distinctive and recently won an award for design excellence.

GLOSSARY

actor (m.)	*actor*
actores (f.)	*actress*
bwyd (m.)	*food*
bwyta	*to eat*
coginio	*to cook*
cyfarwyddwr (m)	*director*
cylchgrawn (m.)	*magazine*
diod (f.)	*drink*
ffasiwn (m.)	*fashion*
ffilm (f.)	*film*
gorsaf radio	*radio station*
gwasg (f.)	*press*
gwyddoniaeth (f.)	*science*
gwyddonydd (m.)	*scientist*
papur dyddiol	*daily paper*
papur dydd Sul	*Sunday paper*
papur newydd	*newspaper*
rysáit (f.)	*recipe*
rhaglen (f.)	*programme*
sinema (f.)	*cinema*
technoleg (f.)	*technology*
teledu (m.)	*television*
teledu digidol	*digital television*
tŷ bwyta	*restaurant*
y cyfryngau (pl.)	*the media*
yfed	*to drink*

Taking it further

Reading

The cinema and the media

Berry, Dave, *Wales and Cinema: The First 100 Years* (Cardiff: 1994)

Blandford, Steve (ed.), *Wales on Screen* (Bridgend: 2000)

Davies, Joanna, *Taff Pac* (Talybont: 2000)

Davies, John, *Broadcasting and the BBC in Wales* (Cardiff: 1994)

Jones, Philip Wyn, *Ffilmiau Cymreig* (Talybont: 1998)

Welsh cuisine

Davies, Gilli, *Tastes of Wales* (London: 1990)

Freeman, Bobby, *Traditional Food from Wales* (New York: 1997)

Websites

www.bbc.co.uk/cymru – information on Wales and the world in Welsh, *Cymru'r Byd* covers a wide range of topics from education to science to entertainment. Links to many related sites such as *Radio Cymru* and *Pobol y Cwm*.

www.s4c.co.uk – official S4C website with interesting film section

www.foodwales.com – details of local Welsh food, food fairs and other events

www.welsh.food.com – a broad range of Welsh produce available online through *Cegin Cymru*

Places to visit

Techniquest – the UK's leading science discovery centre – Stuart Street, Cardiff, CF10 5BW; Tel: 02920 475475 www.tquest.org.uk

Wales Film and Television Archive, Unit 1, Science Park, Cefn Llan, Aberystwyth; Tel: 01970 626007

Sound and Moving Images Collection, National Library of Wales, Aberystwyth; Tel: 01970 632 828 www.llgc.org.uk

Events

International Film Festival Wales is held every November in Cardiff. A two-day animation festival is included in the programme of events. Details: International Film Festival Wales, Market House, Market Road, Canton, Cardiff, CF1 1QE; Tel: 02920 406220 www.iffw.co.uk

08

politics in Wales

In this unit you will learn about
- the political history of Wales
- the Welsh Assembly, Unitary Authorities and recent British and European elections
- some prominent Welsh politicians

The political history of Wales

Liberal hegemony

The first of the modern political parties to gain a foothold in Wales was the Liberal Party whose anti-establishment and reform policies meant that the Liberals dominated Welsh politics from the 1860s until 1922. Up to the 1860s the parliamentary representation of Wales had been the preserve of the predominantly right-wing Anglican gentry. In 1880, however, Wales returned only four Conservative MPs, and none at all in 1906. By the latter half of the nineteenth century, 80 per cent of the population of Wales belonged to a chapel and it was the emphasis Welsh Liberal MPs placed on the rights of Welsh Nonconformists which gave Welsh Liberalism its distinctiveness. This blend of Nonconformity and politics was evident in the Welsh Closing Act of 1881 which forbade public houses to open on a Sunday. Other Liberal policies were the establishing of a degree of self-government for Wales, government support for a distinctly Welsh system of education and legislation to enable Welsh tenants to be freed from the power of their landlords.

The *Cymru Fydd* movement founded in 1886 sought to further an awareness of Welsh nationality and to advance the cause of Welsh devolution. One of the movement's supporters was **David Lloyd George** (1863–1945), who wanted to ensure that the Liberal politics of Wales had a stronger Welsh identity. However, the movement collapsed in 1896 when it became evident that *Cymru Fydd's* ideals were unacceptable to a large proportion of Wales' Liberals. The movement was also not popular in the centres of power in south-east Wales or in the Anglicized towns.

The success of the Liberal Party during this period was due to their appeal to a broad spectrum of the people of Wales. Industrialists approved of the Liberal policy of free trade; tenant farmers saw the Party as the best hope for land reform and Nonconformists hoped for the disestablishment of the Church. The Liberal Party was also seen as a means of furthering the interests of the workingman. This allegiance amongst the voting public in Wales for the Liberals was not to last, however; 1922 saw the beginning of the predominance of the Labour Party in Welsh politics, mainly because of the economic depression and effects of the First World War, but also because of the rise of Trade Unionism.

The effects of the First World War

The First World War destroyed the optimism characteristic of pre-war Welsh society. By the beginning of the twentieth century, with only 10 per cent of its population directly reliant upon agriculture, Wales was manifestly an industrial country with a long tradition of working-class protest (see Unit 1). Liberal fortunes within Wales were also damaged by the party's involvement in total war and by the split in the party caused by Lloyd George's acceptance of Conservative support in his successful bid for the premiership in 1915. Welsh society was plunged into depression in the post-war years, unemployment was rampant amongst industrial workers, particularly in the south Wales coalfield hit by a decline in the foreign demand for coal. Those employed in agriculture were no better off, with many fully employed smallholders and farm labourers earning less than those on unemployment benefit. For some workers, capitalism seemed to have collapsed and support for the Socialists and also the Communists increased. There was industrial unrest in Wales, particularly in the south, there were riots in Tonypandy in 1910 and a year later a riot in Llanelli led to six deaths. During the First World War, the south Wales coalfield was the most militant part of Britain. After the war, hopes for the fulfilment of working-class aspirations and even of social revolution ran high, but they were dashed by the failure of the General Strike and the miners' lockout of 1926.

Trade unionism

The early 1880s saw a marked growth in Trade Unionism, the key development of which was the establishment in 1898 of the South Wales Miners' Federation which was eventually to enjoy the largest membership of any other secular institution in the history of Wales. The Independent Labour Party was founded in 1893 but failed to gain a mass following. The year 1900 saw the founding of the Labour Representation Committee, an organization made up of a combination of trade unionists and members of socialist societies. This organization, which eventually became the Labour Party, had a significant breakthrough when the Committee's candidate for the constituency of Merthyr Tydfil, **Keir Hardie**, was elected. Although a minor party as late as 1914, when only five of Wales' 34 MPs were Labour, the Labour Party won half the constituencies of Wales in 1922. By the end of Lloyd George's term of office in 1922, the political climate in Wales had changed. The First World War had cleared the way for the triumph of the Labour Party. As industrial areas turned increasingly to the Labour Party a gap started to emerge between the largely Welsh-speaking, Liberal rural areas and the Labour-voting, Anglicized south. Wales became increasingly polarized between north and south, industrial and rural.

The triumph of the Labour Party

The Labour Party victory in 1922 was partly the result of the parliamentary reform of 1918 which increased the representation of the industrial areas and granted the vote to young males who were not householders. Liberalism remained strong in rural Wales, and as late as 1945 seven of Britain's 12 Liberal MPs represented Welsh rural constituencies, but support for the party in industrial areas collapsed. Since 1922, the Labour Party has enjoyed an unbroken predominance in Welsh politics. Labour's dominance of the south Wales coalfields began in the 1930s. In 1931, when the Parliamentary Labour Party was reduced to 52 members, the 16 seats it won in the south Wales coalfield constituted its largest stronghold. Support for the party reached its peak in the general election of 1966, when it won 32 of the country's 36 constituencies and 61 per cent of the popular vote.

The Labour Party did not favour devolution for Wales, arguing that it would undermine the unity of the British working class. The establishment of *Plaid Genedlaethol Cymru* (the National Party of Wales – later *Plaid Cymru*, the Party of Wales) in 1925 meant that home rulers, who might otherwise have been active in the traditional parties, found themselves isolated in a new party which, until the 1950s at least, had only a marginal role in Welsh politics. The National Party had been founded with the objective of warding off threats to Welsh language and culture and advocated self-government. The party won some support as a result of the arson attack by its leaders, who included Saunders Lewis (see Unit 3), on a construction hut at the Bombing School at Penyberth in Llŷn in 1936. However, the Second World War, like the First, strengthened the awareness of the British people striving and suffering together. The party had little support outside a small circle of writers and university lecturers. The Labour government, overwhelmingly elected in 1945, was rigorously centralist with its most charismatic figure, Aneurin Bevan, contemptuous of any concession to Welsh nationalism.

The Nationalists gain support

In the immediate post-war years expectations in Wales were high. The Labour government, which came to power in 1945, massively endorsed by the Welsh electorate, established the welfare state and the National Health Service, provided an extensive system of support for agriculture and carried out a programme of nationalization – reforms that enjoyed a high degree of consensus until the 1970s. During the period after the Second World War steady progress was made towards giving Welsh people a greater say in their own affairs and in the 1950s the Conservative government established a minister for Welsh affairs. There was some shift in the opinion within Wales about devolution; the decline of the British Empire removed a central feature of Britishness and many were uneasy that prosperity in Wales lagged behind that of south-eastern England and further behind some of the smaller states of Europe. The successive victories of the Conservative Party suggested that only by winning self-government could Wales be ruled by those that shared the views of the majority of the Welsh electorate. The drowning of the Tryweryn Valley (see Unit 1), unsupported by the vote of a single Welsh MP, indicated that, as a national community, the Welsh were powerless. These were among the factors which allowed *Plaid Cymru* to gain a respectable vote in the general election of 1959.

Welsh Office and Secretary of State for Wales

Partly in order to stave off the nationalist challenge, the Labour government elected in 1964 established the Welsh Office and appointed a Secretary of State for Wales, thus creating a new context for discussion of the government of Wales. In 1964 Harold Wilson's Labour government set up the Welsh Office and gave the Secretary of State for Wales a place in the Cabinet. *Plaid Cymru* made a crucial breakthrough in 1966 when the party's president, **Gwynfor Evans**, was victorious in the Carmarthen by-election caused by the death of the MP **Lady Megan Lloyd-George**, the youngest child of David Lloyd-George. *Plaid Cymru* had gained their first seat at Westminster.

The devolution question

By the 1970s *Plaid Cymru* was contesting every seat in Wales and returning MPs to Westminster at almost every election. Welsh devolution was beginning to make its presence felt on the rest of UK politics. Royal Commissions began looking into devolution in the 1960s as both Labour and the Tories became rattled by sensational electoral victories for nationalists in Scotland and Wales. When the Tories were returned to power with Edward Heath at the helm in 1970 the case for devolution was given another unexpected push. Wales, as ever, had returned a majority of Labour MPs, and many now saw the government in London as having no mandate to rule in Wales. When Heath was forced out of office in February 1974, Labour set up a minority administration. The Labour Westminster majority of three seats meant that they were eager to look for support from any quarter and had to rely not just on the Liberals for help but also on *Plaid Cymru's* three MPs and the 11 returned by the Scottish nationalists.

Referendum 1

The new 1974 Labour government published proposals for Welsh and Scottish assemblies, but Labour was far from united over the issue. Leading critics of the policy, including the future party leader **Neil Kinnock**, would only back the measures if the government agreed to hold referendums on their proposals. The voters of Wales were offered an Assembly. On 1 March, St David's Day, 1979, the people of Wales took to the ballot boxes to decide whether they wanted a measure of self-government. The result was a decisive 'no', with only 13 per cent of those voting in favour, a massive four-to-one against. It is thought that the massive rejection was due to fears in Welsh-speaking Wales that the proposed assembly would be dominated by the Anglicized south and many nationalists did not vote at all fearing that such an assembly would create a permanent Labour majority.

The argument for devolution, however, became stronger during the series of successive Tory governments that followed Labour's 1979 election defeat. Throughout the Thatcher and Major years Wales returned a majority of Labour MPs to Westminster. The subsequent feeling that the Tories had no mandate to govern in the principality was heightened by successive non-Welsh Welsh secretaries including **David Hunt, Peter Walker, John Redwood** and **William Hague**. The Conservative tendency to govern the country through non-elected quangos full of Tory appointees only made things worse. Years of Thatcherite right-wing policies reminded the Welsh that they had to live with political ideas that were not acceptable to many of them.

Referendum 2

When the Labour Party returned to power in Westminster after 18 years on the opposition benches, the question of devolution was revived. The 1997 general election saw not one Conservative being elected in Wales, and Wales was offered a second referendum in 1997. In July 1997, the Government published a White Paper, *A Voice for Wales*, which outlined proposals for devolution in Wales. These proposals were endorsed in the referendum of 18 September 1997. Despite the traditional support in Wales for Labour, turning round the four-to-one votes cast against devolution just 18 years earlier was to be no easy task. In that referendum 559,419 voted for an Assembly for Wales with 552,698 against. Just over half the electorate voted, a much smaller turnout than the general election. The cross-party 'Yes' camp scrambled to victory taking 50.3 per cent of the vote compared to the 49.7 for the 'No' campaign.

National Assembly for Wales

The establishment of the National Assembly for Wales in May 1999 changed the nature of politics in Wales by creating a new style of government in which decisions and policies were focused on Wales. Although the creation of the Assembly was the first measure of self-rule since Edward I defeated Llywelyn ap Gruffudd in 1282 (see Unit 1), Wales remains part of the United Kingdom, MPs from Welsh constituencies continue to have seats in Westminster and laws passed by Parliament in Westminster still apply to Wales. The Assembly develops and implements policy and cannot pass laws or raise taxes.

The powers and responsibilities of the Assembly

The Assembly has considerable power to develop and implement policy within a range of areas including agriculture and industry, culture, economic development, education, the environment, health, highways, housing, local government, social services, sport and leisure, tourism, town and country planning, transport and roads. The Assembly decides on its priorities and allocates the funds made available to it from the Treasury.

Electing Assembly Members

The Assembly has 60 Members who are elected by the people of Wales every four years by a system of proportional representation called the Additional Member System (AMS), a system which ensures that the overall number of seats for each political party reflects the share of the vote they receive. Each elector has two votes, the first vote is used to elect a local or constituency Member – 40 Assembly Members are elected on this basis, one from each constituency in Wales. The second vote is used to elect 20 additional Members from five regional lists which coincide with the former European Parliamentary Constituencies created in 1994. These are north Wales, mid and west Wales, south Wales west, south Wales central and south Wales east, with each region therefore returning four Members. Using this system 28 Labour, 17 *Plaid Cymru*, nine Conservative, and six Liberal Democrat Assembly members were elected in the first Assembly elections in May 1999. With no overall majority for any party, Alun Michael as Leader of the Welsh Labour Party formed a minority government and became First Secretary, Rhodri Morgan succeeding him in February 2000. The title of First Secretary was later changed to First Minister. The First Minister is elected by the whole Assembly and therefore will usually represent the largest political party. In October 2000, a coalition government was formed between Labour and the Liberal Democrats, and the National Assembly entered a period of majority government. In the May 2003 election, the Labour Party secured 30 seats and this increase on the 1999 elections resulted in single-party government for Wales. In the same election, *Plaid Cymru* saw their seats reduced to 12, the Conservative party won 11 seats, the Liberal Democrats six and the Independents one.

How the Assembly works

The structure of the Assembly is a combination of a Cabinet system with a committee structure that enables a wide involvement in policy development among Assembly members. The 60 Assembly Members delegate their executive powers to the First Minister who in turn delegates responsibility for delivering the executive functions to the eight-Member Cabinet known as the Welsh Assembly Government.

The Presiding Officer

The Assembly is chaired by the Presiding Officer who is elected by the 60 Members of the Assembly. The Presiding Officer, who has to serve the Assembly impartially, is responsible for ensuring that the proper procedures of the Assembly are observed. The Presiding Officer is also responsible for support services for Assembly Members and services to the public, such as the visitors' programme which aims to raise the public's knowledge and understanding of the Assembly. The Presiding Officer is the equivalent of the Speaker of the House of Commons. The Deputy Presiding Officer is elected in the same way. Many of the Assembly's day-to-day decisions are made by the Cabinet who are responsible for individual subject areas such as health and education. The Cabinet, under the First Minister, is accountable to the rest of the Assembly, which scrutinizes all its decisions and actions.

The committee structure

Subject committees

Members from all parties can voice their opinions on how the Assembly operates through Subject committees, such as Economic Development and Transport, which deal with policy development. Subject committees can make policy jointly with the Cabinet, or even sometimes overrule the Cabinet. Part of the Subject committees' role is scrutiny of the secondary legislation of the Assembly. Members are elected to serve on these committees to reflect the balance of political groups within the Assembly.

Regional committees convey issues of local concern to the full Assembly and to the Subject committees. There are four Regional committees, which are made up of Members from the relevant constituency and electoral region. All the AMs in the relevant region are entitled to be members of the Regional committee. The Regional committees are only advisory and not decision making.

The characteristics of the Assembly

The style of the Assembly is different from that of either Westminster or the one-party dominated politics that had become the norm in much of Wales. The Assembly aims at being an inclusive institution and a series of checks and balances are in place that ensure inclusivity in terms of the regions of Wales, equal opportunity by gender, disability and race and for all four of the parties. In the Chamber and in committee meetings, AMs have the right to speak in either English or Welsh and simultaneous translation equipment is available to assist non-Welsh speakers. All Assembly papers are also available in both Welsh and English. The Assembly system aims to be open and transparent, papers produced by officials as advice to Subject committees are published, debates on policy issues are held in public, and much information on debates, reports, papers and motions for consideration by AMs is available on the Assembly's website at **www.assembly.wales.gov.uk**. Supporting the aim of open and transparent politics are the permanent broadcasting facilities in the Chamber and in the main committee rooms. Live Assembly business, including some committee meetings, is broadcast on television and there is also a requirement that there must be access to broadcasting facilities in any venue where the Assembly meets. The main Assembly building reflects openness and inclusivity as there is public access to the plenary sessions and the committee meetings, and the foyer of the Assembly provides space for AMs to mix with and meet the public. The Assembly has 'family-friendly hours': debates do not continue long into the night so that Members with families can go home.

The Unitary Authorities

Local government in Wales is undertaken by 22 Unitary Authorities (see map on page xii) who replaced a two-tier County and Borough Council system in 1996. Among the responsibilities of the Unitary Authorities are education, child protection and welfare, housing, leisure and culture, environment, highways and economic development.

Recent British and European elections

The main political parties in Wales are the Wales Labour Party, the Welsh Conservatives, the Welsh Liberal Democrats and *Plaid Cymru*. At the British parliamentary elections in 1997, 74 per cent of the electorate voted. Of MPs elected, 34 were Labour, four *Plaid Cymru*, and two Liberal Democrats. At the 1999 European Parliament elections five members were elected in Wales: two Labour, two *Plaid Cymru* and one Conservative. The Conservatives failed to win any seats in Wales again at the General Election held in 2001 and there were calls from some in the party for the Conservative Party in Wales to become independent of the English organization whilst remaining affiliated to it. Although the *Plaid Cymru* leadership had been predicting that they would win more seats in Westminster, their total number of seats stayed the same at four after they gained Carmarthen East and Dinefwr from Labour and yet lost *Ynys Môn* (Anglesey), part of what some political observers call the 'nationalist heartland'. *Plaid Cymru* did, however, succeed in increasing its share of the vote. The results of the 2001 General Election saw the beginning of two-tier politics in Wales, with differences in voting patterns at Assembly and General elections.

The role of the Secretary of State for Wales

The Office of the Secretary of State for Wales was established in July 1999 when most of the powers of the Welsh Office were handed over to the National Assembly for Wales. As a Cabinet member in the British Government, the Secretary of State ensured that the interests and needs of Wales were fully considered when government policy was developed within the UK Government and consulted and debated the Government's legislative programme with the Assembly. He had the right to attend and speak at sessions of the National Assembly. The Secretary of State for Wales was also charged with making devolution work smoothly and acted as a link between the UK Government and the devolved administrations through membership of the Joint Ministerial Committee. The Secretary of State for Wales was also responsible for taking through Parliament provisions in primary legislation which related particularly to Wales.

In June 2003, the British Labour Prime Minister, **Tony Blair** made some constitutional reforms which included making the Secretary of State for Wales' post a part-time position and amalgamating the Welsh Office into the new Department for Constitutional Affairs. Under the changes, the Secretary will still retain responsibility for taking Welsh legislation through the Commons, negotiate the Assembly's budget allocation and liaise with the First Minister and Welsh Assembly.

Profiles of political figures

David Lloyd George (1863–1945)

Perhaps the best-known Welsh politician is David Lloyd George. He had romantic good looks, which ensured success with women, and, in later life, many of his contemporaries commented on his striking appearance, his collar-length hair and flowing moustache.

David Lloyd George was born in Manchester in 1863 and was brought up by his widowed mother and his uncle in Llanystumudwy, Gwynedd. He trained as a solicitor, seeking to defend people against those in authority. An avid chapelgoer, he soon developed a reputation as a fiery yet eloquent preacher and orator. He joined the local Liberal Party and became an alderman on the Caernarfon County Council. He also took part in several political campaigns including one that attempted to bring an end to church tithes. Lloyd George was also a strong supporter of land reform. He was selected as the Liberal candidate for the Caernarfon Borough constituency and became the youngest member of the House of Commons when he won the by-election aged 27. He fought the election on a programme which called for religious equality in Wales, land reform and free trade.

David Lloyd George

When promoted to the post of Chancellor of the Exchequer, Lloyd George now had the opportunity to introduce reforms he had been campaigning for since he first arrived in the House of Commons. He introduced old-age pensions and National Health Insurance and restricted the powers of the House of Lords. These reforms did not please everyone and the Conservatives accused him of being a socialist. Some Labour MPs thought the reforms did not go far enough and disliked what was later to be called the Means Test aspect of these reforms. He soon emerged as one of the main figures in the government willing to escalate the war in an effort to bring a quick victory. He held the post of First Minister of Munitions and then coalition Prime Minister from 1916 until 1922 and although he continued to campaign for progressive causes, he was never to hold power again. The hegemony of the Liberal Party in Wales belonged to a period of economic prosperity, when Welsh speakers were on the increase, and chapel membership was high. After the First World War, the optimism and hope of many people in Wales vanished and the Liberal Party's fortunes fell.

Neil (1942–) and Glenys Kinnock (1944–)

Two of the most famous politicians in Wales are Neil and Glenys Kinnock, who met at the University of Wales, Cardiff. Glenys trained and then worked as a teacher and Neil became Labour Member of Parliament for Bedwellty and Islwyn in south Wales. He was elected to Labour's Shadow Cabinet in 1980 and became Leader of the Labour Party in 1983 when they were in opposition. He held this position until Labour failed to win the 1992 General Election. In 1995, Neil Kinnock became European Commissioner, with responsibility for Transport. In 1994, Glenys was elected Member of European Parliament for south-east Wales and was re-elected in 1999. She represents Wales and is a member of the European Parliament's Development and Co-operation Committee, and substitute member of the Citizens Freedoms and Rights, Justice and Home Affairs Committee. Glenys is president of One World Action, the Development non-governmental organization. She is also a patron of Saferworld, a council member of Voluntary Service Overseas, chair of the Forum on Early Warning and Early Response (FEWER) and patron of The Burma Campaign. She is co-president of the African, Caribbean and Pacific/EU Joint Parliamentary Assembly and Labour Party spokesperson on International Development in the European Parliament. She has written a number of books which reflect her interests in human rights, ethical trade and fairtrade, indigenous people, gender issues, Third World development and education.

Aneurin Bevan (1897–1960), creator of the National Health Service

Aneurin Bevan, like Neil Kinnock, was born in Tredegar, a mining community in the eastern valleys and a stronghold of the Labour movement. Popularly known as 'Nye', he was originally employed as a coal miner and then turned to politics. In June 1924, as Labour candidate for Ebbw Vale, he entered the House of Commons with a majority of 11,164 over his Liberal and

Conservative opponents. He became the Minister of Health and in 1948 he introduced the National Health Service based on the Tredegar Medical Aid Society. The Tredegar Medical Aid Society was a scheme whereby workers (mainly miners) paid a subscription weekly from their wages to help with their medical costs. He resigned from the Government in 1951 in protest against the use of money raised by Health Service charges for the prosecution of the Korean War. Aneurin Bevan was a popular politician and a great orator, he remained a major force in Labour politics until his death in 1960. Four large engraved memorial stones at the head of Sirhowy Hill, between Tredegar and Ebbw Vale, commemorate Aneurin Bevan. Three of the stones represent Ebbw Vale, Rhymney and Tredegar, the towns comprising the Ebbw Vale constituency he represented for 31 years; the fourth, larger stone represents Aneurin Bevan himself.

George Thomas, Viscount Tonypandy (1909–97)

The flamboyant George Thomas was the 133rd Speaker of the House of Commons and the first Speaker to become well known to a wide public through the broadcasting of Parliament which began during his term of office. The words he used to summon order in the House, 'Order, Order', used to open BBC Radio 4's *Yesterday in Parliament*, and became a household phrase.

George Thomas, whose full name, Thomas George Thomas, earned him the nickname 'Tommy Twice', was born in Port Talbot, the second son of a miner. He was a popular lay preacher and teacher; it was his activity in the National Union of Teachers which would draw him into the political world. He won Cardiff Central in the Attlee landslide in 1945 campaigning successfully for leasehold reform, championing the cause of people whose homes were in danger of reverting after 99 years to former coalmine-owners who held their freeholds.

The peak of George Thomas' ministerial career came between 1968 and 1970 when he served as Secretary of State for Wales under Harold Wilson, during which time he enthusiastically presided over the investiture of the Prince of Wales at Caernarfon in 1969. His anti-devolution stance, while being at odds with Labour's pro-devolution tendencies, was, as seen in the decisive 'no' vote of the 1979 referendum, a common opinion amongst Welsh voters.

Thomas became Speaker in 1974 and was popular with fellow MPs and the media. Some MPs complained that he favoured the opposition: he was a great admirer of Margaret Thatcher and kept a picture of her by his bed. As a Welsh Nonconformist, he opposed Attlee's conscription policy and spoke against pub and cinema opening on Sundays in Wales. The skill with which he kept order in the House of Commons and upheld the dignity and powers of the House, defusing tense situations with his dazzling sense of humour and oratory earned him the respect of politicians on both sides of the House who judged him 'the greatest Speaker in living memory'. One thing which delighted him about his high office was having friends amongst the rich and socially elevated such as the Queen Mother, the merchant banker Sir Julian Hodge and the Saudi Arabian Sheik Yamani. Thomas often made a point of commenting that 'a poor boy from Tonypandy' had ridden with the monarch. His bungalow in Cardiff was crammed with mementos and signed photographs which he had collected during his long career. Critics complained he was inconsistent: he attacked nationalism and language activisits yet while in the Welsh Office he obtained more money for the Welsh language. Although he was a member of the Labour Party, he took an hereditary title and retired to the House of Lords. Once retired, he began a life of lectures, sermons and broadcasts and wrote his autobiography. He celebrated his 80th birthday at a gala birthday party in Cardiff's St David's Hall.

In the 1997 Referendum, the anti-devolution 'Just Say No' campaign had two prominent patrons, the banker Sir Julian Hodge, and George Thomas, by then Viscount Tonypandy. He backed Sir Jimmy Goldsmith's Referendum Party in the general election and even appeared in a video campaign. The 'Just Say No' campaign was to be his last – he died the same year.

GLOSSARY

plaid (f.)	*political party*
gwleidyddiaeth (f.)	*politics*
datganoli	*devolution*
senedd (f.)	*parliament*
cynulliad (m.)	*assembly*
gwleidydd (m.)	*politician*
Ceidwadwyr (pl.)	*Conservatives*
Rhyddfrydwyr (pl.)	*Liberals*

Cenedlaetholwyr (pl.)	*Nationalists*
Llafur	*Labour*
Undeb (m.)	*Union*
ymgyrch (m./f.)	*campaign*
etholiad (m.)	*election*
cefnogi	*to support*
pleidleisio	*to vote*

Taking it further

Reading

Balsom, Denis (ed.), *the Wales Yearbook 2003* (Cardiff: 2003)

Balsom, Denis & Jones, Barry J. (eds.), *Road to the National Assembly for Wales: The Welsh Referendum 1997* (Cardiff: 2000)

Davies, C. A., *Welsh Nationalism in the Twentieth Century* (London: 1989)

Foulkes, D. *et al.* (eds.), *The Welsh Veto* (Cardiff: 1983)

Hannan, Patrick, *Wales Off Message* (Bridgend: 2000)

Herbert, Trevor and Jones, Gareth Elwyn, *Post-war Wales* (Cardiff: 1995)

Morgan, Kenneth O., *Rebirth of a Nation: Wales 1880-1980* (Oxford: 1981)

Osmond, John & Jones, Barry J. (eds.), *Birth of Welsh Democracy – the First Term of the National Assembly for Wales* (Cardiff: 2003)

Osmond, John (ed.), *Welsh Labour Takes Control: Monitoring the National Assembly for Wales March to June 2003* (Cardiff: 2003)

Websites

www.data-wales.co.uk/

www.walesonline.com

www.wales.gov.uk The National Assembly website is an ideal place to visit to read about modern Welsh politics.

09 the basics for living

In this unit you will learn about
- education, housing, health and transport

Education

Welsh people have always placed a great emphasis on education as a means of improving occupational prospects. In the past, qualifying as a teacher or a preacher was seen as a way of escaping the drudgery and hardship of the industrial valleys, or the poverty and day-to-day struggle of rural life. Whilst the spectrum of opportunities is much wider today, education continues to be central to Welsh life.

History and development

Since 1999 education in Wales has been under the control of the National Assembly. Prior to that, the organization of the education system in Wales was virtually identical to that of England. The 1944 Education Act introduced compulsory education for all and raised the school leaving age to 15. It also introduced the intelligence test known as the 11+ taken in the final year of primary school. According to their performance in this test, students went at 11 to one of three types of secondary school – grammar, technical or secondary modern. The proportion going to grammar schools in Wales was much higher than in England, partly because there were very few technical schools.

In the 1960s, Wales responded positively to the British Government's decision to abolish the 11+ examination and to introduce what became known as comprehensive schools. These provided education for all of the children of 11 and over in a certain catchment area, regardless of their ability. Of the 195 comprehensive schools in England and Wales in 1964, there were 76 in the London area and 36 in Wales. By 1979 there were only five grammar schools left in Wales.

The Education Reform Act of 1988 brought about further changes with the introduction of a national curriculum which stated what all pupils between the ages of five and 16 should learn and what they should be capable of. Parents were given the right to choose where to educate their children, with the funding of individual schools based on the number of students on their rolls. The national curriculum also safeguarded the place of Welsh and Welsh history in the education system. At the time, very many schools in Wales, particularly those in Anglicized areas, did not teach Welsh. No Welsh was taught in 97.4 per cent of the schools in Gwent in south-east Wales. As a result of the 1988 Act, Welsh became a foundation subject which had to be studied between the ages of five and 16. In schools where all subjects were already taught in Welsh, Welsh now became classed as a core subject, equivalent to English in English-medium schools.

Not surprisingly, the introduction of Welsh as a compulsory element was not particularly welcomed initially in certain areas of Wales but, by 1997, 65 per cent of secondary schools were teaching Welsh as a second language and 75.2 per cent of primary schools. Also, 17.2 per cent of primary schools and 12.6 per cent of secondary schools taught solely or primarily through the medium of Welsh. If anything, the greatest problem raised by the introduction of Welsh for all was the severe lack of Welsh teachers. Although the situation has now improved somewhat, there is still a shortage today. Generous financial incentives are offered to try and encourage Welsh graduates to enter the teaching profession. To help ease the situation, *athrawon bro* (peripatetic Welsh-language specialists) now offer support and help to classroom teachers and *Canolfannau Iaith* (Language Centres) give intensive language coaching to children between the ages of seven and 11 who have moved into predominately Welsh-speaking areas. Even in such areas, however, there is generally at least one school in every town where English is the main medium of teaching and Welsh is taught purely as a subject.

During the last ten years, the response from parents and pupils to the inclusion of Welsh teaching in the curriculum has become much more positive as the language's profile has increased and teaching materials updated and improved. The majority of incomers, who may be hesitant to learn the language themselves for a variety of reasons, appear to take pleasure and pride from the fact that their children might eventually become bilingual and learn about the history and traditions of Wales. Although a small minority would like to see more emphasis placed on other European languages in Welsh schools, the place of Welsh in the National Curriculum is generally now unquestioned. A knowledge of Welsh is today a distinct advantage, if not a compulsory requirement, when applying for professional jobs in Wales. Welsh is now seen not just as a cultural asset, but a career asset too.

Assessment

As in the rest of Britain, GCSE (General Certificate of Secondary Education) examinations are taken at 16 usually in around ten to 12 subjects. Four or five subjects are then taken at AS level the following summer under the recently introduced Curriculum 2000 programme. These are equivalent to half an A or Advanced Level, which students take before leaving school at 18. Most students take three and sometimes four A levels, although other more vocational qualifications such as GNVQs (General National Vocational Qualifications) are becoming increasingly popular. With 98.2 per cent of all Welsh A Level students obtaining a pass at A Level in 2002 compared with approximately 65 per cent 20 years ago, many critics argue that standards are slipping. Others are in favour of a more general qualification, such as the baccalaureate as taken by the students of Atlantic College near Cardiff, the first United World College, founded in 1962.

Higher education

After successful completion of their A level examinations, a high percentage of young people from Wales go on to university. Rising costs, including the introduction of means-tested tuition fee payments and the lack of student grants in recent years, have meant that more and more Welsh undergraduates are now choosing degree courses in Wales, within easy travelling distance of their home areas. They have more options than one might first realize, in that the federal University of Wales, founded in 1893, is the biggest university in the UK outside of London.

Originally, the University of Wales consisted of three colleges, namely Aberystwyth (founded 1872), Cardiff (1883) and Bangor (1884). Swansea (founded 1920), Lampeter (1822) and the University College of Medicine (1931) later became constituent members, and another six institutions are closely linked to it. Bachelor of Arts and Bachelor of Science degrees are generally three years in length although the demand for part-time degrees is increasing, especially as more mature students return to education. In 2002 the National Assembly introduced learning grants up to £1,500 for those from families on lower incomes, with the aim of widening access to higher education. Whilst similar grants are available in Scotland, no grants are available at present for students in England. In a clear break with government policy in England, the Welsh Assembly Government recently announced they would not be introducing top-up tuition fees until 2007. Variable fees are intended to be introduced in England in 2006. The Welsh Assembly Government is keen to gain powers similar to the Scottish Parliament with regard to student funding in the hope that they can attract more students into higher education in Wales.

The one University in Wales not part of the federal University of Wales at present is the former polytechnic of Wales in Pontypridd which became the University of Glamorgan in 1993. It recently announced a merger with University of Wales Institute Cardiff creating a university of over 30,000 students – the largest in Wales and one of the biggest in the UK. Following this merger in 2004, the new university will join the University of Wales for a trial period of three years.

Welsh-medium education

One of the most significant and exciting developments in Wales during the last 50 years has been the expansion in the use of Welsh as a teaching medium. Thanks to the efforts of hundreds of parents throughout Wales, approximately 25 per cent of children of primary school age now receive at least a proportion of their education through the medium of Welsh.

Primary education

The first official Welsh-medium primary school was founded in Aberystwyth in 1939. The arrival of English-speaking evacuees in the town led to concerns that there would be too many children in the local school and that English would be the principal language of all activities. This private school, set up by *Syr Ifan ab* Owen Edwards, was a tremendous success and as a result parents in other areas began to ask the local authorities to set up similar schools.

The first county to do this was Carmarthenshire, where *Ysgol Gymraeg Dewi Sant* was opened in Llanelli in 1947 with 34 pupils. Other authorities followed suit, including many in Anglicized areas such as Flintshire in the north-east and Glamorganshire in the south. By 1950 there were 14 designated Welsh-medium primary schools with a total of 926 pupils in seven local education authorities. By now there are around 120 such schools in predominately English-speaking areas, along with around 300 traditionally Welsh primary schools in the *Bro Gymraeg* (Welsh Heartland). The success of the Welsh-medium schools ensured that the authorities in many traditionally Welsh areas strengthened their language policies. For example, Welsh is the official language of most primary schools in Gwynedd, whilst most schools in Carmarthenshire and Ceredigion are known as Category A schools, where all subjects are taught in Welsh until the age of seven. This is also the case in the one

Welsh-language primary school to be found in London, which was founded in 1961.

Secondary education

The development of Welsh-language secondary education in Wales tells a similar success story, although one shouldn't forget that the first Welsh-medium secondary school was actually founded in Patagonia in the early part of the twentieth century! Generally known as *ysgolion dwyieithog* (bilingual schools), the first in Wales was Ysgol Glan Clwyd in Flintshire, which opened in 1956 with 93 pupils. There are now 22 bilingual secondary schools in Wales, Powys being the only area without such a school. In the Welsh heartland there are also around 30 secondary schools that call themselves traditional bilingual schools. Within these a certain number of subjects can be followed in Welsh or in English.

Initially those choosing Welsh-medium education for their children were Welsh speakers themselves, but now more and more non-Welsh speakers are choosing to educate their children through the medium of Welsh. This is particularly so in south Wales, where very few of the children speak Welsh at home. As a result of the success of these schools, classes for adults have also mushroomed (see Unit 2). Welsh-medium schools are often considered 'better' schools, more like the old grammar schools, with higher pass rates in public examinations than their English counterparts. A recent survey showed that 50 per cent of parents in Wales would, if possible, wish their children to be educated through the medium of Welsh.

What next?

The 1991 census showed that the number of Welsh speakers under 16 rose in every Welsh county between 1981 and 1991 – 22.3 per cent of Welsh speakers were in this age group. The 2001 census also revealed an increase in young Welsh speakers in all but two of the 22 Welsh Unitary Authorities, namely Gwynedd and Ceredigion in the rural west, where job opportunities for young people are scarce.

Whilst it is clear from these statistics therefore that Welsh-medium education has made a substantial contribution to the perseverance and future of the Welsh language, certain factors still need to be addressed. These include the limited opportunities to use the Welsh language outside school in many

Anglicized areas and the lack of higher education provision through the medium of Welsh. In recent years campaigns have been mounted for a Welsh-medium university college to replace the limited provision offered by Bangor, Aberystwyth and Carmarthen, but as yet they have achieved limited success.

Mudiad Ysgolion Meithrin (MYM)

MYM, the Welsh Nursery School movement founded in 1971, has done a great deal to support and promote education through the medium of Welsh. When it was founded there were 70 independent Welsh language playgroups already in operation attracting less than 1 per cent of the pre-school age group. Now there are nearly 600 *Cylchoedd Meithrin* (playgroups) with about 14,000 children between the ages of two and a half and five attending them. MYM is a voluntary movement, unlike schools it is not run by the local councils. The ownership of each playgroup is in the hands of the parents. They run the groups, along with the help of qualified, paid playgroup leaders and regional organizers.

In 1980 at the request of parents, mother and toddler groups known as *Cylchoedd Ti a Fi* (You and Me Groups) were set up for the under twos. There are now over 400 such groups including four in England. Non-Welsh-speaking parents are encouraged to learn day-to-day words and phrases to use with their children as well as simple songs and lullabies. Through its many groups and various activities such as its Welsh for the Family Scheme, MYM has done a great deal to strengthen and consolidate Welsh as a social language and to highlight the advantages of being bilingual.

Housing

General background

In the 1950s over half of the houses in Wales dated from before the First World War and many lacked basic, modern amenities such as hot and cold water, internal toilets and satisfactory food preparation facilities. The construction of new homes for rent became a natural priority, with the aim of providing good quality damp-free houses with gardens. By 1965, 144,000 of the 225,000 houses in Wales were built by local councils and gradually virtually every town and village in Wales contained

Typical terraced housing in the Valleys

such housing. Between 1955 and 1984, a total of 172,000 council houses were built. People flocked to the new large estates such as Penlan in Swansea and Sandfields in Port Talbot, which was built to accommodate those working in the thriving steel works at Margam.

One unseen problem of many of these early council estates was their location. Many were built in isolation, away from existing communities, shops and recreational facilities and inevitably this resulted in social problems which gave local authority housing a bad name. Estates such as the award-winning Penrhys, built on a mountain top in the Rhondda, were often unfairly seen as ghettos, housing poorly qualified, long-term unemployed people. Escalating costs also meant that later houses were built of far less durable materials than those built during the early stages and gradually the boom faded. In 1990, 610 new council houses were built, in 2000 only 17. Many of the 1960s estates have been considered substandard and knocked down and rebuilt.

The post 1979 Conservative government's emphasis on privatization also contributed significantly to the demise of local authority council building. Council houses were sold off cheaply to tenants, peaking in 1982 with the sale of 15,926 houses. By 1985 over 45,000 houses had been sold. Wales generally has a higher percentage of owner-occupied housing than England – at present 72.1 per cent of all houses in Wales are owner-occupied. Many Housing Associations, offering properties to rent, have also been set up in recent years. For those unable to afford to buy their own homes, these properties are often seen as more socially desirable and in a better condition than the ageing council stocks.

Holiday homes

One particular issue to affect the rural areas of Wales during the late 1970s and 1980s was that of second homes. Houses in the scenic, sparsely populated west were relatively cheap and many were bought by English incomers as holiday homes, as Welsh people moved away to find work. It was estimated that there were 11,000 such dwellings in Wales in 1977–8, 15.9 per cent of all those registered in England and Wales. This led to considerable resentment, especially in Welsh-speaking areas, where such incomers were seen as a threat to the language and culture of Wales. Arsonists under the name of *Meibion Glyndŵr* (Sons of Glendower) bombed many of these second homes in the early 1980s and the slogan, 'come home to a real fire', was plastered on posters and T-shirts everywhere.

'Wales is not for sale'

Whilst some second home owners and potential purchasers may have been discouraged by these arson campaigns, the housing boom of the late 1980s led to the emergence of a different trend. Why have the hassles of a second home, when you could live in Wales permanently – and cheaply? Many took the opportunity to drop out of urban life, with the aim of achieving a better quality of life. The sale of a small suburban semi in the south-east of England could buy a four-bedroomed farmhouse with land in Carmarthenshire or Gwynedd and still provide enough income to live on. Very many of retirement age chose to move to coastal areas such as the Llŷn Peninsula or Pembrokeshire.

At the peak of this movement, it was estimated that the total numbers of people moving in and out of Wales was as high as 1 million, leading to extensive population shifts at local level and an aggressive campaign by *Cymdeithas yr Iaith*, epitomized in the slogan, *Nid yw Cymru ar Werth* (Wales is not for sale). As a result of this and other campaigns, in 1994 the Welsh Office said that local authorities could identify areas which could be considered 'culturally sensitive', where specific restrictions could apply. Although no definition of 'culturally sensitive' has ever been given, most local authorities in the *Bro Gymraeg* now include language clauses in their housing policies. For example, in Gwynedd, if there is uncertainty over the impact of a housing scheme, the developers have to prepare a linguistic impact statement. Proposals with an unacceptable impact are refused as are proposals for holiday homes in areas where more than 10 per cent of the homes are already holiday homes. Ten years' residency must also be proven to build in many areas. *Cymuned* (Community) was set up in 2001, which campaigns for the right for local people all over Wales to buy houses in their own communities, thereby hoping to ensure the continued existence of traditional Welsh-speaking communities. In January 2002, Pembrokeshire National Park became the first Welsh National Park to ban the construction of new homes within its boundaries in an attempt to halt the number of holiday and retirement homes as well as speculative building.

House prices

House prices in the UK rose considerably during the period 2002–3 and Wales was no exception, although in general it still remains one of the cheapest places to buy a house. In the spring of 2003 a terraced house in the north-east of England would on average cost £45,962 and a detached house £123,046. A terraced house in London, on the other hand, would cost an average of £217,600. In Wales the average house price was £73,311, with a detached house being the cheapest in the UK at £115,430.

Averages however are of course deceptive, as prices vary enormously from one part of the country to another, according to a variety of social factors. Whole terraced streets in deprived areas such as the Cynon Valley in south Wales have been known to sell for little more than £50,000, whilst small marina apartments in the likes of Conwy in the north or Porthcawl in the south easily fetch £250,000. October 2002 saw a semi-detached house in Cardiff sell for over half a million for the first time ever. Lack of affordable housing in the capital has resulted in more and more people moving into nearby towns such as Caerphilly, pushing the prices up in these areas.

Homelessness

Whilst inward migration and escalating house prices continue, an equally worrying trend in recent years has been the rise in homelessness in rural as well as urban areas. In 1999, 9,620 people were classed as unintentionally homeless in Wales, rising to 10,920 in 2000. Figures for 2001 indicate a further increase of 24 per cent, proving that many more people are experiencing homelessness across Wales than was previously thought. Statistics also show that over 2,000 people each night live in hostels and other temporary accommodation. Paradoxically, whilst many older people realize their dreams of a more relaxed lifestyle by moving to Wales, many young Welsh people are still unable to find work locally and as a result don't have the means to match the rising prices of local housing. Wales has recently been labelled the new 'grey' capital of Britain, due to the fact that one in nine households are now pensioners. The lack of quality, affordable housing for local people remains a problem and a quarter of those living on the streets in Wales today are under 25 years old. Many of the 98,000 houses in Wales which are unfit for human habitation are in the private rented sector, leaving communities in several of the more scenic areas of Wales in danger of being severely divided between the haves and have-nots.

The Health Service

Everyone in the UK has the right to use the National Health Service established by Aneurin Bevan (see Unit 8) in 1948 and care is provided on the basis of people's clinical need – not on their ability to pay. Today the NHS in Wales spends around 2.6 billion and is Wales' largest employer, representing more than 7 per cent of the Welsh workforce. NHS Wales provides four different levels of care for the people of Wales:

1 Primary care – family doctors, dentists, opticians, pharmacists etc. At present there are around 1,900 family doctors in Wales, 1,000 dentists and 600 opticians. There is an acute shortage of doctors in Wales, particularly family practitioners and a new medical school is to open in Swansea to help alleviate this problem. There is also a dire shortage of National Health dentists is some areas of Wales, particularly in the rural west.

2 Secondary care – hospitals and ambulance services. There are 15 NHS Trusts in Wales, which manage around 135 hospitals. Approximately half a million people will have a stay in one of the 15,000 beds in Welsh hospitals every year. Between 1996 and 2001 the number of new accident and emergency cases rose 6 per cent to 853,700.

3 Tertiary care – through specialist hospitals treating particular types of illness such as cancer.

4 Community care – provided by the NHS and local social services often helping those such as the elderly to live on their own, rather than in a home. Others working in the community include midwives, health visitors and speech therapists.

The NHS in Wales has come under considerable criticism of late due to the fact that almost a quarter of a million patients are waiting anything between 12 to 18 months to see a specialist. As a result, the numbers choosing private healthcare are increasing. During 2000–1, 3,760 patients were treated privately as in-patients or day cases in NHS hospitals, an increase of 55 per cent over the 1996–97 figure. During the same year, there were 8,200 private outpatient attendances in NHS hospitals, an increase of 38 per cent over the 1996–7 figure.

The future of the NHS in Wales

The Welsh Assembly Government is responsible for policy direction and for allocating funds to the NHS and, in an attempt to boost faith in the NHS, they have recently undertaken a radical overhaul of the health system in Wales. The five existing regional Health Authorities have been abolished and Local Health Boards set up in every area. These Local Health Boards which came into operation on 1 April 2003 decide what services are needed for local people and aim to ensure that these are provided. These include family health, community health and hospital services. As these boards include Council representatives, members of the public and representatives from voluntary organizations, it is hoped that this will bring about a more coordinated and effective system, putting the 'power' in the hands of the local communities.

With this in mind, an extra billion is to be spent in the NHS in Wales between 2003 and 2006. Until earlier this year, Wales was the only country in Europe not to possess its own children's hospital. Following extensive voluntary fundraising, which raised over 5 million pounds, construction recently began in Cardiff on a purpose-built children's hospital. The first phase will include three wards, including a cancer ward and family accommodation.

How healthy are the Welsh?

• Around 17 per cent of the Welsh population are now over 65 and the average life expectancy for a woman is 79 and 74 for a man. This has risen considerably over the last ten years and the gap between men and women has decreased slightly. There are however substantial differences between areas – life expectancy in the south Wales valleys is four or five years less than in rural west Wales.

- Many Welsh people inevitably suffer the diseases associated with heavy industries like coal mining along with those associated with poverty as a result of the decline of such industries. Circulatory diseases, mainly heart attacks and strokes, are the commonest cause of death, accounting for 40 per cent of all deaths in 2000. Other major causes of death are cancer, accounting for 24 per cent of all deaths in the same year and respiratory diseases, responsible for two out of every ten deaths. Patterns for men and women are broadly similar, although injuries are a more common cause of death in men than women. In some areas of south Wales, more than a quarter of the population are off work with limiting long-term illness. The 2001 census revealed that there was at least one person with a long-term illness in half the households in Neath Port Talbot, Merthyr Tydfil and Blaenau Gwent. Of the 5.2 million carers recorded in the census, more than 11 per cent came from Wales, many working more than 50 hours per week.

- In spite of the fact that a large percentage of dentists in Wales will now only take private patients who have to pay for their treatment, the proportion of adults who report seeing a dentist regularly has increased from 40 per cent in 1978 to around 60 per cent today.

- Smoking amongst Welsh teenagers showed a steady increase during the 1980s and early 1990s, peaking in 1996 with 29 per cent of 15-year-old girls and 23 per cent of 15-year-old boys reported to smoke on a regular basis. Figures for 2000 remained at 29 per cent in the case of girls but had decreased to 20 per cent amongst boys.

- Adolescents also appear to be consuming less alcohol and taking more exercise than in the last decade; 50 per cent of boys exercise for at least four hours a week outside of school, compared with 20 per cent of girls. Nevertheless, 42 per cent of boys and 41 per cent of girls have used illegal drugs – an increase of 20 per cent on ten years ago.

- Wales is one of the areas of Britain that has very high teenage pregnancy rates which range from 28.6 per 1,000 in Monmouthshire to 69.2 per 1,000 in Blaenau Gwent. The teenage abortion rate for Wales was 36 per cent between 1998 and 2000 ranging from 28 per cent in Blaenau Gwent to 52 per cent in Monmouthshire.

UK and Europe comparisons

- There is a greater percentage of people over 65 living in Wales than in the other UK countries. Indeed, Wales appears to have one of the highest proportions of elderly people of all the EU member states and life expectancy in Wales is two or three years less than the best.

- Coronary heart disease, cancer and asthma are estimated to be more prevalent in Wales than in many EU countries, with death rates from such conditions being inevitably higher than many other countries including England. In the 1991 census 17.5 per cent of the population in Wales reported a limiting long-term illness, but by 2001 that figure had risen to 23.3 per cent. A third of the population of Merthyr Tydfil reported long-term illness, the second highest rate in England and Wales, followed by Neath Port Talbot at 29.4 per cent. Only the former mining community of Easington in Yorkshire was harder hit.

- With an ageing population, it is little wonder that 41 million prescription items were dispensed in Wales during 1999–2000, an increase of 13 per cent over the previous five years. This equates to 14 items for each person in Wales, which is the highest number of prescription items per head of all the four UK countries. The Wales Labour Party have pledged to abolish all prescription charges in Wales.

Transport

Getting around Wales is not always very easy. There are significant gaps in public transport services in mid, west and north Wales and it is impossible to travel by train from north to south Wales without going through England. Most travel by car or public transport is in a west/east direction along both the north and south coastal regions. There is only one motorway, the M4, which enters Wales across the recently opened second Severn Bridge crossing and ends a few miles west of Swansea. In the north, the main road is the A55 dual carriageway, which has been considerably improved in recent years, thereby strengthening communications between north Wales and the rest of the UK. Holyhead on the westerly tip of Anglesey is 476 km from London, whilst Fishguard in Pembrokeshire is 425 km. Aberystwyth is 394 km from London compared with Cardiff which is 249 km. Within Wales itself, the lack of fast and direct road and rail networks means that Aberystwyth, 'the

The second Severn Bridge crossing

cultural capital of Wales', is a more central meeting place than Cardiff and there is a growing tendency for organizations to move out of Cardiff to more rural areas in mid Wales.

The Welsh Assembly Government has direct responsibility for maintaining and improving the 1,708 km of trunk road and motorway network in Wales. Although this is only 5 per cent of all the roads in the country, these roads carry 50 per cent of all Welsh traffic. Local authorities have direct responsibility for the roads in Wales which are not on the trunk road and motorway network, many of which are in a poor condition and impassable in bad weather. Every year about 200 people die, another 1,700 are seriously injured and another 13,000 receive minor injuries on Welsh roads. The casualty rate amongst children is one of the highest in Europe. Increases in road traffic have also had an effect on wildlife – a recent survey estimated that 47,000 badgers, 100,000 hedgehogs and 5,000 barn owls were killed on Welsh roads in the year 2000.

Cars

Compared to some other European countries such as Germany, Britain has relatively low levels of car ownership and Wales has even less than the UK average. Around 30 per cent of households do not possess a car and this figure rises to almost 40 per cent in some deprived communities. At the same time, the level of car ownership has recently been rising slightly faster in Wales than in the rest of the UK. In the affluent border county of Monmouthshire, 6.6 per cent of the population own three cars according to the 2001 census. Those with cars also appear to rely on them more than people in many other areas in Britain. In rural Wales, due to the lack of public transport, 87 per cent of the population use cars to get to work, compared to some 76 per cent in urban areas. More people in the Vale of Glamorgan get on their bikes to go to work than anywhere else in Wales, but this still amounts to less than 2 per cent of the population. The British Government's recent decision to introduce a cheaper road tax for cars under 1200cc helps those with smaller, more economical vehicles, but fuel nevertheless is extremely expensive compared to some other countries in Europe. There are approximately 400 petrol stations in Wales, around 100 of which are open 24 hours a day. In rural areas in mid and west Wales, petrol stations can be very few and far between and here petrol is generally a few pence per litre more expensive than England. The average price of unleaded petrol in 2003 was 78 pence per litre and diesel slightly more. It is little wonder that people from rural Wales were at the heart of recent protests regarding petrol prices that led to the blockading of oil refineries all over Britain.

Driving and the law

According to a recent survey, drivers in Wales are the least law-abiding of all UK drivers. One in five Welsh people has been convicted of a motoring offence, speeding being one of the main culprits. At present, as in the rest of the UK, a fixed penalty of £60 is imposed on those caught speeding and three penalty points are put on their licence. High-speed offences mean an automatic court appearance and usually a period of disqualification with a re-test and higher insurance at the end as well. One of the highest recorded speeds to date was by a motorcyclist in south Wales who was travelling at 250 kph. The fastest recorded car was travelling at 235 kph – while being delivered to its new owner.

Buses

Local buses service most areas in Wales, although in certain rural areas that may mean only one bus a week. There are also 17 Postbuses in operation daily in some of the less-accessible parts of west and mid Wales. During the summer many holiday areas, such as Pembrokeshire, put on extra services. A daily coach service between Bangor in the north and Cardiff in the south takes approximately eight hours. Owing to the inadequacy and unreliability of services and a lack of integration between rail and bus operators, 79 per cent of bus users in a recent report said that they would rather use some other form of transport if at all possible.

To encourage the use of public transport therefore and to increase opportunities for disadvantaged people to access a variety of services, the Welsh Assembly Government decided to introduce free concessionary bus travel in April 2002. Women over 60, men over 65 and all registered disabled people were entitled to free transport on all local buses. In April 2003 free travel was extended to all men over 60. This has proved enormously popular and has improved the provision of public bus services through increased demand in many places.

Railways

Wales' rail network is sparse and the services on it need improving. The two major lines are at opposite ends of the country and are connected only by routes through England. In the north most services are concentrated around the coast, from Holyhead over the border to Chester, whilst in the south there is a regular service between Swansea, Cardiff and London. There is also a reasonable service west of Swansea to Pembroke Dock and Fishguard where, like Holyhead, ferries can be caught to Ireland. Services on the remainder of Wales' lines are less frequent and slower, but worth experiencing if only for the superb scenery. Extremely popular with walkers and birdwatchers is the Heart of Wales line from Shrewsbury to Swansea, whilst the mid Wales line from Aberystwyth to Pwllheli and Shrewsbury is another particularly scenic route.

Privatization means that many different companies operate the various rail services in Wales at present, but it is hoped that soon the railways will all be run by a single operator based in Cardiff. This should bring about enhanced rail services in terms of quality and frequency and better links with local buses. As things stand at present, in spite of recent major initiatives such as the reopening of the Vale of Glamorgan line, rail provision in Wales is woefully inadequate compared to the rest of Europe and fares considerably more expensive than many other European countries.

The age of steam

There are also several steam railways in Wales, and although they now run primarily as tourist attractions, several also operate as public transport. Some of the most well-known steam railways include the Talyllyn, running for 11 km at the base of Cader Idris in mid Wales and the Ffestiniog Railway, 21 km from Porthmadog to Blaenau Ffestiniog. If climbing Snowdon is not for you, why not ascend to the summit of Wales' highest mountain in style on the Snowdon Mountain Railway – Wales' only rack and pinion railway?

Air travel

Wales' largest airport is Cardiff International Airport, which opened in 1942 with flights originally to France and Ireland. The first transatlantic flights took place in 1971 and the growth in the popularity of holidays to the Mediterranean led to the airport being expanded considerably in the 1980s. Charter flights to Florida and Canada were also established and Manx Airlines in the early 1990s began offering daily services to key business destinations within Europe and the UK. In August 1994 the airport celebrated attaining the 1 million passenger mark. Since privatization in 1995, the airport has gone from strength to strength and in 2002 the low-cost carrier BmiBaby established a hub at the airport, which now ranks as one of the UK's most successful regional airports.

GLOSSARY
Education

addysg (f.)	*education*
dysgu	*to learn / teach*
addysgu	*to educate*
meithrinfa (f.)	*nursery*
ysgol gynradd	*primary school*
ysgol uwchradd	*secondary school*
ysgol gyfun	*comprehensive school*
athro (m.)	*teacher*
athrawes (f.)	*female teacher*
prifathro (m.)	*headmaster*
prifathrawes (f.)	*headmistress*
disgybl (m.)	*pupil*
gwaith cartref	*homework*
astudio	*to study*
arholiad (m.)	*examination*

---

prifysgol (f.)	*university*
gradd (f.)	*degree*
myfyriwr (m.)	*student*
myfyrwraig (f.)	*female student*

Housing

byw	*to live*
tŷ teras	*terraced house*
tŷ pâr	*semi-detached house*
tŷ ar wahân	*detached house*
tŷ haf	*holiday home*
rhentu	*to rent*
digartref	*homeless*
digartrefedd (m.)	*homelessness*
cartref (m.)	*home*
cartrefol	*homely*
gartref	*at home*
perchennog (m.)	*owner*
gwerthwr tai	*estate agent*
mewnfudwyr (pl.)	*incomers*

Health

iechyd (m.)	*health*
salwch (m.)	*illness*
meddyg (m.)	*doctor*
nyrs (f.)	*nurse*
meddyg teulu	*family practitioner*
meddygfa (f.)	*surgery*
moddion (pl.)	*medicine*
tabledi (pl.)	*tablets*
poen (f.)	*pain*
deintydd (m.)	*dentist*
claf (m.)	*patient*
apwyntiad (m.)	*appointment*
ysbyty (m.)	*hospital*
llawdriniaeth (f.)	*operation*
arbenigwr (m.)	*specialist*

Transport

cludiant (m.)	*transport*
trafnidiaeth (f.)	*traffic*
car (m.)	*car*
gyrru	*to drive*

parcio	to park
ffordd (f.)	road
traffordd (f.)	motorway
rheilffordd (f.)	railway
trên (m.)	train
bws (m.)	bus
awyren (f.)	aeroplane
maes awyr	airport
hedfan	to fly
tocyn (m.)	ticket
amserlen (f.)	timetable

Taking it further

Reading

Dunkerley, David and Thompson, Andrew, *Wales Today* (Cardiff: 1999)

Parker, Mike and Whitfield, Paul, *The Rough Guide to Wales* (London: 2000)

Williams, Iolo Wyn, (ed.) *Our Children's Language: The Welsh Medium – Schools of Wales 1939–2000* (Talybont: 2003)

Information

The bilingual **Mantais Cymru** information line, operated on behalf of the National Assembly, offers primary access to the very latest traffic and road-user information for travel to, from and within Wales. Tel: 0845 602 6020. Website: **www.traffic-wales.com**

Websites

www.wales.gov.uk The National Assembly website contains detailed information and up-to-date statistics on all the subjects to be found in this unit.

www.wales.nhs.co.uk the official website of the NHS in Wales explains the new health system in Wales in detail and contains useful links to other health-related sites.

www.walesindex.co.uk is a general directory of services in Wales and contains considerable practical information relevant to the topics discussed in this unit.

10 the Welsh at work and play

In this unit you will learn about
- the changing economy
- industry, agriculture, tourism and heritage
- women at work
- the armed forces
- leisure activities

A changing nation

The twentieth century saw great changes in employment patterns in Wales. At the turn of the century, the coal and steel industry dominated the south as did the slate industry in the north. In 1945, 30 per cent of the Welsh male workforce was employed in the coal and steel industries and 10 per cent in agriculture. By the 1950s there was almost full employment in the country yet by the end of the century the old established industries, which once made the port of Cardiff the busiest in the world, had declined to such an extent that the major steel-producing plants at Shotton, Ebbw Vale and Cardiff had ceased to exist and the coal industry had virtually vanished. Employment in agriculture has more than halved and wages are, on average, lower than in both Scotland and England. What was once the cradle of industry was in danger of becoming the cradle of depression but to some extent, coal mining, manufacturing and heavy industry have been replaced by lighter manufacturing industries such as electronics, biotechnology, machine part assembly and the technological industries. Many people in Wales are employed in the service industries and professional and administrative occupations. Tourism and public services have taken over as the main employers within Wales, British governments have attracted English and multi-national companies to Wales with generous incentives but unemployment is still higher than the average for Britain. The unemployment rate, however, has recently shown signs of falling. In 2002, 5.3 per cent of the population of Wales was unemployed, whereas the figure for 2003 is 4.4 per cent. The methods used to calculate the number of unemployed have been changed more than 20 times since the 1980s and it is thought that the actual figure is much higher.

Inward investment

Wales has been able to attract foreign visitors in one key area, however, that of business. Wales has investors from as far afield as the USA, Japan, Canada and Italy. The Welsh Development Agency (WDA), established in 1976, was assigned to attract new business to Wales and succeeded in netting more than 20 per cent of the UK's new inward investors in the early 1990s, partly because of the low wage structure in Wales and the high unemployment levels following the collapse of the traditional heavy industries. Wales' share later fell to 11 per cent as other areas within the UK vied for custom, yet Wales has transformed itself into one of Europe's top locations for Japanese, Korean and American business firms, especially in the automotive and consumer electronics fields. Wales has the greatest concentration of Japanese electronic manufacturing and consumer electronics anywhere in the world outside of Japan or North America. Sony's main European television plant, located in Wales, produces more than 1 million television sets a year and exports these Welsh-made televisions to the United States and other markets around the world. Japanese workers seem to fit in with their new surroundings, Tokyo even has a *Clwb Hiraeth* (the Welsh translates as 'homesickness club') set up by Japanese people who are nostalgic for Wales after having worked there. Although Sony is one of the biggest single private employers in Wales, the largest foreign investors in Wales are from the United States. There are 180 North American firms in Wales, including Ford, General Electric, Dow Corning, Borg-Warner, Allied-Signal and Warner Lambert, employing a total of more than 30,000 people. More than one in three Welsh manufacturing workers are employed by foreign-owned companies. In 1998, there were over 400 overseas companies based in Wales: 179 from Europe, 137 from America and 45 from Japan. These have created 70,000 jobs, particularly in the high-tech and white-collar industries, which have sprung up around Cardiff and Newport on the M4 corridor, and have safeguarded many more. These jobs have been created mainly in areas where the decline in old industries had resulted in serious unemployment problems. Foreign firms include the Italian tyre company Pirelli, Bosch Siemes (Germany) and Matsushita (Japan).

There are a number of reasons why multinational companies invest in Wales and create much needed jobs. One of the key reasons is the presence of a large workforce who are flexible enough to adapt to new working practices. Wales also has the cheapest labour force in the UK: the weekly average gross earnings in 1998 were £354, considerably less than both England and Scotland. The price of setting up and running businesses in Wales compares very favourably with other parts of the world because of the low housing and telecommunication costs, good infrastructure with access to ports and customers and the availability of government grants. The Welsh workforce has other assets as well; when Admiral Insurance wanted an easy-to-understand accent and an accent that raises customer confidence in the company, the Welsh accent scored far higher than other regional accents in the UK. The company employs 600 people in Cardiff selling insurance over the telephone, and is expanding to offer another 300 jobs in Swansea. The new 'call centre' boom is another sector being established in Wales.

The official British Royal Mint is in Llantrisant and all British motoring documents are processed at Swansea. However, despite the relative success of inward investment compared to the rest of the UK, Wales is constantly dropping back in living standards and ranks amongst the poorest part of the UK.

Rejuvenation

The Welsh economy, then, is diverse, incorporating cutting-edge technologies and IT, manufacturing, engineering, telecommunications, media, leisure, tourism and agriculture. Wales is also undergoing a period of rejuvenation, and the old industrial valleys are the focus of new initiatives. Newport Unlimited is the urban regeneration company which has been created to regenerate the newly appointed city and enable it to develop into a thriving and vibrant centre for business, leisure and living. The Broadband Wales programme was announced by the Welsh National Assembly in July 2002. The programme will ensure that the whole of Wales will benefit from access to affordable broadband services and is crucial to the economic and social economy of Wales as building a knowledge-based economy requires access to good telecommunications.

Cardiff Bay

Wales boasts one of the fastest-growing capital cities in Europe and it is hoped to develop Cardiff into a significant financial and administrative centre. The relocation of major institutions to Wales goes some way to achieving that aim, as has the Cardiff Bay regeneration project, Europe's largest urban regeneration scheme. The old dockland is being redeveloped as part of a 10–15 year project to create a city for the future. The project takes over a sixth of the area of the capital, 1,200 hectares and costs over £2.4 billion. Although the city of Cardiff had continued to thrive as the business and commercial centre of Wales, the docks had declined. The multi-ethnic community that had grown up around the docks were suffering just as the valley communities had suffered at the closure of the coal mines. The Cardiff Bay Development Corporation was set up and charged with the task of regeneration. As well as housing and leisure facilities, including the five star St David's Hotel and Techniquest visitor centre, many new fashionable restaurants, cafés and bars, offices and shops have been built. Cardiff Bay will also be home to the proposed new National Assembly for Wales building (see Unit 4). A huge barrage has been constructed and this encloses a 200-hectare freshwater tidal lake. The bay area intends to build upon Cardiff's claim to be 'the multi-media centre of Europe' with over 300 companies based in the capital using latest fibre-optic links across the site.

Industry

Coal mining

There are now only three pits left in Wales. Tower Colliery, near Hirwaun, south Wales, where the workers successfully took over the running of the pit, is the only deep mine left in Wales and employs just 240 people. There are two drift mines in Betws and Cwmgwili employing another 220 men. Some large-scale, open-cast operations are run by Celtic Energy and most coal in Wales is extracted from large open cast sites with the notable exception of the Tower Colliery. There are thought to be about 2,000 coal miners in Wales, most of whom are employed in small private mines. Some former mining towns are now ghost towns, the closure of the mine leading to the closure of businesses dependent on the wages of former miners.

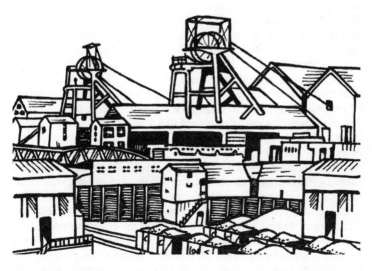

Colliery winding gear

Steel

All steel works in Wales have been either slimmed down, as at Port Talbot, Trostre at Llanelli, Shotton in Flintshire and Newport, or closed down altogether as happened at Ebbw Vale steelworks. It was announced in 2003 that Corus, the Anglo-Dutch group formed with the merger of British Steel and the Netherlands' Royal Hoogovens NV, would be investing heavily in the Port Talbot plant, in spite of this, heavy job losses and the closure of another steel-making plant are predicted.

Slate

Welsh slate from the quarries of north Wales was once widely used for roofing, billiard tables, blackboards and decorative fireplaces. The availability of cheaper alternatives has led to a decline in the industry however and it is nowadays rare to see a new house with a Welsh slate roof. The slate industry does still exist however but on a much smaller scale.

Agriculture

Wales is a land of small farms with sheep farming predominant in the mountains and moorland and dairy and mixed farming concentrated around the coast. Well over half of the land area in Wales is in agricultural use and yet there is a lack of a rich agricultural economy, many of the sheep farms being in isolated communities. Many farmers are leaving farming altogether after suffering from stringent milk production quotas introduced by the European Union, the BSE crisis and outbreak of foot-and-mouth disease. Although agriculture is still relevant to the Welsh economy, fewer and fewer people are employed in the industry. Many farmers have to diversify in order to make a living, opening their farms up for summer visitors or changing their crop to one which can corner a niche market, for instance ostriches. Farmers' markets are growing in popularity and enabling farmers to sell their produce direct to the consumer. Organic farming is increasing (see Unit 11); one organic dairy farming company, Rachel's Dairy, is one of Britain's leading organic dairies and retails yoghurt and cheese. Another company, Organic Farm Foods, operates an extensive packaging and distribution network from Lampeter, Ceredigion. All the company's produce, much of which is home-grown by organic growers in Wales, is certified as organically grown to official national and international standards. The company also imports organic fruit and vegetables. Lampeter has become the UK's largest centre for the preparation, packaging and distribution of organic fruits, vegetables and dairy products. A few hill farmers earn extra money by renting out their fields for wind farm turbines and more and more 'wind farms' are appearing in the Welsh countryside. The highlight of the agricultural year is the Royal Welsh Show, held annually in Llanelwedd near Builth Wells, where farmers come to display and view livestock and view examples of the latest technological gadgets.

Alternative Wales

One early modern windmill in Wales was at the Centre for Alternative Technology, Machynlleth, which was set up as an experiment in environmentally friendly living in 1975 on the site of a former slate quarry and is now one of Wales' main tourist attractions. The centre, or CAT as it is known, has had over a million visitors since it opened to the public in 1976. The centre, which claims to be Europe's leading eco-centre, is built on the foundations of an abandoned slate quarry and covers a 16-hectare site that includes working displays of environmentally sound practices. Its aim is to preserve resources and eliminate waste and pollution and to that end it has its own reservoir, water supply and sewage system and is powered not on mains electricity but by renewable energy resources such as windmills, water turbines, solar energy and biofuels. The centre is reached by an environmentally friendly water-powered cliff railway. Once at the centre, visitors can learn about 'green living' and see cottages built of recycled materials and heated by solar power and wood stoves. The centre offers courses ranging from how to build your own energy-efficient home to organic gardening to organizing a green funeral. Self-catering holidays are also available in eco-cabins. One source of wonder is the organic garden, fertilized by human sewage which has been recycled into organic fertilizer.

Tourism and heritage

Tourism is a key employer and revenue earner for Wales and it is growing in importance to the Welsh economy as the traditional industries decline. Tourism has flourished in Wales since the Victorian era. The first resort to be developed was

Llandrindod. Spas were the first proper tourist resorts in Wales – in their prime, they welcomed 80,000 visitors a year. It was during the Victorian era that 'Wells' was added to Llanwrtyd, Llangamarch and Llandrindod. Victorians flocked to the new seaside resorts in Tenby, Llandudno and Beaumaris. The foundation of the Welsh Tourist Board in 1969 led to an acceleration of attractions in Wales. Each part of Wales possesses a physical feature of its own: the south has sandy beaches, mid Wales boasts gently rolling hills, whereas the north is home to rugged mountains. Tourism contributes to all these areas: rural and urban, coastal and inland. As well as heritage parks, Wales offers activity holidays, castles and theme parks. The first theme park in Wales was Oakwood in Pembrokeshire. It attracts almost half a million visitors a year and has the largest wooden roller-coaster in Europe, Megaphobia. Nowadays tourists come to surf, sunbathe, dive, fish and view the wildlife; half a million people walk on Snowdon every year. Locals and tourists alike use the natural and man-made lakes for watersports. Bala is a popular wind-surfing and canoeing centre, and the national White Water Centre is nearby. Tenby harbour which was built for merchant and fishing fleet is given over to pleasure craft and most of the waterfront houses are hotels and guest houses.

Wales also boasts some striking gardens including Bodnant overlooking the River Conwy, Snowdonia, which consists of 40 hectares of magnificent shrubs and flowers, and the gardens of Powis Castle. Relatively new is Middleton, the National Botanic Garden of Wales near Llandeilo. The Garden of Wales, set in the former eighteenth century regency park of Middleton Hall on the edge of the Tywi valley in Carmarthenshire, was the first national botanic garden to be created in the United Kingdom for over 200 years. A Millennium project aiming to heighten visitors' awareness and understanding of the natural and man-made world, it is dedicated to conservation, horticulture, science, education, leisure and the arts. However, after a promising start, visitor numbers slumped and the Garden faces closure. The Welsh Assembly Government refused a plea for £3 million for the Garden's rescue and it is now hoped that private companies will step in.

According to the Welsh Tourist Board, one in nine jobs in the Welsh economy belongs to the tourist sector, which brings in two billion pounds each year. Welsh tourism is based on the efforts of over 7,000 micro, small and medium sized enterprises, the vast majority of which are indigenous businesses, committed to supporting local suppliers and jobs. Most tourists to Wales are British holiday-makers, and only 3.3 per cent of foreign visitors to the UK come to Wales.

Marketing the past

Industrial history plays a significant role in Wales' own heritage business but critics lament that the workforce of Wales has turned from manufacturing goods to manufacturing heritage. Dotted throughout Wales are a number of establishments based on Wales' industrial past. These establishments, which include folk museums, farm museums, country parks and heritage trails, preserved mills and cottages, slate quarries and mines, act as 'living history' museums, recreating the past in an easily digestible way. Perhaps the first to open was Llechwedd Slate Caverns in Blaenau Ffestiniog which threw open its doors in 1970. The Slate Museum at Llanberis, Gwynedd is housed in the old maintenance workshops of the Dinorwig slate quarry, once one of the world's largest. The museum features a massive working water wheel, a narrow-gauge steam locomotive, a forge and loco shed, craft workshops and demonstrations. Today, the slate mines of Llanberis are a popular attraction, which seeks to preserve the traditions and skills of the Welsh slate miners from two centuries ago. In the 1980s, the Rhondda Heritage Park was opened on the site of the old Lewis Merthyr Colliery near Pontypridd. One of the most popular attractions amongst visiting schoolchildren is Big Pit at Blaenavon. The working mine closed in 1980 and is now a World Heritage site where visitors descend 90 metres to the coal seam and experience the darkness, silence and claustrophobic conditions of life underground. The site includes a range of colliery buildings, blacksmith's shop and pithead baths, and the guides are all ex-miners. The Museum of Welsh Life at St Fagans is devoted to heritage and has a vast collection of buildings showing how people lived in the past including a bakehouse, toll house, school and smithy. The most vociferous critics of such developments claim that Wales is turning into one big museum.

Women at work

The greatest change in Welsh society over the last century is the enhanced role of women in the workplace. In 1936 one out of every three employed people in England and Wales was a woman. However, in Wales itself, despite considerable unemployment amongst men, only 17 per cent of the work force were female. This was to change dramatically with the outbreak of the Second World War. The number of those employed outside the home rose 130 per cent compared to the British increase of 30 per cent. In 1945, less than a quarter of the employed population was female, this proportion has been rising rapidly ever since, partly as a result of the decline in heavy industry – coal, steel and agriculture almost exclusively employed men. The number of women in employment in Wales between 1986 and 1996 grew by 17 per cent. Most new jobs created in Wales are for women, and in many areas, particularly in the south, there are more working women than working men. Women now amount to half the workforce of many of the new electrical companies, which have set up as a result of inward investment. The increase in tourism in Wales has created part-time seasonal jobs, many of which have been taken up by women. In rural areas, farms have been forced to diversify as it becomes more and more difficult to make a living solely from the land. Of the total women of working age, 64 per cent are now in work compared to 72 per cent of men. Although the situation is improving, financial discrimination in the workplace remains a problem. In 1975, women in Wales received only 69 per cent of men's hourly earnings, whereas they now earn on average 13.5 per cent per hour less than men for doing similar jobs. The gap between female and male earnings in general still widens with age and in only one in twelve couples, where both partners work full time, does the woman earn significantly more than the man. The cost and availability of childcare is still proving a problem for many women and it can be an obstacle to returning to work or obtaining employment.

	Women	Men
Part-time employment	85 per cent	15 per cent
Primary school heads	47 per cent	53 per cent
Secondary school heads	12 per cent	88 per cent
Hospital consultants	17 per cent	83 per cent
Members of Parliament	10 per cent	90 per cent
Local councillors	20 per cent	80 per cent

Women also tend to be employed in a narrow range of jobs in such areas as the service sector, often on a part-time or casual basis. The numbers of those in top jobs remains small as indicated in the statistics above. The exception to these examples is the National Assembly where the balance between the sexes is more equal. In the current administration, 50 per cent of the members are women and the Cabinet has more women than men, the only one in Western Europe with a majority of women.

The armed forces

The Ministry of Defence spends over £100 million with firms in Wales each year, thus making a significant contribution to the Welsh economy. A thousand people are employed in the defence industry in Wales, defence manufactures in Wales include Cogent Defence Systems in Newport, which manufactures secure communications equipment and Thales Optics at St Asaph in Denbighshire, which designs and manufactures optical modules for aircraft head-up displays.

The Welsh have been fighting for Britain since the defeat of the last Welsh prince in 1282. At the battle of Crécy in 1346, a third of the English army was in fact Welsh and Welshmen fought in the Wars of the Roses, the English Civil Wars and the Zulu Wars. The Victoria Cross is the highest British award for gallantry in wartime and the greatest number of VCs won in a single action were the ten medals awarded to the Welsh regiment, the South Wales Borderers at Rorke's Drift in 1879 when a detachment of the 2nd/24th held out against 20,000 Zulu warriors. The 82 men manned the small mission hospital and supply depot, earning themselves a Full Battle Honour. The battle at Rorke's Drift was made into a film, Zulu, starring Stanley Baker and Michael Caine. In the First World War 35,000 Welsh soldiers died, convinced that they were fighting for small nations like their own.

Over 8,000 people now work on important defence activities at Ministry of Defence sites in Wales. Wales is home to a number of military bases; Pembroke Dock was for a time the foremost naval shipyard in the world, an ordnance factory was established at Bridgend in 1939 and, during the Second World War, it became the biggest of all British munitions factories with 35,000 women working there – it is still a military base today. The Defence Aviation Repair Agency (DARA) at RAF St Athan, Barry is a centre for the maintenance, repair and overhaul of aircraft for all three services. Almost 4,000 people work at St Athan, 2,500 of whom are civilians. RAF St Athan is the largest station in the Royal Air Force and is now the RAF's only aircraft maintenance unit; it is also where the turf for the Millennium Stadium in Cardiff was grown and it is stored there between games. At RAF Valley in Anglesey RAF pilots undergo fast jet training; the RAF Search and Rescue Sea King helicopters from RAF Valley, supported by the mountain rescue team from RAF St Athan, undertake Search and Rescue in Wales and regularly assist people in difficulty. The headquarters of the Army's 160 Brigade is in Brecon, as is the Infantry Training Centre. The army's Sennybridge training area and the surrounding countryside provide the terrain and conditions needed to train troops ready for overseas missions. There is a tank gunnery range at Castlemartin, in Pembrokeshire, another army range at Epynt, and Aberporth in Ceredigion is home to a missile testing station. The only Victoria Cross won in the Falklands campaign was by Welshman **Colonel H. Jones**, awarded posthumously in 1982. Colonel Jones led his troops to capture an Argentine machine-gun emplacement. Wales is one of the Armed Forces' most important recruiting areas, supplying almost 8 per cent of new recruits each year; it is believed that this is partly the result of there being relatively few employment opportunities in some areas.

Leisure

The latest survey of leisure activities in Wales showed that the most popular leisure activity in Wales is visiting the pub. Of those questioned, 58 per cent cited it as their favourite regular activity. This is ironic given that in 1881 an Act of Parliament was passed, the first ever to legislate specifically for Wales, which forbade the opening of Welsh pubs on Sunday. This was replaced by a referendum held every seven years, which entitled every district to vote for or against Sunday opening. Gradually the dry areas were squeezed into fewer and fewer enclaves of the west and north, until by 1996, the date of the last referendum, every area was 'wet'. Under the old law, if at least 500 registered voters in any Welsh county or county borough requested it, the local authority was obliged to hold ballots in which people decided whether or not alcohol should be sold there on a Sunday. In July 2003, however, this legislation was scrapped meaning that alcohol will be able to be sold throughout Wales on Sunday.

The same poll that discovered the Welsh fondness for drink also found that a third of the adult population engage in sport on a regular basis. The Welsh have always had a fondness for sport.

In 1573, the Lord President of the Council of Marches, the Welsh administrator for Wales, complained that the people disgracefully neglected their archery in favour of tables, dice, cards, bowls and quoits.

Rugby

Rugby Union has always been regarded as Wales' national game, and for some, rugby is a religion. The first rugby organization, the South Wales Football Union, was established in 1874. This organization was to become the Welsh

Rugby players

Rugby Union (WRU) in 1881. That body selected a Welsh team to play England in the same year. The first 'Golden Era' of Rugby Union was from 1900 to 1911 but Rugby Union in Wales was particularly popular after the Second World War. The second golden era was during the 1970s, when players such as **Barry John, Gerald Davies** and **Gareth Edwards** and **J. P. R. Williams** were playing.

Gareth Edwards made 53 consecutive appearances from 1967 until his retirement in 1978 and was voted the greatest rugby player of all time in a 1996 poll organized by *Rugby World*. J. P. R. Williams was capped 55 times and never lost in 11 appearances against England. One of the most memorable tries of the century occurred during a Barbarians versus New Zealand match which involved six players passing the ball from one end of the pitch to the other. Welsh rugby has been in decline since those glory days, and many fans blame the bureaucratic system of the Welsh Rugby Union which until recently has found it very difficult to shake off ineffectual practices prevalent in its amateur heyday, for example taking more committee men than players on international tours. A recent record maker is **Neil Jenkins,** who is the highest scoring player in the game's history. He also holds the Welsh record for the highest number of international appearances – 87 in total. Wales hosted the fourth Rugby World Cup final in 1999 at the Millennium Stadium in Cardiff; the stadium was built on the site of the former National Stadium in the centre of Cardiff and is the most modern sports arena in Europe. It has a seating capacity of 72,500 and is only one of two stadiums outside the USA with a retractable roof. When Wales are playing at home, the area is awash with red scarves, giant green leeks and painted faces singing the traditional songs *Sosban Fach* and *Calon Lan*, as well as the national anthem (see Appendix). Rugby is played between September and May and although the major first-class clubs are all located in south Wales, almost every village and town in the south has a rugby team. Welsh rugby is going through a period of change. In 2003 five regional sides (the Cardiff Blues, Celtic Warriors, Gwent Dragons, Llanelli Scarlets and Neath-Swansea Ospreys) were created to compete in the Heineken European Cup and Celtic League. The nine clubs making up these regional sides will also continue to compete individually on a semi-professional basis in the new expanded Premier Division. Below this level the game will revert to amateur status. The aim of this re-organization is to raise standards at the highest level and improve development opportunities for younger players.

Football

Football is the other main winter sport played in Wales. The oldest football international in the world was **Billy Meredith** from Chirk, whose international career spanned 26 years. He died aged 83. He played for 30 years in English First Division and hardly missed a game until he was well into his 50s. The youngest Welsh cap was **Ryan Giggs** of Manchester United, who played his first international game aged 17. Other famous players include **John Toshack, Mark Hughes, Ian Rush** and **Neville Southall**. The main clubs are Cardiff, Swansea and Wrexham.

Athletics

One of the most famous and popular of modern Welsh athletes is **Tanni Grey-Thompson OBE** from Cardiff who has represented Britain at 100m to 800m distances, as a competitor in the Paralympics in 1988, 1992, 1996 and 2000, winning a total of nine Gold medals. She also competed in the Olympic Games in 1992, 1996 and 2000, and the World Championships, winning five Gold medals. She has broken over 20 world records and won the London Marathon in 1992, 1994, 1996,

1998 and 2001. Since 1996, she has been Development Officer of UK Athletics and is an active member of both the Sports Council for Wales and UK Sport. She has twice been voted Welsh Sports Personality of the Year.

Lynn Davies ('Lynn the Leap') set the still-unbeaten UK record for the long jump of 8.23 metres in Switzerland in 1968, and won the gold medal in the 1964 Tokyo Olympic Games. World champion hurdler **Colin Jackson** set the world record of 12.91 seconds for the 110m hurdles in Stuttgart in 1993, and the world indoor record for the 60m hurdles also in Stuttgart. He retired in 2003. Other famous athletes are **Iwan Thomas** and **Jamie Baulch**. **Steve Jones** won the London Marathon in a record 2 hours 8 minutes and 16 seconds in 1985, and won the New York Marathon three years later.

Every New Year's Eve there is a 6 km race in Mountain Ash, with international athletes, to commemorate the eighteenth-century shepherd and folk hero **Guto Nyth Brân**, who died after running 19 km in 53 minutes. There are many stories about Guto: it was said that he could beat horses in races, keep up with hounds, outrun a hare and that his mother put the kettle on and Guto ran the five miles to Pontypridd to buy tea and back again before the water had boiled. He is buried in the churchyard of St Gwynno in the hamlet of Llanwynno.

Boxing

Boxing has always been popular in Wales, especially in the south Wales valleys where it was traditionally seen as one route out of the poverty and hardship of life there. Wales can lay claim to many famous boxers, amongst them **'Peerless' Jim Driscoll**, featherweight and lightweight champion, who was the first featherweight to win the Lonsdale Belt and whose funeral in 1925 was watched by 100,000 people. **Jimmy Wilde**, known as the Tylorstown Terror, was flyweight champion from 1916 until 1923. In 1907, **F. H. Thomas** 'Freddie Welsh', world lightweight champion, knocked out a lightweight, a welterweight and a heavyweight all in a single day. In one of the great fights in history, another Welsh boxer, **Tommy Farr**, almost beat Joe Louis at Madison Square Garden in 1938. One of the most popular Welsh boxers was featherweight **Johnny Owen**, who died after a world championship fight in America in 1980.

Cricket

Glamorgan has won the cricket County Championship on three occasions, 1948, 1969 and 1997, and the Sunday league in 1993. One of Britain's best spin bowlers, **Robert Croft** from Glamorgan, was picked to tour the West Indies in 1998 and Australia in 1999 with the England team. Glamorgan is the only Welsh county in the county championship. Probably the finest cricketer from Wales was Cardiff's **Maurice Turnbull**, who was capped by the Marylebone Cricket Club and also played rugby for Wales. He was tragically killed in the Second World War.

Other sports

Other sports enjoyed in Wales are golf – the Celtic Manor Resort in south Wales will host golf's 2010 Ryder Cup as well as the annual Wales Open – horse racing, snooker and rally driving. The Network Q rally tours through Wales every year. The Cardiff Devils are one of Britain's leading ice hockey teams and were virtually unbeatable during the mid to late 1990s. Snooker, like boxing, was often played by young men hoping to make their fortune. There are quite a few snooker celebrities from Wales including **Ray Reardon** who was world champion six times between 1970 and 1978 and **Terry Griffiths** who won the title in 1979. The current leader in the world rankings is **Mark Williams** who hails from the small town of Cwm near Ebbw Vale.

DIY and gardening are also very popular pastimes amongst the Welsh. Also popular are short breaks and trips, with a third of the nation taking regular outings to the country or seaside. Other favourite regular activities include bingo, watching sports and visiting the cinema, choirs and eisteddfodau (see Unit 5). Amongst the Welsh-speaking population, *Merched y Wawr* (Women of the Dawn), and the *Urdd* are very popular. Most towns have a *Clwb Cinio* (Dining club) for Welsh-speaking men.

Merched y Wawr

Merched y Wawr is a society for women which operates through the medium of Welsh and has over 250 branches throughout Wales. The various activities they are involved in include cooking, crafts, sports, excursions, aiding charities, singing, quizzes and lectures. They also publish a magazine entitled *Y Wawr* (the Dawn) and campaign for women's rights and for equal rights for the Welsh language. To this aim members have established *ysgolion meithrin* (see Unit 9), campaigned for a new Language Act, supported the campaigns for a Welsh-language channel, raised money for breast cancer research and taped cassettes for the blind.

Urdd Gobaith Cymru

The *Urdd* (Welsh League of Youth) was founded in 1922 by **Ifan ab Owen Edwards** (1895–1970), when 200 boys responded to an invitation to camp at Llanuwchlyn. It is open to girls and boys and now comprises 300 youth clubs and 50,000 members and has two large youth camps, at Llangrannog in Ceredigion where there is a ski slope, and at Glanllyn near Bala. The main aim of the organization is to promote the use of Welsh among children and young adults and many of the schools in Wales have their own *Urdd* branch. The *Urdd* also runs the Urdd National Eisteddfod, which, like the Royal National Eisteddfod, takes place annually and alternates its location from north to south Wales. In the month of May each year a Message of Goodwill is broadcast to the countries of the world and it also produces magazines and organizes events throughout Wales.

Outdoor activities

Wales' landscape makes it an outdoor pursuit hotspot. Many water sports such as dinghy sailing, fishing, surfing and windsurfing are carried out along the many kilometres of rivers, lakes and sea coast. Mountaineering, hillwalking, rock climbing and caving activities occur in the more rugged parts of the country. The International Outward Bound Movement was founded in Aberdyfi in 1941 and the National Centre for Outdoor Pursuits is located at Capel Curig. Other popular outdoor pastimes are cycling, pony-trekking and quad biking, particularly among the young. Llanwrtyd Wells, which claims to be the smallest town in Britain, has a reputation for outdoor activities and offers an imaginative programme of events including, as well as the more usual mountain biking and pony-trekking (which locals claim they invented in the 1950s), a 'man-versus-horse' marathon which takes place over a hilly 35 km course every June. Llanwrtyd Wells is also famous for its International Bog Snorkling competition held in a local peat bog. It also holds a Mountain Bike Festival including Bog-Leaping (August). Not all the events hosted by Llanwrtyd Wells could be classed as sports competitions; it also hosts the mid Wales Beer Festival in November and also holds Real Ale

Rambles. On December 31, the New Year Walk-In is a torch-lit procession that calls in on many of the pubs in the town.

Crafts

Crafts have a long tradition in Wales and craft items, in particular rural crafts, are still made today, both for pleasure and for commercial reasons. As well as wood-carvers making love spoons (see Unit 6) and other wooden objects, Wales is also home to potters, textile artists and painters. One example of an old rural craft being turned into a souvenir for the tourist market is the *caseg fedi* (harvest mare) or corn maiden/corn dolly. The *caseg fedi* was a means of celebrating the last sheaf of corn to be harvested. This last tuft of corn, symbolizing the forces of natural growth, was plaited carefully and a contest followed where the workers took it in turns to throw their reaping hooks at the tuft in order to cut it. After shouting a rhyme, the successful reaper would try to carry the *caseg fedi* into the harvest feast without it being soaked by women throwing water. If he succeeded in reaching the feast with a dry *caseg fedi*, he sat in a place of honour and could drink as much beer as he wanted. If he failed in his task, he was scorned and was not offered beer. The *caseg fedi* would adorn the house until the next harvest.

Coracles

Roman visitors to Wales wrote of the coracles used to fish on Welsh rivers. The coracle is a traditional small round craft which is so light it can be carried on the fisherman's shoulders. Its lightness makes it easy to handle in the water by those with experience. The coracle is made of canvas over wooden laths and is ideal for netting sewin (see Unit 1) and salmon. Once a familiar sight on rivers, coracling is now severely restricted and licences are not being renewed. In 2002, only 12 fishermen possessed hereditary licences to net salmon. Fishing by means of a coracle is now only practised on three Welsh rivers, the Teifi, Tywi and Taf. Like much else in Wales, this former craft has become the domain of tourism. Every year in August there is a coracle regatta in Cilgerran. The National Coracle Centre at Cenarth Falls in Carmarthenshire includes, among its exhibits, examples from Vietnam, Iraq, India and North America.

Festivals and shows

Many festivals and shows are held in Wales, particularly during the summer months. The Welsh people flock to eisteddfodau, country fairs, agricultural shows, sheep dog trials and arts and craft exhibitions.

Selection of annual events

March	Wrexham Science Festival
April	Cambrian Arts Festival, Llanddewibrefi, Ceredigion
May	Crafts in Action, St Donats; Llangollen International Jazz Festival
May/June	Hay Festival of Literature attracts top writers to the book capital of Europe; Old May Day Celebration Fair, Museum of Welsh Life, Cardiff; Urdd National Eisteddfod
June	Gregynog Festival – a classical music festival which takes place at Gregynog Hall near Newtown *Gŵyl Ifan* – Welsh folk dancing in Cardiff Three Peaks Yacht Race, Barmouth
July	*Gŵyl Gwerin y Cnapan* – a popular Celtic music and folk festival, in Newcastle Emlyn; Welsh Proms, St. David's Hall, Cardiff Fishguard International Music Festival; Snowdon Race (fell running); Llangollen International Music Eisteddfod Royal Welsh Agricultural Show, Llanelwedd *Sesiwn Fawr*, music festival held at Dolgellau
July/August	Cardiff Street Festival
August	Brecon Jazz Festival which attracts major talents from all over the world; Menai Strait Regatta; Anglesey County Show, near Llangefni; Royal National Eisteddfod; United Counties Agricultural Show; Pembroke County Show; Llandrindod Wells Victorian festival week; Faenol Festival
September	Tenby Arts Festival
September/ October	Cardiff Festival, one of the UK's largest festivals, with music, the arts, drama, literature and opera events
October	Swansea Cockle Festival – a seven-day food festival celebrating local produce
November	International Film Festival of Wales, Cardiff; Dylan Thomas Festival, Swansea; *Gŵyl Cerdd Dant* (see Unit 5)

GLOSSARY
Industry

diwydiant (m.)	*industry*
cyflogaeth (f.)	*employment*
electroneg (f.)	*electronics*
diweithdra (m.)	*unemployment*
pwll glo	*coal mine*
gwaith dur	*steelworks*
gweithlu (m.)	*workforce*
gweithio	*to work*
gweithwyr (pl.)	*workers*
ffatri (f.)	*factory*
byddin (f.)	*army*
llechi (pl.)	*slate*
cwmnïau (pl.)	*companies*
buddsoddi mewnol	*inward investment*

Agriculture

amaethyddiaeth (f.)	*agriculture*
arallgyfeirio	*diversification*

Tourism

twristiaeth (f.)	*tourism*
crefft (f.)	*craft*
marchnata	*marketing*
Bwrdd Croeso Cymru	*Welsh Tourist Board*
treftadaeth (f.)	*heritage*
amgueddfa (f.)	*museum*

Leisure activities

chwaraeon (pl.)	*sports*
chwaraewyr (pl.)	*players*
clwb (m.)	*club*
rygbi (m.)	*rugby*
hamdden (f.)	*leisure*
paffio	*boxing*
criced (m.)	*cricket*
pêl-droed (f.)	*football*

Taking it further

Reading

Welsh industry

Gildart, Keith, *North Wales Miners: A Fragile Unity, 1945–1996* (Cardiff: 2001)

Sport and leisure

Billot, John, *History of Welsh International Rugby* (Cardiff: 1999)

Jackson, Peter, *Lions of Wales: A Celebration of Welsh Rugby Legends* (Edinburgh: 1998)

Johnes, Martin, *The History of Welsh Sport 1850–1999* (Cardiff: 2002)

Websites

More details about sports in Wales can be found at:

www.wru.co.uk

www.millenniumstadium.com

www.walesopen.com

www.network-q.co.uk

www.wda.co.uk You can learn more about the Welsh Development Agency

www.visitwales.com For more information about the Welsh Tourist Board

Places to visit

Big Pit: The National Mining Museum of Wales, Blaenafon, Torfaen, Gwent NP4 9XP; Tel: 01495 790311

Museum of Welsh Life, St Fagans, Cardiff, CF5 6XB; Tel: 02920 573500

Centre for Alternative Technology, Machynlleth, Powys SY20 9AZ; Tel: 01654 702400. **www.cat.org.uk,** the website of the **Centre for Alternative Technology** contains a wealth of information on environmentally friendly living and includes a free consultancy service and details of appropriate publications.

For details of over 50 arts festivals: 'Festivals of Wales', Red House, Newtown SY16 3LE.

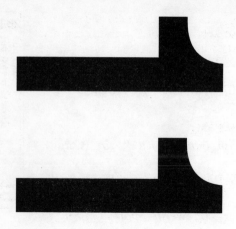

the Welsh people

In this unit you will learn about

- stereotypical images of the Welsh
- demographics
- minority populations
- popular names
- women in Wales
- religions
- the environment

So far we have looked at many aspects of Welsh life and culture, all of which have an effect on the people who live in the country. But what of the people themselves? What is the average **Cymro** (Welshman) or **Cymraes** (Welshwoman) really like? Indeed, is there such a thing as a national character?

The 'typical' Welsh person

Positive images

Many of the stereotypical images that we have of Welsh people go back a long way. **Gerald of Wales** (1146–1233), otherwise known as **Giraldus Cambrensis,** wrote a detailed account of the nature of Wales and the Welsh people in 1193. He himself was the son of the Norman Lord of Manorbier Castle in Pembrokeshire and nephew to the Bishop of St David's. In Book 1 of his description, entitled *Descriptio Kambria,* he concentrates on the good points of the Welsh people and in his second book he looks at what he calls the 'less good points'.

He comments with approval on the importance given to the family in Wales, the skill and courage of the Welsh in war, their love of choral singing and of poetry and their hospitality and generosity. He also commends the Welsh for their devotion to the Christian faith and says that they pay greater respect than any other nation to their churches. At the same time however he says that they are not a serious and dull race, he praises their sense of humour and their quick-wittedness and their bold, confident attitude even 'in the presence of their princes'.

Certain of these statements hold true today. Whilst by no means everyone can sing in harmony, singing, particularly choral singing, already strong in Gerald's day, was refined by the chapels in the nineteenth century (see Unit 5). Today choirs flourish both in rural and urban areas, even if the chapels do not. The phrase 'Land of Song' is more than merely a commercial tourist invention.

Equally so Wales could be called the Land of Speech, for as noted by Gerald, Welsh people love talking. The English poet Rudyard Kipling once wrote 'The Celt goes talking from Llanberis to Kirkwall, but the English, ah the English, don't say a word at all!' It is true that many Welsh people are eloquent, articulate talkers, full of what's known in Welsh as *hwyl*. Naturally warm-hearted and friendly, they are often as emotional and ebullient in their speech as in their singing. Many great political orators in recent history have been Welsh, such as Lloyd George and Aneurin Bevan (see Unit 8).

When referring to their sense of humour, Gerald notes that the Welsh love 'sarcastic remarks, libellous allusions, play on words and equivocal statements' and it is this sort of humour that is still appreciated today. Present-day literature, particularly Welsh poetry, contains much tongue-in-cheek humour, although Wales is not particularly well known for its comedians. Whilst the English are the butt of many Welsh jokes, the Welsh also frequently poke fun at themselves, as in the following example which is just one of the endless sheep-related jokes to be heard in Wales!

> *Some sheep farmers in west Wales have formed a society of teetotallers. There is a clause in the rules however that permits the use of alcohol at sheep-dipping time. One member keeps a sheep at home, which he dips every day.*

Other jokes overplay the differences between north and south Walians, with the north Walians frequently cited as dour and humourless. Natives of Cardiganshire in west Wales, on the other hand, are frequently considered stingy, with short arms and deep pockets:

> *English tourist: 'I'm sorry I ran over your hen. If I give you £5 would that be all right?'*

> *Cardiganshire farmer: 'Better make it £10. I've got a cockerel that was very attached to that hen and the shock might kill him.'*

Negative images

What therefore of the 'less good points' of the Welsh character? One weakness of the Welsh according to Gerald of Wales was their inconsistency, their instability and inability to keep their word, even when it was given on oath! Whilst Welsh people are not generally seen in that light now, it does partly explain how the verb 'to welsh', which means to go back on one's word, has entered the English language. Gerald also considered the Welsh to be greedy, enjoying vast quantities of food and 'intoxicating drink'. Partly due to the rural nature of much of Wales, Welsh people today still tend to be rather traditional in their eating habits, cooked dinners remain popular and beer consumption high! In the more urban areas, workingmen's clubs still thrive, many only recently allowing women into the bar area as well as the lounge.

Gerald was also critical of the enjoyment the Welsh had of living well by stealing from other people, even from each other as well as foreigners. Whilst this again is not something that one thankfully associates with Welsh people today, many anti-Welsh rhymes based on this theme have been passed down through the ages, including the rhyme *Taffy was a Welshman*, cited in Unit 12.

Feuding and fighting were commonplace amongst the Welsh according to Gerald, although whilst criticizing this, he did indirectly praise their tenacity saying that 'they are very difficult to defeat in a long war'. Some may argue that it is due to their tenacity and determinedness to continue that the Welsh people have survived over the centuries. A sense of nationhood and identity has always been important to the Welsh, whether or not they speak Welsh.

For many this feeling is expressed today through sport, particularly rugby. It has been said that rugby is the closest thing the present day offers to Wales' traditional national sport, namely war, and that it gives the Welsh the chance to humiliate the English at the game they invented, particularly since England's victory in the 2003 World Cup. Indeed the Welsh national football team has been much more successful recently than the rugby team. In rugby, as in so many other aspects, one negative aspect of the Welsh character is their tendency to dwell too much on the past, thereby making themselves prisoners of their own history.

Extremes

So is there a typical Welsh person? Probably not, any more than one could agree on the characteristics of the typical Englishman, German, Spaniard or Chinese. But as Gerald of Wales concluded: 'You may never find anyone worse than a bad Welshman, but you will certainly never find anyone better than a good one.'

Demographics

Population trends

The rate of growth of the Welsh population has been more erratic than that of England during the last hundred years. Up to 1921 the population of Wales grew at a faster rate than that of England, but declined sharply up until the Second World War, whereas the English figure increased during the same period.

Since 1945 the Welsh population has steadily increased with the 2001 census showing a 1 per cent increase since 1991. The population of Wales now stands at 2.9 million. Overall numbers in the north-west and north-east of England fell during these years, whilst the increase in the rest of England, with the exception of the affluent south-east, was comparable to Wales.

Young and old in Wales

Although the population of Wales is growing, it is however also ageing. The recent census revealed that, for the first time ever, Wales now has more people aged 60 and over than under 16. Women outnumber men in virtually every age range. Very many of those moving into Wales during the last 20 years have been over 50, whilst many younger people have left the country in search of better jobs. As a result of this, along with declining mortality, 9 per cent of homes are made up of pensioners. Gwynedd in north-west Wales has the highest proportion of retired people at present – over 35 per cent of the population there are retired. This also means that north Wales has a high number of people living alone. Although slightly lower than the rate in England, 29.1 per cent of people in Wales now live alone.

Overall however, the breakdown of households at present across Wales is broadly in line with England, with 24 per cent married with children and 13 per cent being childless couples; 28 per cent of people in Wales are single and have never been married. The annual numbers of childbirths in Wales rose steadily from the 1970s to a peak of 38,866 in 1990. By 2001 this figure had fallen to 30,616. This decrease has been coupled in recent years with a trend for women to have children later in life. The average age that women now have their first child is 29. Since the 1970s marriage has become much less popular, regardless of whether or not the couple has children.

Minority populations

Whilst the proportion of ethnic minorities living in Wales has more than doubled in the last decade, it still remains well below the British average. The 2001 census showed that ethnic minorities now make up 2.7 per cent of the population of Wales, compared to 1.2 per cent in 1991. There have been increases in the proportion of Indian, Pakistani, Bangladeshi and Chinese people living in Wales as well as those of mixed race. Very few live in the Welsh-speaking heartlands as most have settled in the urban south, particularly the Cardiff area. Around 5.5 per cent of people living in Cardiff at present were born outside the European Union, twice the percentage of any other local authority area in Wales.

Popular names

Christian names

In recent years Welsh-language names have gained in popularity in Wales, even among non-Welsh speakers. The Welsh language has a wide variety of *enwau cyntaf* or Christian names that reflect various aspects of Welsh history, religion and culture. Many are the names of saints and poets and kings and queens and date as far back as the fifth century. Others reflect aspects of nature and the countryside of Wales, whilst many can be traced to the *Four Branches of the Mabinogi*, some of the oldest Welsh folk tales (see Unit 3).

Some of the most popular Welsh Christian names today include:

Boys

Rhodri – *rhod*, a circle + *rhi*, a ruler. Rhodri Mawr was king of Gwynedd in the ninth century whilst Rhodri Morgan is First Minister of the Welsh Assembly Government. Both Rhodri and **Rhydderch,** another native Welsh name, have close connections with the Germanic name Roderick.

Rhys – this popular name, meaning 'ardour' in English, is often Anglicized to Rees, Rice and Reece. Rhys ap Gruffudd was Lord of south-west Wales in the twelfth century. Rhys Ifans is a well-known Welsh actor.

Huw – the Welsh version of the Old German Hugi. It means 'mind' or 'heart' and is popular in English as Hugh. Huw Edwards reads the BBC Ten o'Clock News.

Llŷr – the father of Branwen and Bendigeidfran in the second branch of the *Mabinogi*. The English version 'Lear' is seldom heard today. Llŷr Evans is the brother of Rhys Ifans and is also an actor.

Owain – derived from Old Celtic, this popular name and its alternative **Owen** can be translated as 'well born'. Owain Glyndŵr led a revolt against English rule in Wales in the early fifteenth century. Owain Arwel Hughes is a distinguished Welsh conductor.

Aled – a river in Denbighshire in north-east Wales. Tudur Aled was one of the greatest Welsh poets of the fifteenth century. Aled Jones is a successful singer and broadcaster.

Girls

Rhiannon – a Celtic horse goddess and wife of Pwyll in the first branch of the *Mabinogi*. Rhiannon Evans is an original and innovative designer of Celtic jewellery whose work is popular worldwide.

Heledd – sister of the seventh-century prince Cynddylan. Poems composed around AD 850 express her feelings at his death. The Hebrides are known in Welsh as *Ynysoedd Heledd*.

Angharad – *an*, intensifying prefix + *car*, 'loved'. The name is sometimes Anglicized as Ankret and Anchoret. The mother of Giraldus Cambrensis was called Angharad. Angharad Mair is a popular presenter on the Welsh-language channel S4C.

Gwenllian – *gwen*, white + *lliant*, stream. The mother of Lord Rhys (see p. 209), Gwenllian was a twelfth-century queen who led an attack against the Normans. The daughter of Llywelyn ap Gruffudd, the last Welsh-born Prince of Wales, was also called Gwenllian. She lived all her life a captive in an English convent. *Cymdeithas* Gwenllian, a society to commemorate her, was formed in 1996.

Catrin – from the Greek, then Latin meaning 'pure'. The sixteenth-century aristocrat Catrin of Berain was known as 'the Mother of Wales' owing to the fact that she married four times and had many children. Catrin Fychan is a well-known Welsh actress.

Sioned – a comparatively new name compared to some of the others, this is a feminine form of **Siôn** (John) or a diminutive of **Siân** (Jane), which translates as Janet. Sioned Davies recently became the first ever female Professor of Welsh at the University of Wales.

Surnames

It is also becoming increasingly popular amongst Welsh speakers today to revert to the Old Welsh system whereby children took their father's Christian name as a *cyfenw* or surname. For example, Aled the son of Rhodri would be Aled *ap* Rhodri. *Ab* is used before a vowel, so that Aled the son of Owain would be Aled *ab* Owain. *Vch*, a shortened form of *verch* (*merch* – daughter) was used originally when referring to daughters, but was gradually replaced by *ap/ab*, which of course corresponds to *mac* in Ireland and Scotland. This system was used up to the Act of Union with England in 1536 (see Unit 2), but gradually Anglicized surnames were adopted, which resulted in Christian names such as David, John, Huw and William becoming Davies, Jones, Hughes and Williams. It is little wonder that Jones is the most common surname in Wales today! Other common Welsh surnames were created as a result of the demise of this form, for example *ab Owen* gradually became Bowen, *ab Evan* became Bevan and *ap Prys* became Price/Pryce.

Rather than reverting to *ap/ab*, other Welsh people today choose just to reverse an Anglicized surname to its Welsh form, for example Angharad Griffiths would become Angharad Gruffudd, Dewi Jones would become Dewi Siôn. Another alternative is to use the father's Christian name as a last name. For example, Gwenllian and Sioned, the daughters of Owen Burt, would be Gwenllian Owen and Sioned Owen.

There is also a growing trend amongst Welsh speakers to omit a surname altogether. For example Rhiannon Eluned whose parents may be Mr and Mrs Jones can be named just Rhiannon Eluned if her parents so wish or as an adult she can choose to use these two names alone. The name of a district, river etc. is another popular surname choice today, for example Gomer Powys after the county of Powys or Watcyn Teifi after the river Teifi. Like the other possibilities mentioned, this alternative reflects a growing pride amongst Welsh people in their national identity and heritage.

Women in Wales

You will have noticed that many of the units in this book dealing with Welsh history, politics and so forth do not contain many references to individual Welsh women. The Welsh national anthem (see Appendix) begins with the words 'Land of my Fathers', and this sums up the position and status of women in Wales until relatively recently. Instead, particularly from the period of the Industrial Revolution through until the mid- to late-twentieth century, people's perception of Welsh women was dominated by two very distinct and very different images.

The first of these was the Welsh *mam* as depicted in novels like *How Green was my Valley* (1939) and films such as *Proud Valley* (1938). She was the wife and mother of miners, pious and devout, a regular chapelgoer who managed the family finances, scrimping and saving and going without if necessary. Her sphere of power was the home, outside of this she had no power. Inevitably, this image of the 'ideal Welsh woman' had a tremendous influence on both what Welsh women expected of themselves and of what men expected of them.

The second image, still pushed by the tourist trade, was that of a Welsh woman in the national costume, invented by Lady Llanover and described in Unit 6. By the late-nineteenth century the tall black hat, heavy cloth skirt and shawl were rarely worn. Although the costume was modelled on the rough and heavy clothes of country servants, the image it still presents through the sale of Welsh lady dolls, china Welsh ladies, postcards etc. is of a sweet, demure and genteel woman who is little more than an ornament herself. Interestingly there is no male equivalent. Welsh national costume is only worn nowadays on St David's

Traditional Welsh costume

day – and then usually only by girls under the age of around ten. Whilst these images can be said to be stereotyped and misguided, it is true that the role played by women in Wales has been largely defined by the fact that Wales was, until very recently, a very religious country. Chapels stressed the importance of a high moral code. As late as the 1950s pregnant unmarried women were thrown out of chapels, as were married women who committed adultery. Nonconformity also promoted the idea of the woman as a sort of 'domestic goddess' and very few married women were in paid employment at the start of the twentieth century. A court action in the Rhondda Valley in 1923 established the legality of the marriage bar that allowed councils to sack married women teachers in order to 'increase efficiency'.

Work, the Welsh language and Women

More and more jobs in Wales now require that employees are able to speak and write Welsh or that they are prepared to learn it. A recent report from the Equal Opportunities Commission has also shown that women who can speak Welsh are more likely to be in better-paid jobs than those who cannot speak the language. The report stated that a quarter of Welsh-speaking women were in professional jobs compared with 17 per cent of Welsh-speaking men and only 15 per cent of non-Welsh-speaking women. However, it also indicated that Welsh-speaking women were less likely to return to higher education than those who couldn't speak the language and were less likely to choose to be self-employed or to run their own businesses. It has been suggested that Welsh-speaking women lack confidence in their own ability and therefore are more likely to give up courses and choose not to work for themselves.

Women's voices

Whereas there may be an element of truth in the above view, in general, recent years have seen women in Wales rid themselves of the passive Welsh doll image. One of the positive side effects of the 1984–5 Miners' Strike was that women in Wales gained a new confidence and realization of their worth as they rallied around to support the miners. More and more organizations developed to meet women's needs and to give them a voice. European Commission funding set up initiatives providing women with the training and support needed to help them compete for jobs, whilst the organization *Chwarae Teg* (Fair Play) was founded to raise awareness amongst employers of problems facing women in the workplace. A women's press entitled Honno which publishes books by and for the women of Wales was set up in 1986 and a women's film co-operative Red Flannel Films was established in 1988. The leader of the Anti-Nuclear Campaign in Wales during the 1980s was a woman and many women walked from Wales to the Greenham Common air base in the south of England to set up peace camps. In the mid 1970s, the social/cultural group *Merched y Wawr*, the Welsh language equivalent of the Britain-wide Women's Institute (see Unit 10), was founded. A sister organization for the thirty-somethings called Gwawr was set up in the late 1990s. Another recent development has been the founding of *Mewn Cymru* (In Wales), a black and ethnic minority women's network.

This varied array of organizations highlights the fact that women in Wales have come a long way in the last 100 years. Women are now represented in all walks of life, but there is still however a considerable way to go before complete equality is reached within Wales and before Welsh women can truly be said to be on a par with their sisters in England.

Religions

Chapels

During the nineteenth century, the chapel in Wales was the focal point of the community (see Unit 1). By the First World War the total number of chapelgoers was estimated to be more than 500,000. Since then however the history of Nonconformity has been a chronicle of continual decline. There are many reasons for this. For example, in urban areas the lack of employment opportunities, due to the collapse of heavy industry, has resulted in close-knit communities becoming dispersed and fragmented. Nonconformists tend to feel that they belong to a particular chapel and not to the denomination to which it belongs and on moving to new areas are often very reluctant to join another chapel.

Along with the decline in strong residential stability, the twentieth century also saw a severe drop in the number of Welsh speakers from nearly 55 per cent of the population in 1891 to 18.6 per cent in 1991. This too has obviously been another critical factor in the decline of traditional Welsh Nonconformity. Establishing links with the non-Welsh-speaking population has always proved difficult and the increase in inward migration in recent years, especially into rural areas, has weakened the fortunes of the chapels still further. These rural areas have also ironically been hit by the emphasis placed by Nonconformity on education. Many rural areas have been denuded of their natural leaders as many young people have gone away to University and have inevitably found jobs elsewhere. Chapels have become increasingly isolated and thousands have sadly been closed and sold off during the last 30 years.

The Church in Wales

Until 1920 the Church in Wales was part of the Church of England but it is now totally independent with its own Archbishop and administrative offices based in Cardiff. It sees itself as the direct successor of the ancient Celtic Church and, due to its bilingual tradition, it has been better able to adapt to the cultural and linguistic changes of the last century in Wales than has the Nonconformist movement. However, once again the number of those attending Churches has declined considerably and due to this, along with a shortage of candidates wishing to enter the ministry, there has been much regrouping of parishes, particularly in rural areas. This situation has been eased somewhat by the ordination of women priests since 1996, although there is still a lack of Welsh-speaking clergy and the Church in Wales is frequently criticized for being too English in its outlook.

Religious observance

The most recent survey of religious observance to be undertaken in Wales (apart from the 2001 census) was in 1995. This survey, just of Christian denominations, revealed that an estimated 8.7 per cent of the population attended a church or chapel in Wales:

Denomination	per cent church attendance
The Church in Wales	28
Roman Catholics	21
Presbyterians	10

All other groups achieved single figures only. The Roman Catholic church was the only one to increase its percentage since an earlier survey in 1982. As is still the case today, church/chapel members tended to be over 45, 35 per cent were actually over 65 and approximately two-thirds of them were women. At that time 24 per cent of churches/chapels in Wales had no minister and 22 per cent shared a minister – today the figure is probably significantly higher. More people in rural areas attended a church or chapel than in urban areas.

The 2001 census presented a similar picture, revealing that the area with the highest number of families that practised no religion was Rhondda, in the former industrial south, where the figure was 25 per cent. The census also reveals interesting comparisons with England:

	Wales	England
No religion	18.5%	14.6%
Non-Christian religion	1.5%	6%

The census records that there are in Wales: 21,773 Muslims, 5,500 Hindus and Buddhists, 2,500 Jews and 2,032 Sikhs. There are mosques and synagogues in Cardiff, Newport and Swansea. The Muslim community in Wales consists of many who are students in the University of Wales, which partly explains the fact that there is also a mosque in Chepstow near Newport as well as those in the more rural university towns of Lampeter and Bangor in the west. Buddhism has often attracted Welsh people, particularly in rural areas.

The environment

Rural Wales, particularly west and mid Wales, has also in recent years become a haven for those seeking an alternative lifestyle, particularly English people escaping from high-pressured jobs in built up areas. Many have been inspired by the Centre for Alternative Technology based near Machynlleth in mid Wales and described in Unit 10.

Going organic

Many of those searching for 'the good life' have set up successful businesses, particularly selling organic produce. There are countless cheese and yoghurt producers in these areas, whilst others sell organic meat or vegetables through local shops and farmers' markets. The University of Wales, Aberystwyth, was the first University in Britain to offer a year-long course on organic farming and now is home to Organic Centre Wales, which was formally opened in the year 2000. This centre coordinates the provision of advice and information to farmers under the National Assembly's Welsh Agri-Food Partnership Organic Action Plan. The aim of this plan is to have 10 per cent of Welsh agriculture organic by 2005.

The National Assembly has also led the way in Europe in acting to prevent cross-pollination from genetically modified 'GM' planting in order to safeguard organic production and has put a great deal of money into the agri-environment scheme *Tir Gofal* run by the Countryside Commission for Wales. Under this scheme, which in 2002–3 received a budget of £16 million, farmers are encouraged to manage their land in a more environmentally friendly way. Grants are given to farmers to protect wildlife and existing habitats, create new habitats, encourage public access and protect the landscape including historical and archaeological features.

GLOSSARY

Cymry	*Welsh people*
poblogaeth (f.)	*population*
tref (f.)	*town*
cefn gwlad	*countryside*
trefol	*urban*
gwledig	*rural*
dyn (m.)	*man*
menyw (f.)	*woman*
gŵr (m.)	*husband*
gwraig (f.)	*wife*
mam (f.)	*mother*
tad (m.)	*father*
mab (m.)	*son*
merch (f.)	*daughter*
brawd (m.)	*brother*
chwaer (f.)	*sister*
geni	*to be born*
priodas (f.)	*marriage*
gwahanu	*to separate*
ysgariad (m.)	*divorce*
teulu (m.)	*family*
crefydd (f.)	*religion*
capel (m.)	*chapel*
eglwys (f.)	*church*
gweddi	*to pray*
Duw (m.)	*God*
amgylchfyd (m.)	*environment*
ailgylchu	*to recycle*

Taking it further

Reading

Aaron, J., Rees, T., Betts, S. & Vincentelli, M. (eds.), *Our Sisters' Land: The Changing Identities of Women in Wales* (Cardiff: 1994)

Beddoe, Deirdre, *Out of the Shadows: A History of Women in Twentieth Century Wales* (Cardiff: 2000)

Gruffudd, Heini, *Enwau Cymraeg i Blant, Welsh Names for Children* (Talybont: 1980)

Richards, John Winterson, *Xenophobe's guide to the Welsh* (London: 1993)

Stephens, Meic, *Welsh Names for your Children* (Cardiff: 2000)

Websites

www.wales.gov.uk/statistics A wide range of statistics relating to Wales, which include education, health, local government, housing and agriculture.

12

Wales in the wider world

In this unit you will learn about
- Welsh identity
- early migrations
- Wales and her Celtic neighbours
- Wales and England
- immigration into Wales
- the future for Wales

Identity

Wales cannot boast to have had an impact on the international stage; it has not spread its culture and language throughout the globe or influenced the history and development of other countries. Many people in the world do not realize that Wales is a separate country from England. Wales is not a state, it has no embassies and ambassadors, it does not have its own currency, and there is no Welsh passport. Yet despite lacking the external trappings of a nation state, Wales still has its own separate identity. The question of 'Welshness' is a hotly debated subject in Wales, particularly with the 'language question' as some people maintain that one must be Welsh-speaking in order to be Welsh.

Wales' population has undergone many waves of change over the centuries with many inward and outward migrations of population. The turn of the twentieth century saw lots of people coming into Wales to work in the new thriving industries. The south Wales coalfield was a magnet for immigrants from all parts of the United Kingdom, and the rural areas were characterized by massive out-migration as workers went south to enjoy better employment prospects. By the end of the century the situation had shifted to a predominantly outwards migration from around 1910 to 1960, as the heavy industries declined and people had to look further afield for work. The trend for outward migration reversed in the 1960s and 1970s, and has continued with an inwards trend so that today well over 80 per cent of the inhabitants of the old industrial areas of the south are Welsh by birth whereas, in rural areas, the proportion is below 50 per cent. The relative cheapness of Welsh land and rural housing, the rise of the self-sufficiency movement and the growth of electronic communications, which permits a living to be made even in the remotest areas, are all factors in the increase in the number of rural immigrants (see Unit 9). Migration leads to considerable strains in the country as many Welsh-speaking communities feel overwhelmed by the monoglot English influx.

Emigration

The Vikings were early visitors to Wales and they raided and settled in Wales, leaving the trace of their language in place names like Swansea, Bardsey, Flat Holm and Great Orme. Welsh people have been emigrating for centuries and, with the possible exception of Patagonia, the Welsh were quickly assimilated into the culture of their new country and Welsh communities of expatriates overseas hardly exist. Some 430,000 Welsh people left during the Depression of the 1930s, but a high proportion returned, mainly to retire. There are no strong Welsh communities abroad like those of the Irish and Scottish in America and Australia, a fact lamented by the chief executive of the Wales Tourist Board, whilst citing that there are about 40m Irish–Americans and 10m Scottish–Americans but only 1.7m Welsh–Americans. One of the most popular ceremonies during the National Eisteddfod is the one which welcomes the 'exiled Welsh' or '*Cymry alltud*'.

Wales and America

One of the countries that has witnessed much emigration from Wales is the United States of America. Wales has many connections with the USA, and the Welsh are said by some Welsh historians to have shaped American history. According to legend, America was discovered by the Welsh prince **Madog ap Owain Gwynedd**, son of **Owain Gwynedd**, in 1170. Madog is said to have taken to his ships to escape the feuds and fighting between his brothers in Wales. Owain Gwynedd's 32 year reign was marked by constant warfare between the Norman barons and the Welsh chieftains. Owain was said to have had 17 sons, including Madog, and at least two daughters, which led to a bitter dispute as to who among his sons would succeed him. On his death in 1169, Gwynedd was plunged into the civil war from which Madog fled. Madog's tales of a wondrous, fertile new country on his return convinced many other Welshmen to return with him to the wondrous new land far across the sea. The presence of a series of pre-Columbian forts on the banks of the Alabama River, which are unlike any known Indian structure, coupled with the tradition handed down by the Cherokee Indians of the 'White People' who built them, has led to the opinion that Madog's wondrous new land is modern day Mobile Bay, Alabama. Most archaeologists agree that the forts date several hundred years before 1492 and that they were built by the same group of people within the period of a single generation. The forts are said to bear striking similarities to the ancient fortifications of Wales. The Welsh settlers were believed to have travelled to Ohio in order to escape hostile Indians and to have been eventually assimilated by Indians. Although several tribes have been considered as possible descendants of the Welsh settlers, the most likely candidate is the Mandan tribe, who once inhabited villages along tributaries of the Missouri River.

European visitors to the Mandan tribe during the eighteenth century described the Mandans as being white-skinned people who fished using coracles (see Unit 6) and buried their dead in Celtic mounds. The Mandan language was said to be proof that the tribe had been in contact with Welsh settlers as there are many similar words in both languages including the word for valley: *cwm* (*koom* in the language of the Mandan), and *prydferth* (beautiful) (*prydfa* in Mandan). Early visitors commented on the customs and lifestyle of the Mandans and noted that these differed greatly from other native Indians. The Indian settlements consisted of forts, towns and permanent villages laid out in streets and squares, the menfolk had beards. The Mandans had been repeatedly driven out of their villages and forced up river by their continual conflicts with the Sioux. Like so many other Indian tribes, they were wiped out by the smallpox epidemic introduced to them by traders in 1837. Now considered extinct, the Mandans claim the distinction of being the only Indian tribe never to have been at war with the United States.

Throughout the centuries, scholars and historians have argued for and against the Madog story. In November 1953 a memorial tablet was erected at Mobile Bay, Alabama by the Virginia Cavalier chapter of the Daughters of the American Revolution, which reads: 'In memory of Prince Madoc, who landed on the shores of Mobile Bay in 1170 and left behind, with the Indians, the Welsh language.' Madog was never to return to his homeland and he is commemorated in the Triads (a mixed collection of triadic sayings found in early manuscripts that recount personages, events or places in Welsh history, thought to have been designed as mnemonic structures to aid the bard's recollection) as 'one of the Three who made a Total Disappearance From the Isle of Britain'. During the reign of Elizabeth I, John Dee cited the legend of Madog when claiming America for the Queen, thus exerting a claim to sovereignty in the New World which preceded that of Spain. Some say that America was named after **Richard ap Meurig**, otherwise known as Richard Amerik, a merchant from Glamorgan who sponsored John Cabot's second voyage from Bristol.

Later emigrations to America

There is more concrete historical evidence for later emigrations to America by the Welsh. A colony of Welsh and Cornishmen dating from 1607 still survives on the islands around Chesapeake

Bay in Maryland and in 1617 a Welsh poet, **William Vaughan** (1575–1641) established a colony in Newfoundland. In 1636 **Roger Williams** (c.1604–84) founded Rhode Island colony upon the basis of democracy and complete religious freedom. Religious intolerance in Wales forced many Welsh people to emigrate to America from the seventeenth century onwards. A trial at Bala in north Wales in 1679 for non-payment of tithes to the church had convinced many Welsh Quakers to emigrate and the 1680s saw many of them sail to America. They were the founding fathers of Pennsylvania after William Penn promised they would be able to establish a Welsh-speaking colony 'New Wales'. The name of this new haven, 'New Wales' was not to be, however, as William Penn was overruled by the King. The new so-called 'Welsh barony' consisted of 40,000 acres and the newly established settlements were named after places the settlers had left behind in Wales – Bannog, Narberth, Radnor, Berwyn, St Davids, Haverford, Bala and Bryn Mawr. Large tracts of Pennsylvania today are still called Gwynedd, Uwchlyn, Llanerch, Meirion, and St Davids. By 1700, it is estimated that a third of the 20,000 European settlers in the area were Welsh. **Dr Thomas Wynne** of Caerwys planned the layout of Pennsylvania, and his house, Wynnewood, the first stone-built house in the state, still stands. The Welsh Society of Philadelphia, dating from 1729, is the oldest ethnic language society in the USA. The Welsh Quakers flourished in their new environment, and Welsh men became an influential force in their new country.

The twentieth-century Welsh historian, **Gwyn A Williams** (1925–96), described American Independence as the first modern Welsh political cause, as it was the first to excite the interests and arguments of all educated Welshmen. There were fourteen Welshmen among the generals of the Revolutionary Army and 18 of the 56 men who signed the Declaration of Independence were of Welsh descent. The Declaration of Independence itself was written by Thomas Jefferson who claimed his father was born within the sight of Snowdon; a US State Department official unveiled a plaque at Llanfair Ceiriog in 1933, which bore the commemoration 'to the Memory of a Great Welshman, Thomas Jefferson.'

John Thomas Evans of Waunfawr, Gwynedd, explored the Missouri Valley in 1792 in an attempt to locate Prince Madog's Welsh Indians. Evans, who was in the service of Spain, reached the Mandans and spent a terrible winter with them. He helped to establish the current American–Canadian border by successfully holding the Mandans for Spain against the

Canadians. Evans died in New Orleans aged 29 after succumbing to alcoholism. John Evans' maps were later used by **Meriwether Lewis** (1774–1809) who commanded and completed the first overland expedition to the Pacific coast and back, at the beginning of the nineteenth century. It was Lewis, and his fellow explorer, **William Clark** (1770–1838), who opened up the American west. They encountered many Indian tribes and noted many different species of flora and fauna. Lewis followed the Missouri to its source, crossed the Rockies aided by an Indian woman called Sacajawea and followed the Columbia River to the Pacific Ocean. Lewis was the first white man to cross the Continental Divide.

Three of America's first six presidents claim Welsh descent and in total, 11 of America's presidents have Welsh ancestry, one of whom was **John Adams** (1735–1826) who negotiated the treaty with England that ended the American War of Independence. He was the father of the sixth president, John Quincy Adams, and their ancestral home is Penbanc farm, near Llanboidy, Carmarthenshire.

The Welsh were also prominent in education, as well as politics. The name Yale derives from Iâl, the village of Llanarmon-yn-Iâl, near Wrexham in north-east Wales. The leading female college in the USA, Bryn Mawr, has Welsh origins and Brown University, Rhode Island, was founded by a Welshman, **Morgan Edwards** of Pontypool. Both Johns Hopkins University and Morgan State University in Baltimore have strong Welsh connections. **George Jones**, whose parents emigrated from Llanwyddelan, co-founded the New York Times in 1851. The first registered distillery in the USA was that of **Jack Daniels**, the family firm of the Daniels family from Cardigan.

In the nineteenth century another flood of Welsh emigrants sailed from Welsh ports to America; sometimes whole families would make the voyage. Thousands of people left the rural west and mid Wales to make new lives for themselves in New York, Pennsylvania, Ohio, Wisconsin and Illinois, where they were mainly employed in agricultural work. Most Welsh people headed for the towns of Scranton and Wilkes-Barre in Pennsylvania and at the turn of the twentieth century, there were 19,000 Welsh speakers in Scranton. Many Welsh people from north-east Wales and the industrial valleys of the south sailed for America, with some joining the California Gold rush. By 1872, there were 384 Welsh language chapels in the USA and 24 Welsh periodicals. The Welsh language newspaper *Y Drych* (The Mirror) is the oldest ethnic language newspaper in America.

The relationship between America and Wales continued into the last century, during the Cold War there was an American tracking station at Brawdy in Pembrokeshire. **Frank Lloyd Wright** (1867–1959), the architect responsible for designing the Guggenheim Museum of Modern Art, was so proud of his Welsh heritage that he called the Wisconsin home he built for himself 'Taliesin', after the legendary Welsh bard (see Unit 3).

Wales and Argentina

It is estimated that there are around 7,500 Welsh speakers in Welsh communities in Patagonia, Argentina. In 1865, 153 Welsh people sailed from Liverpool aboard the ship Mimosa, bound for a new life in a Welsh colony in Argentina. The colony founder, **Michael D. Jones** (1822–98), who is today regarded as the founder of the Welsh Nationalist Movement, was concerned about the Anglicization of Wales and wanted a place where settlers could live independent lives in Welsh. The new settlers were prominently Nonconformist, and the first sermon preached in Patagonia had as its text the story of the Israelites in the wilderness. The colonists landed at Port Madryn, and trekked 65 km to found a settlement near the Chubut river. The group established a settlement that developed into the town of Rawson, now provincial capital of Chubut province. Until the colonists perfected irrigation methods, the Chubut valley was very dry and forbidding. For ten years, this Welsh state was completely self-governing, with its own constitution written in Welsh, and Welsh was the language of parliament and education. The Welsh owned their own land and farmed their own farms, and were free from the tyranny of the landlordism rampant in Wales. The colony at Patagonia was the first democracy in the world to give the vote to all people over the age of 18 and voting was by means of a secret ballot. The Welsh on the whole

The Mimosa heading for Patagonia

lived in peace with the native Teheulche Indians who taught them how to catch rhea from prairies. The Sabbath was observed and daily Welsh newspapers published. In 1885, some families migrated inwards crossing 400 miles of desert to establish another settlement at Cwm Hyfryd at the foot of the Andes. For a time, it seemed that the Welsh colonists had found a haven in Patagonia. Nonconformism and the Welsh language dominated life in *Y Wladfa* (the colony) as the colony came to be known. Back home in Wales, the use of Welsh was forbidden, and Nonconformists were still obliged to pay tithes to the Church of England. Butch Cassidy and the Sundance Kid were alleged to have formed a gang comprising of Welshmen in Patagonia, and to have been helped by the Welsh to breed horses. The haven for the Welsh in Patagonia was not to last, however, as the colony gradually came under the control of the Argentinian government. Immigration by the Welsh continued until around the time of the First World War. The language, while still spoken in Patagonia, is on the decline and the native Welsh speakers are elderly (see Unit 2). The colony at Patagonia has been the most successful colony as far as retaining the cultural identity of the Welsh is concerned. Ironically, during the Falklands Conflict, the Argentinian pilot who fired the Exocet missile that killed 23 Welsh Guards was a Welsh Patagonian.

Other emigrations

There is a sizeable Welsh population in Durban, South Africa and in Canada. A Welshman, **James Evans** (1801–46), invented the Cree alphabet in nineteenth-century Canada.

Australia and New Zealand proved attractive to many south Walians. New South Wales was named by **Captain Thomas Jones** of Llanddewi Skirrid. From 1870, many Welsh took up the offer of a free passage to Australia as Australia wished to develop its mineral resources. One Welsh emigrant, **William Morris Hughes** (1862–1952), held the office of Prime Minister from 1915–23 during a parliamentary career spanning 58 years. New Zealand's massive sheep farms proved a magnet to Welsh farmers and nowadays the tide has turned and young sheep shearers from Australia and New Zealand come to Wales every summer to work. There are still big Welsh communities in Sydney and Auckland. Although exiled Welsh Catholics made their home in Italy during the Protestant Reformation, there is no significant ex-pat population there now. Other countries to become home to Welsh people were Chile, where miners went to work in the copper mines, and Cuba, where there is a Swansea Cemetery. The first steel mills in Tsarist Russia were built by the nineteenth-century industrialist, **John Hughes** (1815–89) of Merthyr who founded the town of Hughesocka. Hughes provided a hospital, schools, bath houses, tea rooms, a fire brigade and an Anglican church dedicated to the patron saints St George and St David. Hughesocka has now been renamed Donetsk yet is still home to citizens of Welsh descent.

Celtic neighbours

Wales and Brittany

Of all the Celtic countries, Wales perhaps enjoys the best relationship with Brittany. This relationship began during the Age of the Saints in the sixth century, when there was much travelling between the two countries. Some Bretons came over with the Normans and the garrison at Monmouth was populated by Bretons, including the writer Geoffrey of Monmouth who was responsible for introducing the Arthurian legend to Europe. A common sight until relatively recently was the Breton onion sellers who cycled throughout south Wales selling their onions from their bikes. Many Welsh people learn the Breton language in Wales and the University of Wales, Aberystwyth, offers MA degrees in Breton and teaches the subject at undergraduate level. In 1996, **Rita Williams** from Fishguard was awarded the Silver Collar of Brittany, a cultural award which dates back to the Middle Ages. Rita has translated Breton short stories and plays into Welsh and compiled both a Welsh–Breton and a Breton–Welsh dictionary. She was the first Briton to receive the award.

Wales and Ireland

The Irish have been coming to Wales to settle since very early on. Some bilingual memorial stones have been found in Wales bearing both Latin and the Irish Ogham script. There are Irish names in the *Mabinogi* (see Unit 3), and some stories display themes common to both countries. The Llŷn peninsula bears the same name as Leinster. Celtic Christianity was an early link between the two countries and Irish saints travelled to Wales to establish monasteries during the sixth century. In more recent times, the Irish settled in Wales in large numbers during the nineteenth century. The Irish were not always particularly welcome in Wales; during the long industrial strikes they were seen as strike breakers and the memory of poor Irish workers who were willing to work for a fraction of that earned by Welsh workers still remains in the coal mining valleys of the south.

Transport between Wales and Ireland is relatively easy nowadays, there are regular ferry trips to Ireland from the ports of Holyhead, Fishguard, Pembroke and Swansea and there is a fast catamaran service from Fishguard to Rosslare which takes just 1 hour 50 minutes. Irish radio stations are easily received along the west coast of Wales – and sometimes give a better reception than Welsh! There are many schemes supported by the European Union which are designed to encourage partnerships between member states, particularly with a view to stimulating regional development and fostering an integrated approach to economic, social and environmental development. Many public bodies, educational establishments, voluntary organizations, community groups and private sector businesses in Ireland and Wales have benefitted from one of these schemes called Interreg in which funding is available for organizations who work in partnership with another organization across the Irish Sea. Both the Irish Government and the National Assembly for Wales have declared their commitment to partnership in this area.

Wales and Scotland

There is an historic link with Scotland. South-west Scotland was once a Welsh kingdom, and the earliest poem in Welsh is centred in the old kingdom of Gododdin (see Unit 3). The Scottish national hero William Wallace hails from this region; his surname means 'Welshman'.

Wales and England

Taffy was a Welshman
Taffy was a thief
Taffy came to my house
And stole a leg of beef
I went to Taffy's house
Taffy was in bed
So I upturned the chamberpot
And put it on his head!

This rhyme recalls the days of cattle raids between Wales and England when territory was passed back and forth between the Welsh and the English rulers. England has always been inextricably concerned with affairs of Wales, dominating its economy and powerfully influencing its social progress. The border towns of Chester, Shrewsbury and Hereford have always had a Welsh-speaking enclave, and the town of Ludlow became important when the Council of Wales was established there under the Tudors. For many in north Wales, Liverpool is the real capital of the north and the nearest thing to a north Wales daily newspaper is Liverpool's *Daily Post*. The nearest international airport to north Wales is Liverpool's John Lennon airport. The thriving Welsh population has produced many Welsh scholars, including **Saunders Lewis** (see Unit 3). In Bristol, every merchant ship had Welshmen in its crew. London has had its Welsh enclave and societies since the time of the Tudors, even today there are Welsh churches, chapels, a Welsh school, and rugby club. Societies of London exiles were founded, one of which, the *Cymmrodorion*, still exists. The list of Welsh people who found success in England include bishops, writers, statesmen, lawyers, scholars, actors, musicians and television personalities. Welshmen have held the offices of Prime Minister, Foreign Secretary, Home Secretary and Chancellor of the Exchequer.

In 1995, a new society was formed in London entitled SWS (Social Welsh and Sexy) when the entertainer and producer **Stifyn Parri** invited 40 Welsh friends for drinks at the Groucho Club, Soho. The club, which lists many celebrities amongst its 4,000 members such as the actors **Siân Phillips** and **Catherine Zeta Jones** (see Unit 7), hurdler **Colin Jackson** (see Unit 10), is open to all who are interested in being with Welsh people and regularly organizes parties and dinners.

Immigration

Cardiff has a more cosmopolitan population than any other British city apart from London and was home to the first large black community in Europe yet the rest of Wales has few immigrants from outside Europe. Norman kings established a colony of Flemings in Pembrokeshire. At the point where the Normans advancing from the southern coast were held by the Welsh, a no man's land was established running from coast to coast of the Pembrokeshire peninsula. South of the line, known as the Landsker, was predominantly Norman and then English speaking. Even now, that area is known as 'little England beyond Wales' and most of southern Pembrokeshire hardly regards itself as Welsh at all and is suspicious of everything north of the Landsker. During the great coal rush of the nineteenth century, Americans, Germans, Italians, Frenchmen, Spaniards, West Indians, Greeks, Arabs, Indians, and Scandinavians all flocked to work in the Welsh mines or docks. During the nineteenth and early twentieth centuries, whole families of Spanish ironworkers and miners settled in south Wales. At Merthyr a street was built especially to house Spanish immigrants, called King Alphonso Street. Many Spaniards learnt Welsh in the mines. Many of these nineteenth-century immigrants were to become assimilated and to regard themselves as Welsh. A Greek Orthodox Church still thrives in Cardiff which is also home to several Islamic centres and Mosques. The Italians were also very much a part of Welsh valley life in this period. In 1890, the Bracchi brothers came from the Po valley in Italy to open a café in the south Wales coalfield. Soon all the valleys had Italian-run cafés and ice cream sellers, which became known generally as 'Bracchis' after the first café opened. Polish refugees and German former prisoners of war also remained in Wales after the war, with many a Catholic church holding a Polish-language mass for the Polish members of their congregations.

Jews were early settlers in Wales and have been in the country since Roman times. There is a significant Jewish population in south Wales; there was a Jewish mayor in Swansea during the 1940s. One prominent Welsh Jewish family is the Abse family: the politician Leo Abse and Dannie Abse (see Unit 3), the Anglo-Welsh poet. A prayer was said for the first time in the Welsh language in a synagogue in 1982 after Rabbi Kenneth Cohen had learnt the language with the help of a *Teach Yourself* cassette and book.

Gypsies

Just outside the porch of the church at Llangelynnin in Gwynedd there is a stone which commemorates **Abram Wood,** the patriarch of the Wood family, a clan of Romanies who settled in Wales at the beginning of the eighteenth century and who called themselves The Welsh Gypsies. Abram Wood came to Wales from Somerset in England. He died in 1799 at Llangelynnin, where he was entered in the parish register as 'Abram Wood, a travelling gypsey'. The descendents of Abram Wood prospered and learnt to speak Welsh. They travelled the length and breadth of Wales and were employed on farms at busy times of the year until they married into Welsh families and abandoned their Romany way of life. The family were noted musicians, harpers, and fiddlers.

The future

At the beginning of the third millennium, the future looks secure for Wales as a nation. Wales has gained some measure of political control over its affairs with the establishment of the National Assembly and its powers may well be increased at some stage. The growth of Welsh institutions, particularly during the twentieth century, has ensured that a significant amount of the political, economic, sporting and cultural life of Wales is organized on Welsh national lines. The Welsh literary and music scene continues to evolve and contribute to the Welsh cultural identity and yet there are some fears that although the future for Wales as a nation will survive, the Welsh language might become less important in the definition of what it is to be Welsh. There are, in spite of the national institutions in Wales, so many similarities and connections between Wales and England, both economically and administratively, in some respects the Welsh language could be said to be the principal distinguishing feature between the two nations. In this way, the health of the Welsh as a nation is bound with the survival of Welsh as a modern spoken language, as noted in Unit 2. Welsh is now more visible as an official language than it has been for some time; however, it is losing ground as the language of the home and community as the number of Welsh speakers are reduced in the Welsh-speaking heartlands. If the language, one of the features which distiguishes the Welsh as a nation, does not thrive, one must question the future of the Welsh people as a distinct nation.

GLOSSARY	
allfudo	*emigration*
gwladfa (f.)	*colony*
cymuned (f.)	*community*
gwlad (f.)	*country*
byd (m.)	*world*
Llydaw	*Brittany*
Cernyw	*Cornwall*
Iwerddon	*Ireland*
Yr Alban	*Scotland*

Lloegr	England
mewnfudo	immigration
cysylltiadau (pl.)	connections
hwylio	to sail
ymsefydlu	to settle
perthynas (f.)	relationship

Taking it further

Reading

Betts, Clive, *Culture in Crisis* (Upton: 1976)

Chatwin, Bruce, *In Patagonia* (London: 1977)

Greenslade, David, *Welsh Fever – Welsh Activities in the US and Canada Today* (Cowbridge: 1986)

Jarman, A. O. H. & Jarman, Eldra, *The Welsh Gypsies. Children of Abram Wood* (Cardiff: 1986)

Jenkins, Geraint H., *The Foundations of Modern Wales* (Oxford: 1993)

Morgan, K. O., *Rebirth of a Nation, Wales 1880–1980* (Oxford: 1982)

Morgan, P. and Thomas, D., *Wales: The Shaping of a Nation* (Newton Abbot: 1984)

Petrie, Pamela, *Travels in an Old Tongue – Touring the World Speaking Welsh* (London: 1997)

Williams, Gwyn A., *Madoc: The Making of a Myth* (Oxford: 1987)

The Welsh national anthem is *Hen Wlad fy Nhadau* (Land of my Fathers). It was composed in Pontypridd in 1856 by Evan James (1809–78) and his son James (1833–1902). It is believed that Evan James was responsible for the words and his son for the music. Though there are three verses, the last two are very rarely sung. A Breton version – *Bro Gozh ma Zadoù* – was adopted as the Breton national anthem in 1902.

Hen Wlad fy Nhadau

Mae hen wlad fy nhadau yn annwyl i mi,
Gwlad beirdd a chantorion, enwogion o fri;
Ei gwrol ryfelwyr, gwladgarwyr tra mâd,
Tros ryddid gollasant eu gwaed.

Cytgan (Chorus)
Gwlad, gwlad, pleidiol wyf i'm gwlad,
Tra môr yn fur i'r bur hoff bau,
O bydded i'r heniaith barhau.

Hen Gymru fynyddig, paradwys y bardd,
Pob dyffryn, pob clogwyn, i'm golwg sydd hardd;
Trwy deimlad gwladgarol, mor swynol yw si
Ei nentydd, afonydd, i mi.

Os treisiodd y gelyn fy ngwlad dan ei droed,
Mae hen iaith y Cymry mor fyw ag erioed,
Ni luddiwyd yr awen gan erchyll law brad,
Na thelyn berseiniol fy ngwlad.

Land of my Fathers (words by A. P. Graves)

O land of my fathers, O land of my love,
Dear mother of minstrels who kindle and move
And hero on hero, who at honour's proud call,
For freedom their life-blood let fall.

Chorus
Wales, Wales! O but my heart is with you!
And long as the sea your bulwark shall be,
To Cymru my heart shall be true.

O land of the mountains, the bard's paradise,
Whose precipice proud, valleys lone as the skies,
Green murmuring forest, far echoing flood
Fire the fancy and quicken the blood.

For tho' the fierce foeman has ravaged your realm,
The old speech of Cymru he cannot o'erwhelm,
Our passionate poets to silence command
Or banish the harp from your strand.

teach
yourself

welsh dictionary
edwin c. lewis

- Do you want to be able to look up words quickly and easily?
- Would you like to check your grammar at the same time?
- Do you want words that will be useful for life in Wales today?

Welsh Dictionary will get you out of trouble fast. You can use it as a quick-and-easy way to check spellings and definitions and at the same time improve your pronunciation.

teach
yourself

welsh
julie brake & christine jones

- Do you want to cover the basics then progress fast?
- Do you want to communicate in a range of situations?
- Do you want to reach a high standard?

Welsh starts with the basics but moves at a lively pace to give you a good level of understanding, speaking and writing. You will have lots of opportunity to practise the kind of language you will need to be able to communicate with confidence and understand Welsh culture.